C0046 32896

D1582220

To Jane, Ella, Tess and Daisy for their love and support.

First published in January 2011

A catalogue record for this book is available from the British Library

ISBN 978 1 84425 946 5

Library of Congress catalog card no. 2010934889

Published by Haynes Publishing,
Sparkford, Yeovil, Somerset BA22 7JJ, UK

Tel: 01963 442030 Fax: 01963 440001
Int. tel: +44 1963 442030 Int. fax: +44 1963 440001
E-mail: sales@haynes.co.uk
Website: www.haynes.co.uk

Haynes North America, Inc.,
861 Lawrence Drive, Newbury Park,
California 91320, USA

Printed in the USA by Odcombe Press LP,
1299 Bridgestone Parkway, LaVergne, TN 37086

WARNING!

Some of the information and techniques shown in this book should only be used in dire circumstances where survival depends on it. The publisher cannot be held responsible for any injuries, damage, loss or prosecutions resulting from the use or misuse of techniques described. Respect the rights of private landowners and all laws protecting certain animals and plants.

OUTDOOR SURVIVAL

A STEP-BY-STEP GUIDE TO PRACTICAL BUSH CRAFT AND SURVIVAL OUTDOORS

Foreword by Bear Grylls

DAVE PEARCE

CONTENTS

FOREWORD 4
INTRODUCTION 6

1 ESSENTIAL EQUIPMENT 10

Essential Equipment 12
Survival pack 14
Rucksacks 16
Overhead cover 18
Footwear 20
General clothing 22
Sleeping bags 24
Taking food 25
Cutting tools 26

2 FINDING YOUR WAY 28

Maps and map-reading 30
Compass and bearings 32
Without a map or compass 34
Using the stars 36
Guidance from nature 38
Improvised compass 41
Speed and distance 42
Crossing rivers 44
Building a raft 47
Building a sea raft 48

3 CAMP CRAFT 50

Making fire 52
Bamboo fire saw 56
Friction fire 57
Using knives 58
Tying knots 60
General shelter 66

4 FINDING FOOD 68

Living off the land 70
Bugs and grubs 72
Animal tracking 74
Traps and snares 76
Spear construction 83
Fishing and fish traps 84
Field preparation 86

5 FIRST AID & RESCUE 90

First aid 92
Recovery position 95
Rescue helicopters 100

6 SURVIVING THE COLD 102

- Cold environments 104
- Building a shelter 106
- Cold basics 108
- Cold travel 110

7 COASTAL SURVIVAL 112

- Coastal environments 114
- Protection 116
- Finding water 118
- Finding food 121
- Rescue 124
- Maritime survival tips 125

8 DESERT SURVIVAL 126

- Desert environments 128
- Finding shelter 130
- Desert basics 131
- Finding water 132
- Desert travel 136
- Signalling and rescue 137

9 JUNGLE SURVIVAL 138

- Jungle environments 140
- Building a shelter 142
- Jungle basics 144
- Jungle travel 146
- Jungle hazards 148

10 MOUNTAIN SURVIVAL 150

- Mountain environments 152
- Building a shelter 154
- Mountain basics 156
- Mountain travel 158
- Avalanches 161

APPENDIX 164
INDEX 166

Foreword

The key to survival is the combination of skills, ingenuity and determination and there are few men with whom I have adventured who display these qualities as comprehensively as Dave Pearce.

This book is the sum parts of all of Dave's extensive experience, condensed into a book that is both simple to read and simple to apply. If used correctly, it will empower you to survive the harshest of conditions.

I have travelled to all four corners of the earth with Dave, and together, we have had to work out ways to survive in some truly horrible conditions. That means that the techniques here are proven to work. At times we have had some serious struggles on our hands, and at times we have learnt as much about how not to do something as we have about how to do it – but that is what survival is all about. Improvise. Adapt. Overcome.

Ultimately, whether a person makes it out of the wilds or not will come down to spirit – and on that front this book has been written by the best.

Bear Grylls,
January 2011

Introduction

There are many people, including myself, who have been pushed to painful limits in order to cope with challenging environments and situations. On occasion it has felt like life itself was threatened. This sensation of peril can be almost instant or can creep up on you over a period of hours or days until the realisation becomes suddenly stark and clear. It is at those times that I have really come alive – determined to survive, to find a way out and back to the things I value most. On many of these occasions I have been in the company of exceptional individuals; and within that team fortitude, guile, determination, humility and friendship have thrived. It is these values, learnt from fine people during difficult times, that carry me through so much else in life, not just the risky, life-threatening situations that I've faced in the past and continue to face today.

I don't regard myself as an expert survival practitioner, but in the course of many pleasant, grim, uplifting, horrible and dirty experiences I've learnt the value of knowledge, clear thinking and the respect that all extreme and challenging environments should be shown. There is order to the natural world, and attempting to understand it will put you more 'in tune' with your surroundings and thereby give you hope. I love the great cities of the world and enjoy being in them, but I probably wouldn't survive as a businessman. It is my lack of business knowledge that makes me think so. But with some understanding I think I might just muscle through. The natural world seems equally intimidating to many because of their limited understanding of it, but I hope that this book will provide sufficient knowledge for more of them to go and experience our natural playground.

I have been extremely privileged and fortunate to have operated, travelled and been thrust into tough locations alongside great and extremely knowledgeable individuals. Many of the lessons I've learnt from them will live with me forever. To these people I'll be forever grateful. In all my encounters with people and environments, I've found a common thread that appears to be applicable to all survival and demanding situations. I have formed it into an acronym that I use as a mantra even today, when confronted by any challenge:

B-PRO – Be Proactive, Resourceful and Opportunistic

About the Author

Dave Pearce is a former Royal Marines Commando. He is an adviser to the TV and film industries and has worked with outdoor adventurers Bruce Parry and Bear Grylls. Dave's greatest mountaineering achievement came in May 2003 when he reached the summit of Mount Everest by its challenging North Face.

• WISE WORDS •

I remember the very first night I spent in the jungle. I had spent many nights sleeping in wild locations in the mountains, but that first night in the jungle was so different. I had no jungle knowledge and had the idea that it was full of snakes, spiders, ants, mosquitoes and wild biting crawlies! For me, that night was sensory overload, and I hardly slept a wink in my crudely constructed hammock. I recall our instructor looking so comfortable, not seeming to bother about the battle to prevent even one ant getting into his hammock. I asked him about his carefree jungle persona. He said: 'You'll be lucky if you ever get bitten by anything venomous or big! And there's only a ten per cent chance you'll see anything impressive. Wild animals and reptiles just move on unless they're threatened or cornered, so don't do that. There are more eyes watching us than we will ever see, and the more you resist the harder it becomes.' I now have some of my best sleeps in the jungle.

Proactive

Take control of the situation and don't sit with your head in your hands. It's important to keep a clear head. Being proactive is about taking action. You'll not get any results if you don't take any action. A shelter won't build itself and a survival plan won't get created without taking action; and heat and warmth aren't found created by sitting down. In a team, be proactive in building a positive, robust and cohesive team spirit that's underpinned by determination.

Fear and panic can be early states of mind in precarious situations. But they're only a state of mind. Being proactive can turn fear into the edge you need to survive, and panic can be transformed into focus. Being proactive is not about running about like the proverbial headless chicken. The headless chicken dies; in fact, it's already dead. Instead you should gather your thoughts and take stock of the situation; this alone is being proactive. Make or agree on a plan, but be flexible as to how you achieve it.

Seizing the opportunity and collecting good vine. This could be useful for all manner of things – B-PRO!

Resourceful

Almost all environments provide the necessary materials for survival. Resourcefulness is about using what's around and on you to your advantage, and to support your efforts to survive, travel, protect and get rescued. Any equipment you have with you is an advantage and should be valued.

Use all available materials to your advantage. I recall a time when, as part of a small team of Commandos, we were obliged to survive a number of nights and days in the open with just the limited clothes we had on. The nights were cold and wet. We huddled together for warmth, built overhead cover and stuffed ferns and grass down our clothes and all around our bodies for insulation. We may have looked overweight, but we were warm!

If you're with a wrecked mode of transport, use what you can to create a bigger 'footprint' of your location, and to enhance the main elements needed for survival: water, rescue, protection, food, fire and navigation. Place these in whatever order suits your needs and, more importantly, the environment. Resourcefulness promotes success.

Opportunistic

Seize the moment or be prepared to seize the moment. Opportunities for rescue, food, water, protection, fire and navigation may present themselves at the unlikeliest of moments. These elements of survival may also be some time or distance away and form part of your survival plan. In either case be 'at the ready' and fully prepared to jump on any of these opportunities. It's they who strike first that will prevail. As soon as you're thrust into a survival situation, look for opportunities in your immediate area that will support the key elements of survival. It may be that the dread of what initially seems a desperate situation can be relieved by making positive use of an early opportunity.

Use the power of teamwork to find opportunities that may not have revealed themselves to you. No one person will have all the answers. A good, positively functioning team can increase the chance of finding opportunities that will aid survival.

Opportunists defy desperation and cultivate chance.

Lost

It's possible to get lost when travelling, to lose awareness of your location, or to find yourself in an unplanned location where you weren't expecting to be. Disorientation can be scary. Before deliberately entering an extreme environment or departing on a journey in the wilderness, leave a rough plan of your intended itinerary with someone. Even if you're in a familiar area, tell someone where you're going. Take a mobile phone that's fully charged. Have it switched off unless you need it. When travelling, make regular map and location checks. Guard your map and compass as valuable and indispensable survival resources.

If you don't have a map and compass and are entering terrain that may disorientate you, then 'way mark' your route. This means that the route you've travelled can be reversed to your last known location. Way marking your route is about making the natural look unnatural. This can be done by:

- Piling stones and rocks into cairns.
- Snapping small trees at about chest height so that they catch your eye and the fresh break is visible.
- Turning over large leaves so that the paler underside contrasts with the darker upper side of the surrounding foliage.
- Cutting large sections of bark from a living tree.
- Cutting nicks and chevrons into the bark of living trees.
- Placing flags and/or marker sticks if the resources are available.
- Noting key natural land features that are distinct. For example: obvious large trees, river junctions, distinctly shaped hills and mountains, waterfalls and large boulders.

Turn over a leaf to mark your route.

Even in the arctic wastes, the sun is an excellent indicator of direction.

Ensure your way marks are visible when you turn to follow them back – for instance, markings in the bark of a tree should be made on the side of your preferred direction.

Don't leave marks that can be affected by the elements. For instance, shapes made in the snow will disappear over time.

If you get lost:

- STOP. Don't keep wandering aimlessly – things will only get worse and your anxiety level will rise. Conserve your energy.
- If the weather has disorientated you then build a shelter and wait for an improvement in the weather to reorientate yourself.
- If you've made way marks then retrace them to your last known position.
- Use the techniques described in Chapter 2 to orientate yourself.
- If you're in a team get a consensus on your location. Get everyone to try and establish their position and use a 'unit average' to determine your approximate location.
- If necessary, get to a high point to see the terrain about you. This can sometimes be achieved by climbing a tree.

ESSENTIAL EQUIPMENT

Whether you are in the hottest or coldest climates, having purchased or improvised protective equipment and clothing will save your life. We are all constantly bombarded by the environment when we step outside. We may all cope in the short term but survival can often mean you are in it for the medium to long haul. It is essential to have some understanding of the effects of the environment on the body. It is also key to know how materials, fabrics and equipment offer some protection against the elements. Armed with information on both these factors, you will be able to select or improvise essential equipment.

Essential Equipment

Choosing the most appropriate equipment for any journey or expedition can appear daunting. Surviving in challenging environments requires both good use of the essential equipment that you've chosen to take with you, and making the best use of your natural surroundings.

First consider the basic factors that will affect both the amount and type of equipment you pack:

- **Budget** – can you spend what it takes? Duration of the expedition – how long do you plan to be away?
- **Type of expedition** – is your expedition by foot, land transport or boat?
- **Location** – would you take thermal underclothes to the jungle, or flimsy tents to the Arctic?
- **Weather conditions** – how much are local weather conditions likely to vary?

Keep it simple and functional.

- **Team size** – the team size will mean some equipment can be carried by one person and used by all.
- **Medical support** – this could be internal or external. External is whatever medical support has been arranged 'in country' to be called upon, internal is what you take with you. What level of knowledge do you require for your medical plans?
- **Fitness** – your fitness will enable you to take on greater challenges in more remote environments and for longer periods, both of which may require giving more thought to what you take.

If you're fit and reasonably experienced, don't think that you can therefore carry more equipment. I've seen capable, super-fit people suffer because they've been carrying too much equipment and tried to go too fast. If you try to do this in the Arctic, for example, you'll sweat, and sweating too much in cold environments can seriously wick your body heat away, leading to hypothermia.

Our ancestors travelled and survived in extreme environments with none of our modern-day protection from the elements. All they had were natural materials derived from the harvest or the hunt.

Today, equipment designed for outdoor environments is varied and specific. Far fewer natural fibres tend to be used and this has allowed equipment to become more versatile and lightweight. But planning your equipment well doesn't necessarily mean discounting less than up-to-the-minute materials. Arguably, modern equipment and clothing aren't always more effective or robust than the equipment of our ancestors.

When deciding to take equipment into any environment to sustain yourself, and possibly others, there are a few basic rules that need to be observed:

- **Protection** – the clothing and equipment you select should protect you from the environment in which you're operating. Some materials will work better in specific environments than others.
- **Durability** – clothing and equipment must be able to withstand intense conditions over long periods of time, usually without the opportunity for it to be repaired or washed effectively.

In cold climates, so you don't sweat too much, start with minimal layers. Add layers as you require.

- **Multi-functionality** – it's always worth considering clothing and equipment that has the potential for more than one use; this increases the effectiveness of the item and reduces the load you carry. For instance, a compressed foam sleeping mat can have a small section cut off to use as insulation under your cooker when cooking on ice and snow; it can be used as extra insoles for your boots; and foam smokes well when you need to do any signalling.
- **Weight** – modern clothing and equipment is generally much lighter than in the past. Choose items that are light but don't compromise their durability, effectiveness or protection. Taking too much equipment that's heavy and ineffective reduces your ability to function.
- **Simplicity** – too many zips, straps and fasteners increase the possibility of breakage. All that's required is simple, fit-to-function clothing and equipment, elementary and uncomplicated.

• WISE WORDS •

I spent three months in Greenland re-enacting Captain Scott's journey to the South Pole, in conditions similar to those of Antarctica. Our team travelled and lived in period clothing, slept in period tents and ate period food. We used boots, sleeping bags and gloves all made from reindeer skin. We had tweed trousers, canvas tents and bamboo tent poles in which to endure months of freezing conditions and storms. Our film crew had modern, up-to-date equipment and food. During one major three-day Greenland storm called a pittorach we were pinned down and could hardly leave our canvas tent. But when the storm subsided the only damage that had been sustained was a small tear in the green canvas, whereas the modern tents of the film crew were trashed. Even in temperatures as low as minus 50° we never got really cold.

Survival pack

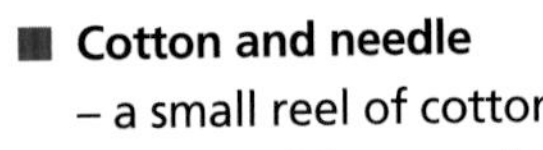

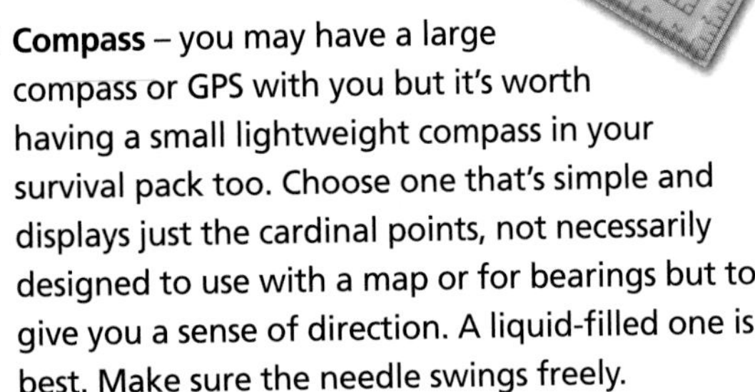

Keep it simple, small and waterproof. For example, in the military we would pack our first line survival equipment in a tobacco tin, of which the inside of the lid was polished to double as a signalling mirror. Essentials are:

- **Compass** – you may have a large compass or GPS with you but it's worth having a small lightweight compass in your survival pack too. Choose one that's simple and displays just the cardinal points, not necessarily designed to use with a map or for bearings but to give you a sense of direction. A liquid-filled one is best. Make sure the needle swings freely.
- **Flint and striker** – these can be used when it's raining, but you'll need cover for your fire. Make sure you've removed the protective paint off the flint after purchase. You may even be able to discard the striker, as a knife can be used to the same effect.

- **Condom** – as well as keeping tinder dry, a heavy-duty condom can protect an injury (particularly to a finger or toe). A condom will hold about 1.5 litres of fluid. It can be used as the rubber for a small catapult too.

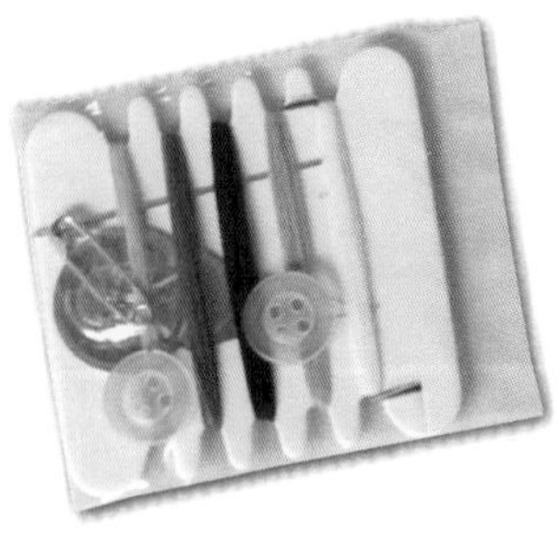

- **Cotton and needle** – a small reel of cotton is required for mending material and to fabricate small rodent snares. The needle can be used to remove splinters before any infection sets in. Needles can be used as hooks too. It's even possible to magnetise a needle to point north.
- **Small candle and matches** – using a candle saves precious matches. Melting a small amount of wax on to match heads will waterproof them (break the wax off before you strike the match). A candle is also useful to start fires and provides a constant light source should you need it.

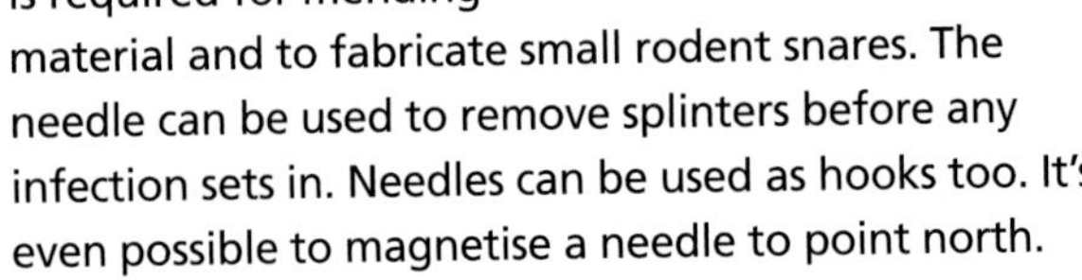

- **Tampon** – tampons often come wrapped in plastic so are waterproof until the plastic is removed. The compact yet fine cotton takes a spark well and makes good tinder. Designed to absorb liquid, they're also useful as a wound dressing.
- **Water sterilisation** – it's best to carry the tablets rather than filter pumps, as tablets are lighter and there's less to go wrong! One small tablet will sterilise about a litre of water, so budget accordingly. Be mindful that the sterilisation will kill bacteria but won't eliminate contaminants such as oil. Purified water will taste of chlorine, but at least it's drinkable.
- **Razor blades** – a razor blade or two will be useful for medical purposes and for some fine skinning, gutting and cutting. Tape the sharp edges for protection. Use them on materials and body parts that won't blunt them too much, so prolonging the life of the blade. If necessary, fabricate a handle out of wood.
- **Wire saw** – these are tough and can cut through bone, wood and other materials. A wire saw will cut through a 4–5in diameter branch, although harder woods may be less forgiving. The saw can be used as a snare by passing one end through the ring on the opposite end.
- **Whistle** – a loud whistle is useful for attracting attention, and for keeping track of other members of your party. A plastic whistle won't rust. The range of the whistle will vary depending on conditions and terrain, but line-of-sight on a clear day will give you an approximate range of a kilometre.

- **Fish hooks and gut** – pack small to medium hooks as you'll be able to catch medium to moderately large fish with these: large hooks will only be good for large fish. A good length of gut is also useful, for snares and for possible suturing of a wound.
- **Wire** – brass wire that's thin and flexible is useful for a range of applications but mainly for snares. Take as much as possible and cut it to different lengths. Always have one long section of a metre or two.
- **Para cord** – para cord (parachute cord) is extremely useful and the more you can take the better. It can be used for snares, lashings for shelter, and repairs. The cord can be stripped down for other uses such as fish line and alarms. It's very strong, with a breaking strain of around 250kg. Use black or green cord for camouflage.
- **Magnifying glass** – although it has its limitations (you need sunlight), a small lens helps in fire lighting. It's also useful for treating wounds. Many compasses include a magnifying glass to magnify small detail on maps, and I've used this to start fires on a number of occasions. It does take some patience to get the heat of the light intense enough, but it does work.
- **Head torch or mini-light** – modern head torches are light and compact and deliver a good spread of light. They're useful for travelling at night, for hunting in caves and for signalling. If you're packing your survival kit then look for small 'finger-sized' lights or even smaller ones that take wrist watch batteries. Although more expensive, lithium batteries work the best and last the longest. Many head torches have different lighting applications – a bigger and stronger spread of light will need more power. Take spare batteries as necessary, and remember that cold conditions limit the life of batteries.
- **Butterfly sutures** – these take up no space and are extremely useful to close a wound and limit infection. Take at least 20.

Additional items

Adapt and modify your survival tin or pack to suit the environment or your needs. The list above will apply to any environment and is suggested as the standard minimum for any situation. Other small non-essential items that are undoubtedly useful include:

- **Waterproof notebook and a pencil** – useful for recording, planning and sketching.
- **Altimeter and barometer** – many outdoor watches have these functions, and are usually very accurate. They usually have to be calibrated at known heights whilst you're on your journey. Since they generally derive altitude from air pressure, readings may be less accurate in changeable weather systems.
- **Global Positioning System (GPS)** – extremely accurate, but, like any complex equipment, subject to breakage.
- **Zip ties and duct tape** – these are useful for lashing and repairing. Use zip ties that can be released once they've been used.
- **Tin mug** – this is multi-functional. You can boil water in it, eat from it, cook in it and drink from it.
- **Plastic spoon** – this is all you need to feed yourself with; you'll have a bush knife for cutting anyway.
- **Sunglasses** – with a high UV protection rate. Wraparound shades are best for eliminating refracted sunlight.
- **Hat** – a sun hat or baseball cap provide good protection for the face and for the head, especially if you're thinning on top!
- **Lip salve and sun lotion** – lips are very exposed to the elements, so reapply a high-protection salve frequently. Apply lotion to head, neck, any exposed areas. Harsh UV light in sunny, snowy or icy conditions will affect areas of the body you wouldn't think of – I've had sunburn inside my nostrils, on the backs of my ears and under my chin.

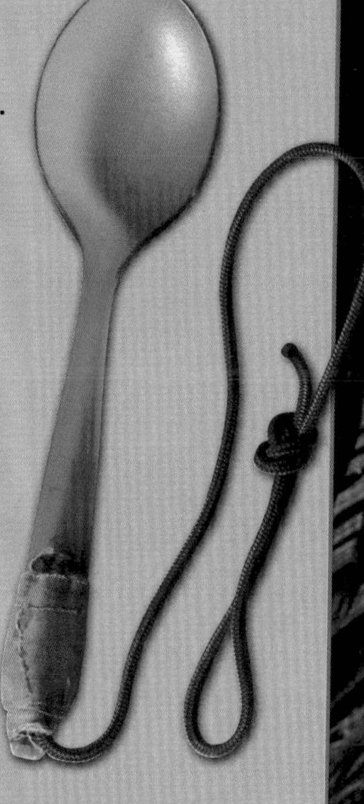

Rucksacks

Choose a rucksack that will be functional in your intended environment. As with all equipment, keep it simple. It's worth considering a rucksack that has a good few external pouches. These pouches can be used to carry essentials for the day: food, navigational equipment, water and protective clothing or equipment. The inside of your rucksack can then be used for overnight equipment – spare clothing, cooker, first aid kit and further food.

Pick a suitable-sized rucksack to just meet your needs. If you buy too big a rucksack you'll just fill it up with equipment that you probably won't use. Make sure it fits well and sits comfortably on your back. You want it to be high up your back rather than low. A low-slung rucksack causes you to lean too far forward to counter the weight: an inefficient and uncomfortable position.

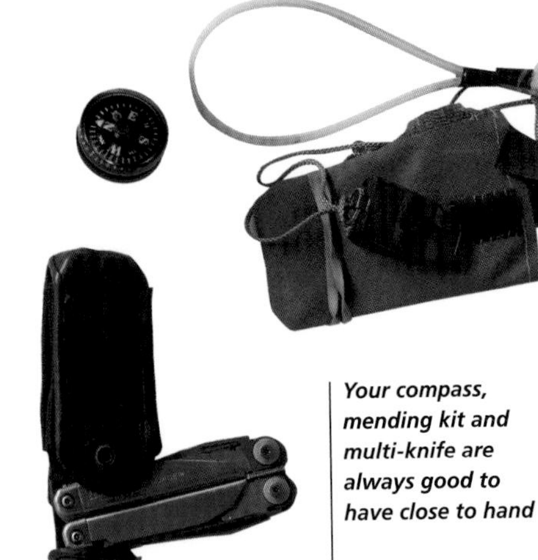

Your compass, mending kit and multi-knife are always good to have close to hand

Have some food that is easily accessible for the day's work and to graze on

Pack less essential daily equipment deep in your rucksack but have waterproofs at the top ready to go!

If you carry one lighter – then take two – always essential!

Keep awkward-shaped objects and fuel in the outer pouches

Packing your rucksack

Spend time packing your rucksack well, efficiently and appropriately. You'll be glad you did!

- Pack your rucksack with the lightest items at the bottom and the heavier items central and towards the top. Having all the weight at the bottom or on side will cause you to lean awkwardly.
- Waterproof everything regardless of the climate – it can rain even in the desert. Waterproof some items individually or in blocks (for instance, have spare clothing waterproofed in one sealed bag and your sleeping bag in another). Use good quality resealable bags, not plastic shopping bags!
- Pack useful items likely to be needed during the day in the outside pouches. Waterproof these if necessary.
- Make sure fuel is in an outside pouch.
- Pack your rucksack so that all the space is filled with the equipment you have. Aim not to have empty spaces underneath what you've packed on top.
- Don't hang items on the outside: they can be snagged and pulled off. Everything that you have is essential, so losing anything at all is not an option.

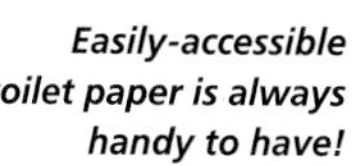

Easily-accessible toilet paper is always handy to have!

Know where your head torch is – nightfall can happen very quickly

Keep water, safety kit and the odd luxury in a handy place

Water carriers

The inside of a wine box is a great and robust carrier and collector

Water is one of the single most important commodities in any environment. Without it you die very quickly. Choose a good water carrier that won't split or break. Carry a couple of water containers, especially in hotter more humid environments. The average person will need at least four litres a day to stay in good shape. Use a container with a large opening that's easy to fill should you come across a water source.

Insulate water containers to prevent freezing in cold climates. On a number of occasions I've seen individuals curse at the frozen water tube coming from their camelback water container. The small amount of water in the exposed drinking tube freezes easily, and you're then carrying water around that you can't drink. So insulate the tube with the adhesive grip tape used for tennis and squash racket handles.

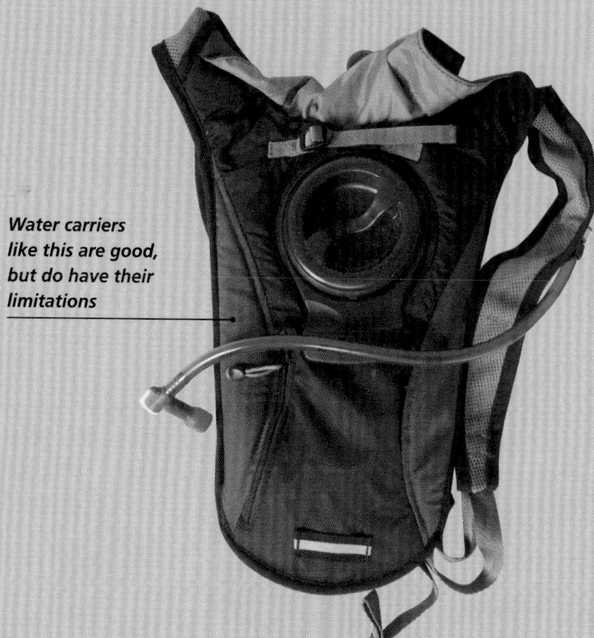

Water carriers like this are good, but do have their limitations

Overhead cover

There are no climates in which overhead cover won't be at least useful to counter the depleting effects of the elements; usually it'll be a life-saver.

Tents

Tents provide the best all-round protection; but even though modern tent materials are light and strong they're still a noticeable extra weight to carry. They may also need mending after a time – zips may fail, holes get burnt or poles bent – and conditions can sometimes make it very difficult to perform any repairs. Make sure your tent has a built-in groundsheet and adequate stowage space inside.

A lightweight tent will provide some shelter in extreme conditions, but beware of relying on a low-rated tent.

Ponchos

If well placed and well erected, with a good spine and well-secured sides, an overhead cover the size of a poncho will offer some protection against the wind and keep off non-driving rain. If you place your overhead cover in a well-selected location with natural cover at the sides and above, the shelter will then become adequate against driving rain and wind. Buy ponchos that clip or button together.

During my military career it was important to be able to operate for weeks whilst only having a lightweight poncho for overhead protection. It was always uncomfortable, unpleasant and challenging, and nights could be long and wet, but though it was a crude form of protection it did allow you to 'lie up' for short periods of time.

In fact poncho bivouacs can be very versatile; they're light, easily packed and very quick to erect if the terrain and foliage allow:

- They can be stretched out flat and close to the ground so you can just crawl underneath. Have the cover at a slight angle so the rain runs off, or rig a line from the centre of the cover to an overhead attachment such as a branch to lift the centre up slightly.

Ponchos can provide quick, simple and lightweight protection – but they do have their limitations.

A well-placed and constructed hammock can provide a dry and comfortable place to shelter.

- One edge can be fixed to the top of a suitable bank whilst the other is fixed close to the ground. This offers natural shelter on one side and a good incline for rain to run off.
- The use of bungee straps on attachment points can provide flexibility and speed in construction.
- A couple of three-foot lightweight tent poles will allow you to erect reasonable overhead cover in areas devoid of trees and natural banks. Use the poles at either end and create a tent-like shelter from your poncho. Take six to eight light pegs for the sides and corners.
- Beware of constructing your overhead cover over a natural dip – if it rains the dip will probably accumulate water.
- If there are two of you, clipping two ponchos together allows for a bigger area to be covered.

Disadvantages:

- Ponchos don't provide completely enclosed protection.
- They provide no extra warmth and are therefore of limited use in cold conditions.
- Strong winds will affect you, as the ends and sides are open.
- It's difficult to stay completely dry, especially in driving rain.
- They're only good for one person unless you carry two for yourself.
- Bugs, beasts and insects can easily get in.

Hammocks

These are the best form of shelter in a jungle environment, since it's important to get off the jungle floor at night away from the bugs, insects and beasts. Hammocks are lightweight and easy to erect. Many come with an integral overhead cover that can be pulled out and attached to surrounding trees, but if not then use your poncho for overhead protection. When it rains in the jungle you'll know it!

• WISE WORDS •

On many occasions I've lived for short periods in a tent holding one more person than the manufacturers recommend. In an effort to cut down on weight and travel faster I've taken a two-person tent for three. If your tent drills, routines and personal administration are excellent then this can work.

Footwear

I've learnt from years of Commando 'yomping' in many environments that you'll not get anywhere without a good set of feet. Look after your feet and they'll look after you and get you places.

There are many good brands of boots on the market but many people suffer years of pain and hard slog to find the ones that work best for them. Break your boots in well before you head out on a long trip, especially if you're walking long distances. Make sure the sole will give the grip you require. Vibram soles give good grip on any surface, and especially on wet rock.

There are specific boots for every environment, so search around for a specialist pair. Some considerations for specific environments are:

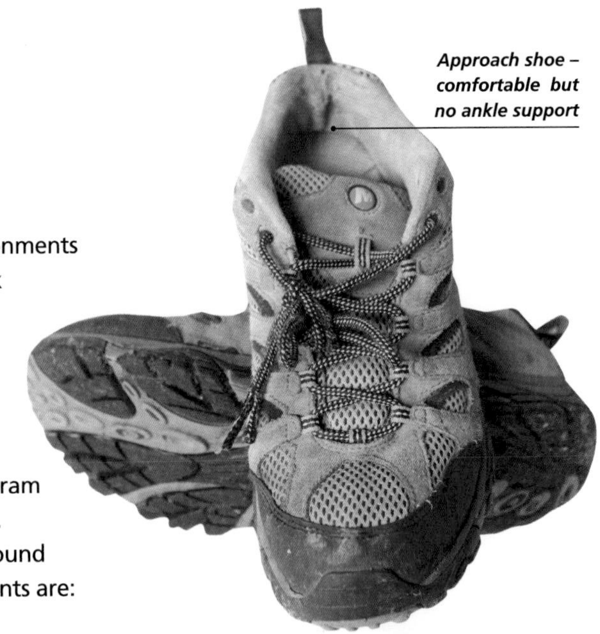

Approach shoe – comfortable but no ankle support

Arctic

Buy a boot that's a size and a half too big. This will allow you to get two pairs of socks on and to put in an extra thermal insole. Buy a boot with a good Vibram sole. It's useful to have an easy, practical and quick lacing system that can be undertaken successfully while you're wearing gloves. A double tongue gives comfort, protection and warmth. Arctic boots should have good ankle support and possibly be able to take a crampon.

Integral gaiters – useful for keeping the snow out and the warmth in

Thick thermal lining and a double boot

High uppers keep most mud out

Wide, deep studs provide grip in mud and on wet ground

Jungle

Look to have high ankle support and vent holes at the in-step to allow water out. Jungle boots are often made of soft, treated canvas. This provides a tight seal around the ankle without restricting while still allowing movement and preventing the 'beasties' getting in!

The jungle sole allows wet mud to be pushed out from under the foot for better grip. Be aware that jungle boots and the sole can be extremely slippery on wet rock, and they're not good for climbing. Most things can rot quickly in the jungle too, so look after your boots and treat the leather.

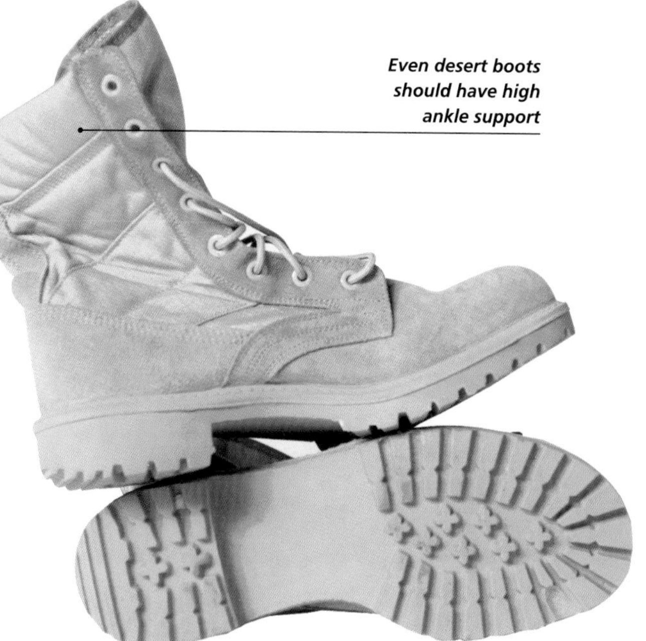

Desert

High ankle support and soft suede are good for desert boots. Ensure they have a reasonably stiff sole and are well sealed to stop the sand getting in as much as possible.

Temperate

Treated leather boots work well as do good ankle-supporting fabric boots, although in very wet, cold temperate conditions fabric boots won't always provide adequate protection. Always have good ankle support and a Vibram sole.

Seawater will rot boots very quickly, so if you're operating for long periods in or by the sea spend time treating your boots so that they look after you.

Socks

The choice of socks to match your needs is very important. The wrong sock made from the wrong fabric will make you suffer. As a rule you should never wear nylon socks in any environment: the fabric creates friction and in turn blisters. Nylon also offers very little in terms of warmth and function. Instead, choose wool and loop stitch socks that reach high up above the ankle. Loop stitch offers the best thermal qualities.

I wear a single pair of wool loop stitch socks in the jungle and desert. They're comfortable and they work. In the jungle your feet are going to be wet, so choose something that's comfortable when wet.

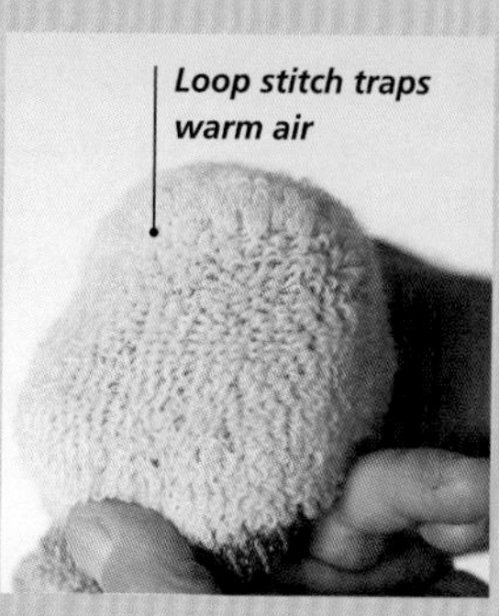

In Arctic conditions I tend to wear one thin base layer sock and then two pairs of wool loop stitch socks. Layering for the feet works well – it traps warm air between the layers as well as wicking perspiration away through the base layer to the next. This allows for a near dry sock next to the skin.

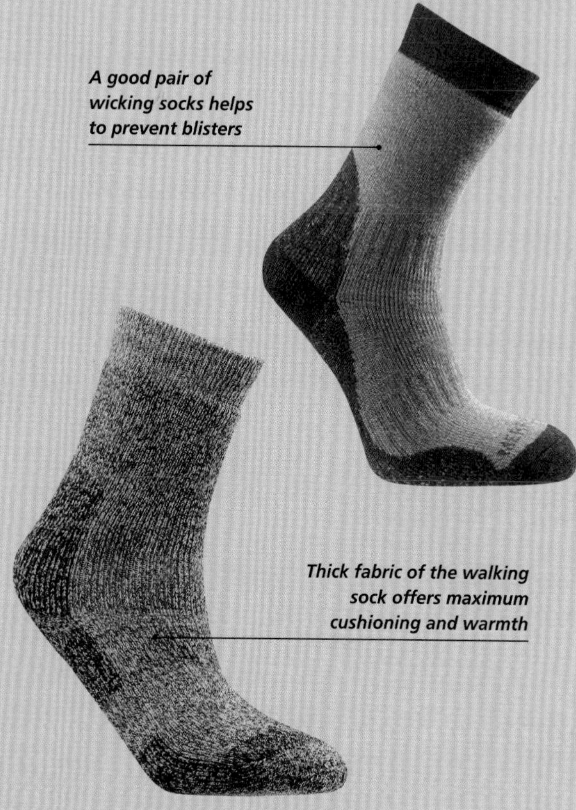

General clothing

Adhere to the following principles when selecting clothing for the climate you're expecting to face.

Extreme cold

- Choose natural fibres and fleece.
- Use the layer principle, so that warm air is trapped between the layers. It's better to have five thin layers than two thick ones.
- Don't have your clothing too tight fitting. You want warm air to be trapped in the cavities.
- Wear good thermal underpants.
- A good windproof outer layer limits the loss of the warm air you've generated.
- Wear a good hat or balaclava. Much body heat is lost through the head.
- Glove material should have windproof qualities. A lot of blood flows through the wrists to the hands, so make sure these are also covered and protected by your gloves and jacket.

Layering

Base layer

Thin, natural fibres that are comfortable and wick away perspiration, including socks as a base layer

Mid layer

Loose fitting and ventable mid layers that are a little thicker than the base. Loop stitch socks.

Outer bottom layer

Loose fitting, windproof and waterproof bottom layer. Ideally, zips should run the length of the leg so they can be put on with boots on.

Outer top layer

Strong, windproof and ventable. Top layer that is well fitting

Waterproof layer

Wear a loose, wind and waterproof top layer with a large hood and accessible, zipped pockets.

Base layer

Mid layer

Jungle

- Wear baggy, loose-fitting clothes so that the air can flow around your body.
- Choose tough material that won't tear easily. A canvas type material works best.
- All cuffs should be sealable, to keep out the beasties!
- Choose clothing that's quick-drying. You will get wet!

Desert

- Wear baggy, loose-fitting clothes so that the air can flow around your body.
- Choose colours that reflect light.
- Have something warm to wear at night. Desert nights can be very cold.
- Wear good headgear that protects your neck, ears and nose from the sun.

Clothes that dry out quickly are advisable.

Outer bottom layer	Outer top layer	Waterproof layer

Sleeping bags

There's a vast range of sleeping bags on the market from which the survivalist can choose. The filling will be either a natural fibre (eg duck or goose down) or synthetic (eg holofill).

A good 'stuff-sack' allows you to pack and compress the sleeping bag down to its smallest possible size, but, if possible, you should try to air your sleeping bag as often as you can. This will dry it through and keep the filling 'puffy' for maximum effectiveness.

Most sleeping bags will have information on how many seasons they operate effectively in: 'one season' means summer only; 'four seasons' includes winter. For more extreme temperatures labelling will indicate to what low temperature the bag will function.

Natural fibres

Advantages:

- Warmer than synthetic materials.
- Lighter.
- Pack easier.
- More comfortable.

Disadvantages:

- Dysfunctional when wet.
- Hard to dry.
- Filling can drop to the outer edges, leaving areas with no down.
- Often need airing for the best possible performance.
- A rip in the lining can leave a tent full of feathers.

Synthetic fibres

Advantages

- The fill doesn't shift or drop so doesn't leave cold gaps.
- Easy to clean and maintain.
- Continues to perform even when wet.
- A tear in the lining will not leave your tent full of fibres.

Disadvantages:

- Bulky and harder to pack.
- Less comfortable.

Large area to cover your head

Draw cords to close gaps

Zip – robust and protected by insulation, only travelling down half the sleeping bag length

Small sized quilts separated by stitching gives even distribution of warmth

Large area for feet to breath and capture warmth

A further sleeping system can include a bivouac bag that acts as an external barrier, and a roll mat for comfort and insulation. Bivouac bags are lightweight and pack down to a reasonable size, but if you're going to a very dry climate it may not be worth packing one. Although you may be confident that the environment you're entering has enough natural foliage to make a comfortable ground mattress unnecessary, most of your body heat is lost through the ground, so in cold climates a good insulating roll mat is essential. Avoid blowing too much moist air into an inflatable mattress in very cold conditions as it may later freeze.

In cold to extreme cold climates your chances of survival without a warm sleeping system are limited. It's the one thing that allows you to rest, warm up and shelter, so take care of it!

Taking food

Should you plan an expedition or journey to a challenging environment then food will be a critical factor in performance and morale. The environment you're venturing into will have an impact on the food you take along. For instance, if you take 'wet' food to a freezing environment it will freeze. Fuel energy is then required to defrost and cook it. So consider dehydrated or dry food in cold environments. Balance the food you take with your nutrition requirements, weight, size and age. Add some 'treats' of your own to boost morale and take the boredom out of a repetitive menu.

The food triangle

The food triangle shows the proportions of food groups the body needs to sustain itself

> **• WISE WORDS •**
>
> **As I mentioned earlier, I was once part of a team that re-enacted Captain Scott's ill-fated expedition to the South Pole for a television production. We journeyed on the Greenland Ice Cap using period equipment and clothing and following a diet very close to that of 1911. This included a main meal of Pemmican, an extremely high fat mixture that was so difficult to eat and digest it made many of the team wretch. We ate this for close to three months. Eating Pemmican day in and day out was very demanding and we rarely looked forward to dinner.**

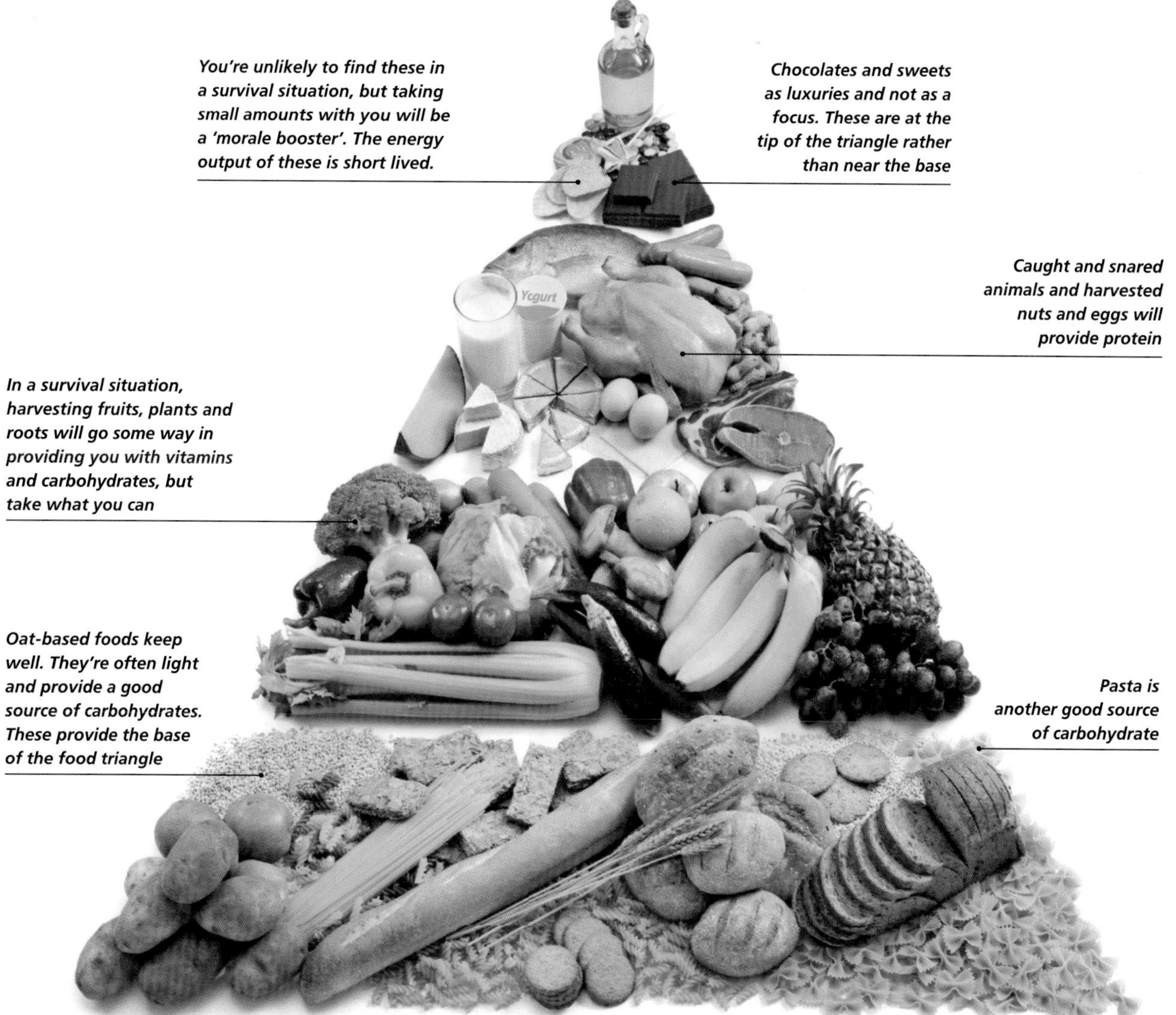

You're unlikely to find these in a survival situation, but taking small amounts with you will be a 'morale booster'. The energy output of these is short lived.

Chocolates and sweets as luxuries and not as a focus. These are at the tip of the triangle rather than near the base

Caught and snared animals and harvested nuts and eggs will provide protein

In a survival situation, harvesting fruits, plants and roots will go some way in providing you with vitamins and carbohydrates, but take what you can

Oat-based foods keep well. They're often light and provide a good source of carbohydrates. These provide the base of the food triangle

Pasta is another good source of carbohydrate

Cutting tools

A knife is an invaluable item in any survival situation. Having any sort of knife will make performing most tasks easier and will increase your chances of survival. A knife is without doubt one of the first items that comes into my mind when packing for any expedition, adventure or trip. Operating in an extreme environment or when on an expedition, a knife should always be close to hand. In all but a few cases I take only one knife, but I care for that knife and safeguard it. 'Have a knife, save a life.'

The jungle is the only environment in which I would carry a machete in addition to a smaller blade. In the mountains I would have a multi-blade knife with pliers. The pliers are useful to adjust crampons and touring skis, as well as for unlocking frozen karabiners.

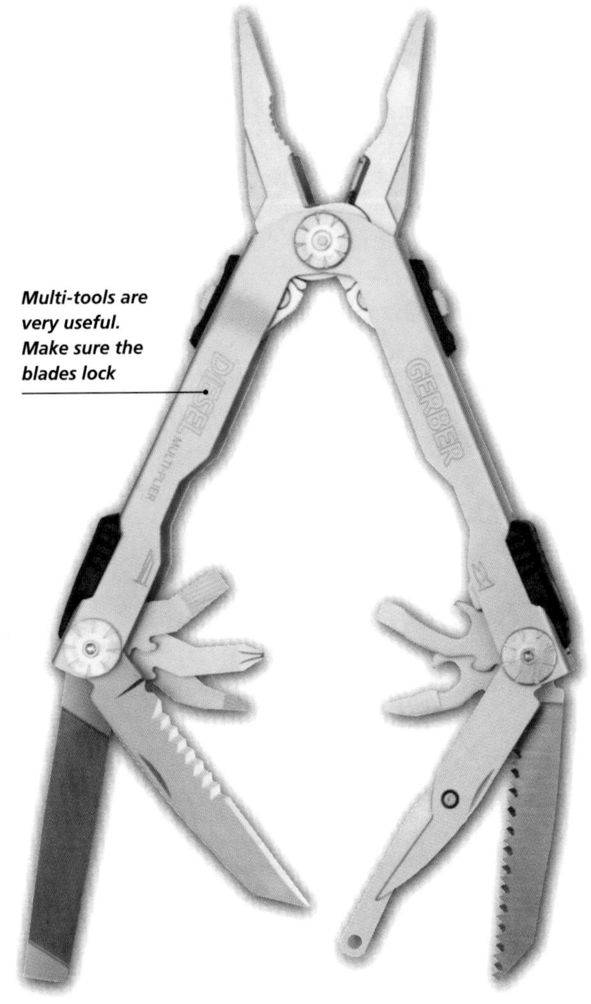

Multi-tools are very useful. Make sure the blades lock

Choosing a knife

There are many knives on the market, but beware showy knives with huge blades or overcrowded with too many functions: these can become rapidly less functional after sustained periods of hard use, and how much use is a corkscrew in a survival situation anyway? Simplicity is often the key, so choose a knife that's robust and functional; one that will hold its

Serrated edge – good for cutting rope

Good solid blade that doesn't corrode easily

Protective scabbard that locks the knife/ blade when housed

Well-constructed body that locks the blade in position

Tether hole

Well-shaped constructed handle that grips well and is non-slip

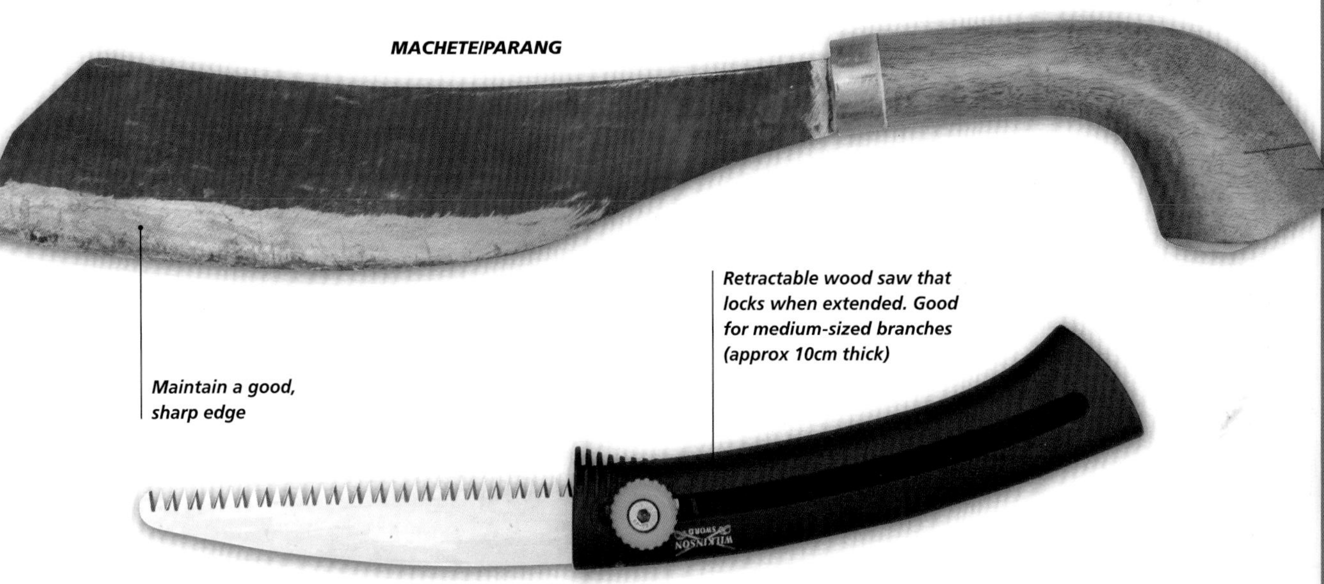

edge for a good period. A medium-length blade is usually enough for most eventualities. That said, any knife is better than nothing.

Before you purchase a knife, check that it feels comfortable in your hand. This is important, as prolonged use can cause blisters. Folding knives are valuable as they can be safely stored, but they're also intrinsically weaker, as the blade doesn't extend into the handle. Make sure the blade locks into position when it's open – some knives don't, and can collapse in use and cause serious injury.

The opening and closing of the blade should feel secure, and a rubber outer is often better than plastic. Check the blade is easy to open as this could be a factor with cold hands. Also ensure the knife has a strong attachment point for a tether. Fixed blades need to have a good sheath and a means of securing the knife inside it.

A serrated edge on all or part of the knife is sometimes useful to take the scales off fish, but in a survival situation you won't be confining your diet to fish, so you need a blade that can cut anything. Again, serrated edges can cut fibrous plants and rope but they're difficult to sharpen in the great outdoors. Having a miniature saw is a more practical option, especially if you're in an environment where you'll need to cut medium-sized branches and trees. If you do take a miniature saw you should still also have a knife.

If you're heading for the jungle, then in addition to a knife a machete or parang is essential. You're best buying these 'in country'. A wooden handle is best and the blade need not be any longer than about 30cm. The shape gives some protection to the hand, as when hacking the blade comes into contact with what you're about to cut before your hand does. You can also cut with some finesse by using the narrow part of the blade where it meets the handle.

Stainless steel blades don't corrode easily but you'll not get as good an edge as with other metals. However, other metals may corrode quicker. (See Chapter 3 for information on safely using knives).

WARNING!

It is the responsibility of each individual to understand and be aware of the law of the land regarding the use and carrying of knives. Not all sharp things are illegal and those knives that are ideal for the purposes described in this book should not contravene any laws. However, be sensible and mindful when you purchase a knife for practical survival and journeys to extreme environments. A flick knife – banned in the UK – is in any case of little use in a survival situation. Nor is a 12in blade much good for a day foraging in the local forest. Use common sense.

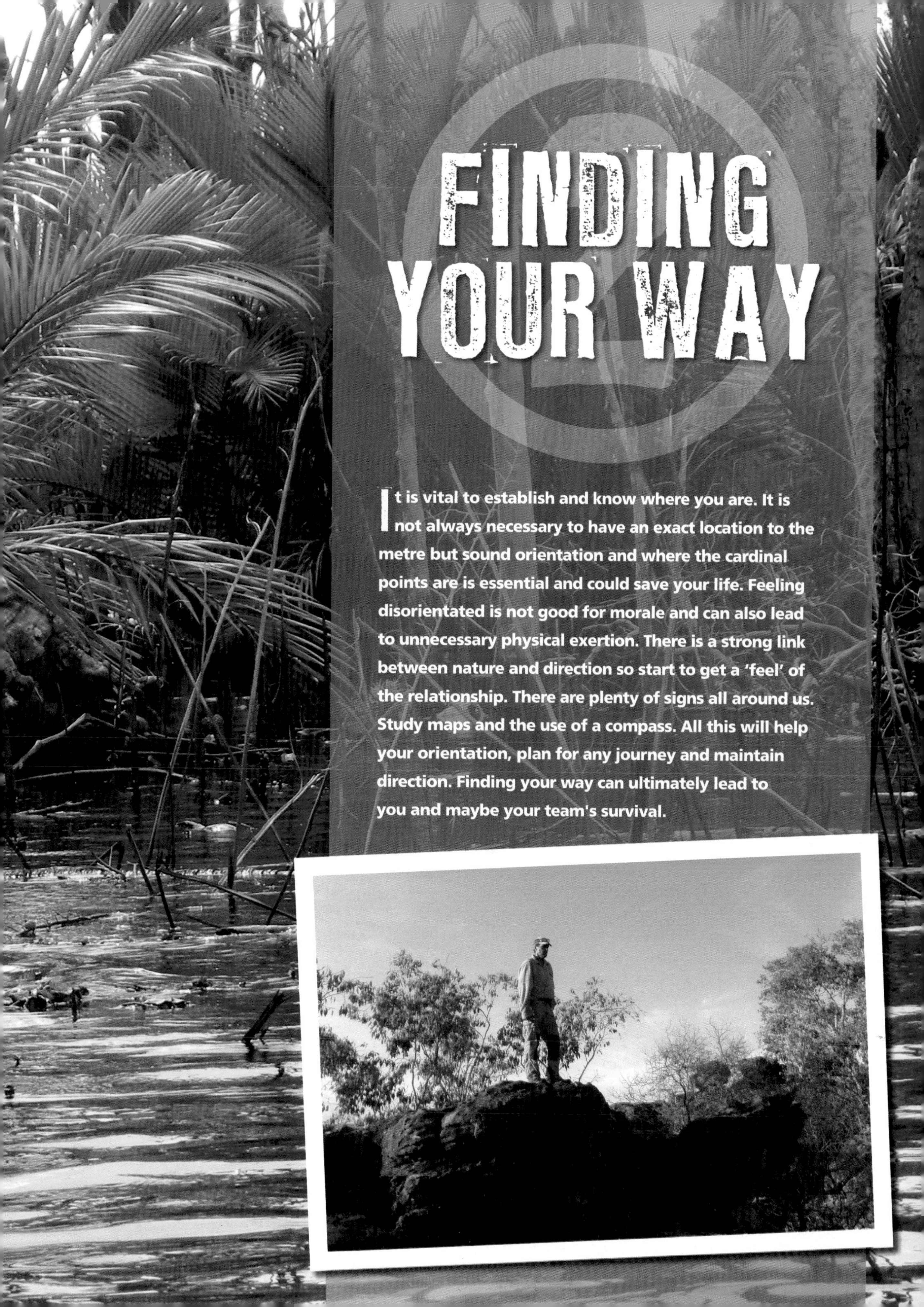

FINDING YOUR WAY

It is vital to establish and know where you are. It is not always necessary to have an exact location to the metre but sound orientation and where the cardinal points are is essential and could save your life. Feeling disorientated is not good for morale and can also lead to unnecessary physical exertion. There is a strong link between nature and direction so start to get a 'feel' of the relationship. There are plenty of signs all around us. Study maps and the use of a compass. All this will help your orientation, plan for any journey and maintain direction. Finding your way can ultimately lead to you and maybe your team's survival.

Maps and map-reading

A map is a bird's eye view of a piece of land drawn to scale. Study your map well and understand the symbols and markings. Check the scale. Commonly maps use a 1:50,000 scale, meaning that a centimetre on the map represents 500m on the ground. Maps for specific purposes may use a very different scale, but there will always be a black scale bar on the map – in miles and kilometres – and you should use this when measuring distance.

Contour lines (usually drawn in brown) link points with the same altitude: they therefore show relief. The closer the contours are, the steeper the ground will be, as each contour marks the vertical elevation; sea level is the zero contour. The intervals between each contour can

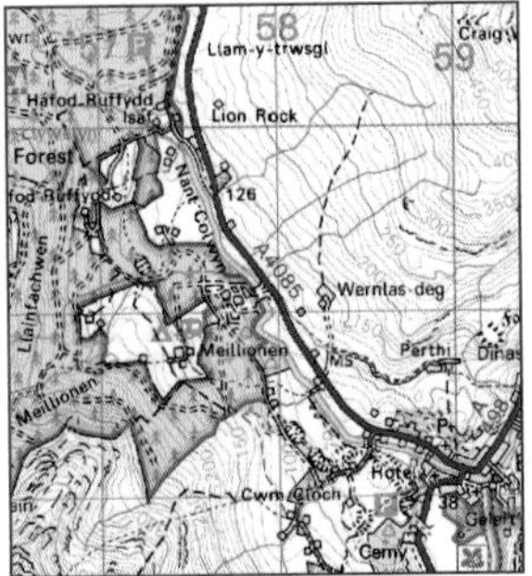

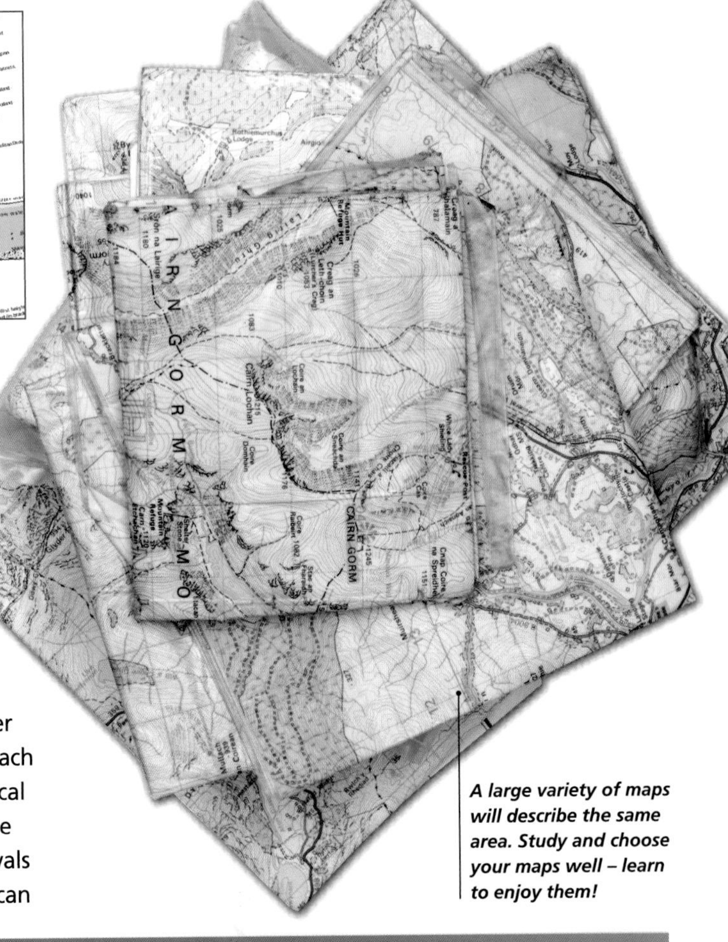

A large variety of maps will describe the same area. Study and choose your maps well – learn to enjoy them!

Survival tips

- Fold your map in such a way as to show only the area in which you intend to move: this makes handling the map easier and focuses your attention on the essentials. It may be that you can fold your map down to a 15–20cm square.
- Cut off any blank or non-essential paper.
- Waterproof your map well. A soggy map is useless and could cost you dearly.
- If you're in a team ensure that each individual has a map, and carry a spare.
- Never put your map down on the ground to perform another task. One gust of wind and you could lose it.
- Always secure your map.
- Continually study maps. This is the best way to become familiar with them.

vary from map to map, so check the map key. Every fifth contour will be drawn as a thicker line with the elevation indicated on it. This is an 'index contour'.

Most maps are marked with grid lines. These are thin black lines crossing the map from left to right and top to bottom, breaking it up into uniform squares. The lines running to the top of the map are pointing to grid north. This is not magnetic north and these lines should predominantly be used only to plot grid references and to set your compass.

• WISE WORDS •

In the Second World War, Allied military pilots carried silk maps of the enemy territory over which they were flying in case they were shot down and needed to find their way to safety. The maps were often sewn into the linings of the pilots' flying jackets to conceal them from enemy soldiers if they were captured.

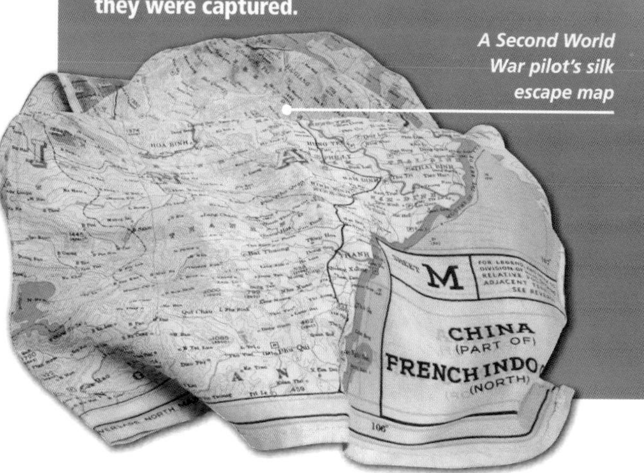

A Second World War pilot's silk escape map

Making your own map

In a survival situation where you're caught out map-less, consider making your own. Once you've established availability of the essentials – water, shelter, food and protection – consider plotting potential rescue routes. Should you abandon your base for any length of time, in search of food, water or rescue, leave a map or 'model' at your base for anyone who may come across it. Also leave something that indicates when you expect to return.

Try to get to as high a vantage point as possible and note down key landmarks, obstacles, dangers and life-saving recourses. Make a drawing on paper whenever possible but always ensure you have a good mental map inside your head before you depart.

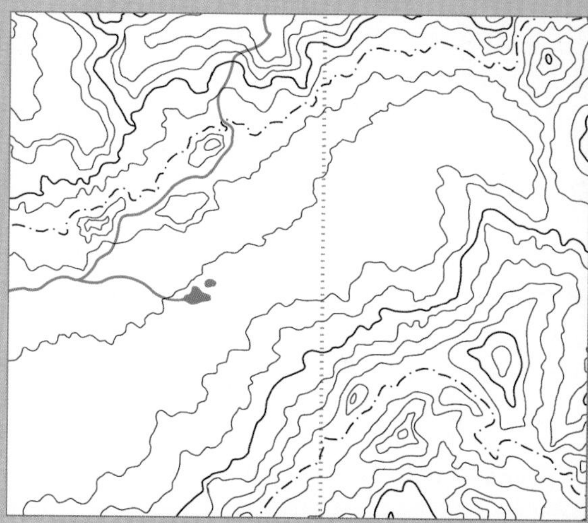

- Work out your own scale and estimate distances.
- Mark key features and approximate altitudes.
- Create some approximate contour lines.
- Mark rivers, obstacles, cliffs, forests and unusual features such as huge trees.
- Mark water, food and recourse locations.

In the military we would generally use such natural features to create a 'model', piling up soil to represent relief, using strips of vine to represent river courses, piles of small stones as cliffs, green leaves as forests and small sticks to denote the shapes of key features. This was made on the ground and was crudely to scale. The model was destroyed post-brief, but in a survival situation you could keep it and add to it as you discover more.

Compass and bearings

Accurate use of a compass (particularly in conjunction with a map) will allow you to navigate and travel efficiently. Compasses come in all shapes, sizes and models so choose one that best suits your needs. Keep it simple but ensure it has key luminous features for use at night. The main needle will usually have one end tipped red – this will always point to magnetic north and is the key to your navigational accuracy. When using your compass be aware of influences that can disrupt the needle and affect its accuracy. These include:

- Anything that is magnetised.
- Some metals.
- Some rock types that have high iron content.
- Some electrical sources.

Taking a bearing

- On the map, place the side of the compass along the line you want to travel. The direction of travel arrow must be pointing the way you're going.
- Rotate the bevel so that the lines of orientation and the north pointer on the lines point to grid north. Use the grid north lines to set the bevel accurately.
- Take the compass off and add the magnetic variation if necessary. Currently in the UK and Europe this is approximately 4°. (Magnetic variation is the angular difference between true north, magnetic north and grid north. All good maps will have a variation diagram on the map.)
- Hold the compass flat and into your stomach so that you're looking directly down on to it.
- Turn your body until the magnetic north needle aligns with the north pointer on the orientating lines marked on the base of the bevel.
- The arrow of direction is the line you travel on. Look directly up and pick a feature that won't move and isn't too far away. Walk to it, then hold the compass to your stomach and turn to repeat the process.

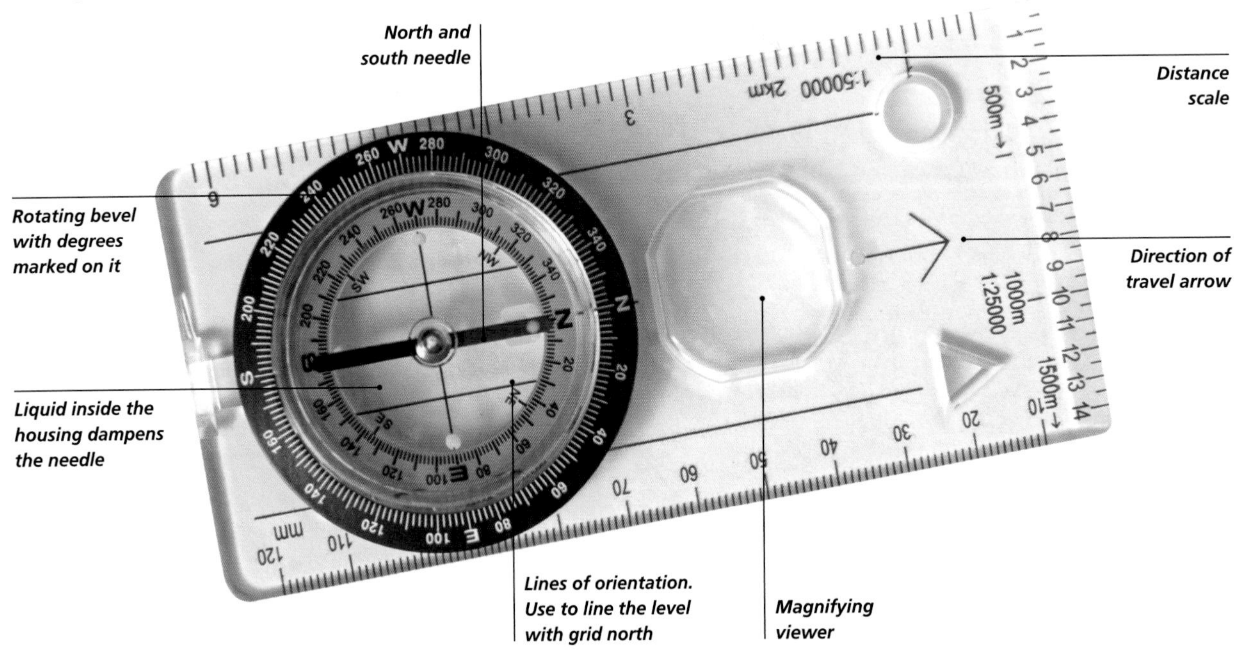

A button compass is small enough to carry around in a pocket at all times.

Orientating the map to the ground

Orientating the map to the ground allows you to pick out key features on the map or key features on the ground that the map is representing. It's good practice to orientate your map before you set off. It puts the ground you're going to cover in perspective and paints a better mental picture of what lies ahead.

- Lay the compass on the map however you want.
- Turn the bevel until the lines of orientation and arrow on the base of the bevel line up with the grid lines on the map and all are pointing grid north.
- Keeping the compass in this position turn the map until the north pointer lines up with the grid north arrow on the base of the bevel.
- Lift the compass off. The map is now orientated to the ground. This is not exact but is sufficiently accurate.

Survival tips

- **Keep each leg of the journey short: the margin of error will be less. Check direction at regular intervals during each leg.**
- **Be careful not to accidentally move the compass bevel.**
- **Be as precise as you can when setting your bearing.**
- **Pick features to walk to that won't move and aren't too far away.**
- **Using the map, check what sort of ground you're going to encounter when travelling on the leg.**
- **Confirm and collaborate, if you're not alone.**

• WISE WORDS •

I have been lost as both a military man and a civilian. Neither is pleasant; sometimes it's life-threatening. But why stumble about when you can hit the mark exactly? Take stock of your situation, think practically and get in tune with your surroundings and environment. The geography, environment and topography that surround you can throw up many clues to help your navigation.

Notes and warnings

- The bearing you've set is a straight line ignoring any sizeable features. If you have to walk around a feature then take another bearing from a known point once the feature has been negotiated.
- Be aware of tracking off the line of the bearing. This can happen when traversing a steep slope, as there may be a tendency to drift downhill. A strong wind hitting you on one side may inadvertently make you lean into the wind and cause you to drift off your bearing.
- At altitude, air bubbles may form in the liquid suspending the north/south pointer needle. These air bubbles can distort the needle.
- In white-out conditions or areas devoid of landmarks use a team member as a marker. Direct him or her out on the bearing line and instruct them to stop when still easily visible. Walk to the person and repeat the process.
- During the night pick shapes and outlines that are prominent. Pick landmarks that are close. Use another team member with a head torch.
- Learn to trust the map and the compass!

Without a map or compass

Shadow tip method

Many living creatures use the sun to navigate from. It's one of the most reliable ways to find direction. In the northern hemisphere the sun rises in the east and sets in the west. So in the morning the eastern sky will be brighter and in the evening the western sky will be brighter. At midday the sun in the Southern Hemisphere is to the North, whilst in the Northern Hemisphere it is in the South.

The 'shadow tip method' works in the northern and southern hemispheres. You need sun, a stick approximately a metre long and a flat piece of ground.

1 Place the 'shadow stick' vertically in the flat piece of ground.
2 Mark the tip of its shadow with a mark or pebble.
3 Wait 10–15 minutes and mark the second shadow tip.
4 Draw as straight a line as you can through the two marks. This is your east–west line. The first point is the west marker. This is true in the northern and southern hemispheres.
5 A line perpendicular to the east-west line will be the north–south line. In the northern hemisphere the side where the shadow stick is will be south. In the southern hemisphere the stick will be on the north side.
6 If you plot the shadow tip in the morning and regularly mark each shadow tip throughout the day the shortest shadow will be at noon and due north in the northern hemisphere.

Survival tips

I find it useful to work out how much sunlight I have left in the day. If I know how much travel time is left before nightfall I can plan for shelter. Each finger represents approximately 2.5° and the sun moves approximately 15° every hour. One finger therefore represents ten minutes. Hold your outstretched arm towards the sun: with your fingers horizontal, see how many fit between the sun and the horizon. It's best not to use the thumb. If six fingers fill the gap between sun and horizon it's approximately one hour until sunset.

The sun is one of the best indicators anywhere in the world for direction. Learn to use it!

7 In Arctic and Antarctic regions above the latitudes 66.5° south and 66.5° north, the sun may be above the horizon all the time. In this case when the sun is at its lowest or highest point it will be at true north in the northern hemisphere or true south in the southern hemisphere.

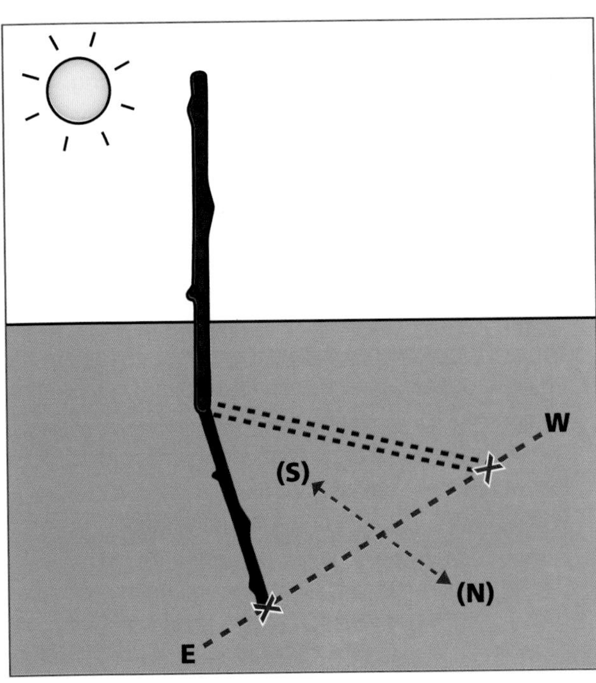

Tracking time

A more accurate method, and a way to track time, is a variation on the shadow tip method. It requires you to record shadow tips from the moment when the first shadow is cast until the time that the last shadow disappears.

1. Place your 1m stick as above before first light. As the first shadow is cast mark the tip. This will be approximately 06:00 and due west.
2. Mark as accurate an arc as possible from the first shadow and past 180° degrees on the approximate west–east line. The shadow stick to the first shadow tip mark is the radius.
3. Regularly mark the shadow tips throughout the day.
4. When the shadow tip crosses the arc, mark this point. This will be approximately due east and 18:00.
5. The shortest shadow tip mark will be approximately noon and due north in the northern hemisphere.
6. Divide the arc into 12 one hour segments from 06:00 through the arc line to 18:00.
7. The season is an important factor, as sunrise and sunset change with the seasons. But noon will always be a reasonable constant.

Even if you think there's no sun to cast a shadow try placing your knife or a small stick on a piece of paper or a light coloured surface and you may be surprised to see a faint shadow cast, enough to be a useful direction indicator.

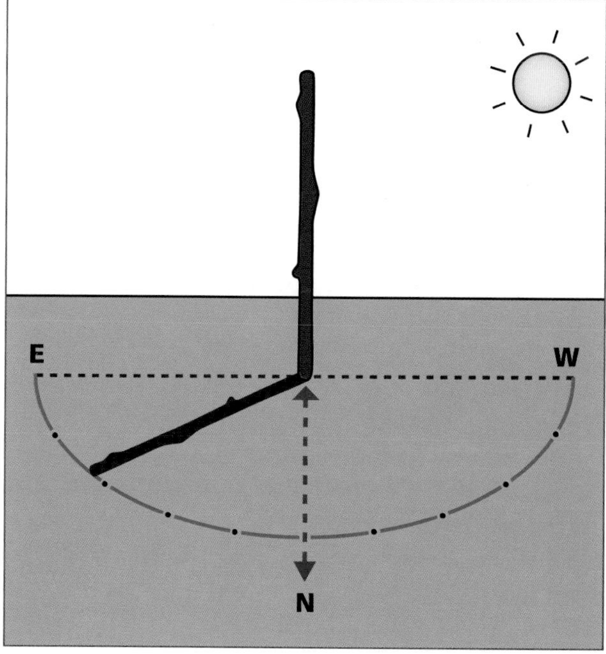

Finding North

This is a useful and quick way to determine direction but is less accurate than the shadow tip method. It works only with a conventional watch. Ignore any time zones, as they don't match real time.

Northern hemisphere

Hold your watch flat and point the hour hand at the sun. Bisect the angle between the hour hand and the 12:00 noon mark on your watch. The bisected angle between the hour hand and the 12.00 noon mark will point south. The opposite direction is therefore north, and from this you can work out west and east.

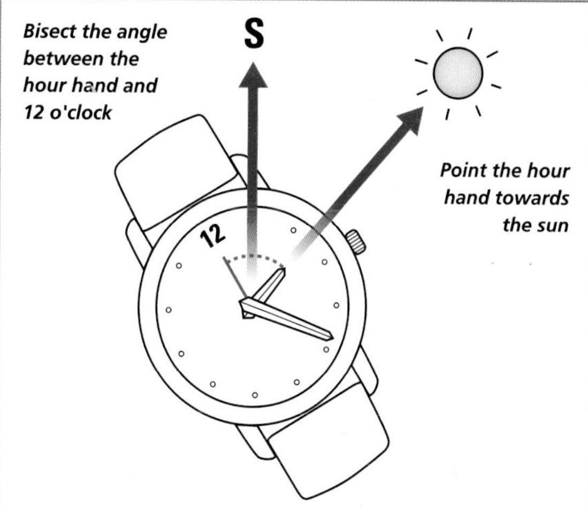

Southern hemisphere

Point the 12:00 noon mark on your watch at the sun. Bisect the angle between the 12:00 noon mark and the hour hand. This points north.

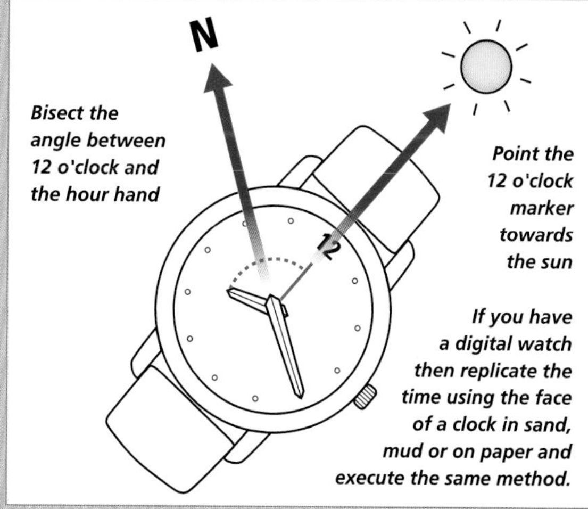

Using the stars

On a clear night the stars can help you find and maintain a direction. Although the sun and moon fluctuate somewhat, the stars move in a more uniform sphere. In the northern hemisphere groups of stars rotate around the Pole Star. The Pole Star, which is the last star in the 'handle' of the Little Dipper constellation, is less than 1° off true north and is in almost the same place every night. Only visible in the northern hemisphere, the farther north you go the higher the Pole Star gets in the sky, until at extremely high latitudes it can no longer direct you.

Even when the constellations are low on the horizon (one or two may even be below the horizon) there's a good chance one of these three major constellations will be visible, so it's worth knowing them all. Orion also gives a rough indication of the direction of the Pole Star. This constellation consists of three stars quite close together (the 'belt' of Orion) and four outside of this in a very rough square. One star, at the top left, is brighter and bigger than the others. Draw a line through the bottom left star and the bright top left and these will point somewhat towards the Pole Star and in a roughly northerly direction.

Once you've located the Pole Star imagine a line directly down from it to the horizon, pick a landmark not too far away, and travel to it. Once you get to that landmark repeat the process. Keep the legs short and be mindful of the stars getting obscured: if this looks likely then pick a landmark as far away as possible. If the night is clear and the Pole Star is at a good angle in the sky it may be just as easy to follow the Pole Star itself.

Stars in the southern hemisphere

In the southern hemisphere the constellations of Ursa Major, Cassiopeia and Orion don't appear and, unlike the Pole Star in the northern hemisphere, no single star points north or south. The most obvious constellation to use is the Southern Cross and the pointer stars close to it (the Southern Cross is also visible some 25° north of the Equator). There's also a 'false' Southern Cross, so look for the two pointer stars close to the true Southern Cross. The 'false' constellation is less bright, larger, the stars are more widely spaced, and there's a star in the centre.

To find south, draw an imaginary line through the long axis of the Southern Cross towards the horizon and an imaginary line from the middle of, and at right angles to, the two pointer stars towards the horizon.

Key constellations

Perhaps the easiest way to locate the Pole Star is using the Big Dipper constellation (Ursa Major). A straight line drawn through the two end stars at the 'bowl' will point to the Pole Star, which is the first star that this straight line will hit and is brighter than many other stars in the sky. The distance to the Pole Star is about five times the distance between the two end stars of the Big Dipper. It's also about the width of six fingers on outstretched arms from the two end stars of the Big Dipper.

Directly across from the Big Dipper is the constellation Cassiopeia, which resembles a 'W' or 'M'. A line drawn from the first star of the 'W' to the first star of the Big Dipper will approx cross the Pole Star, it is about half way.

These constellations and the constellation Orion are obvious when learnt and always rotate close to and in an anticlockwise direction to the Pole Star.

Ursa Major

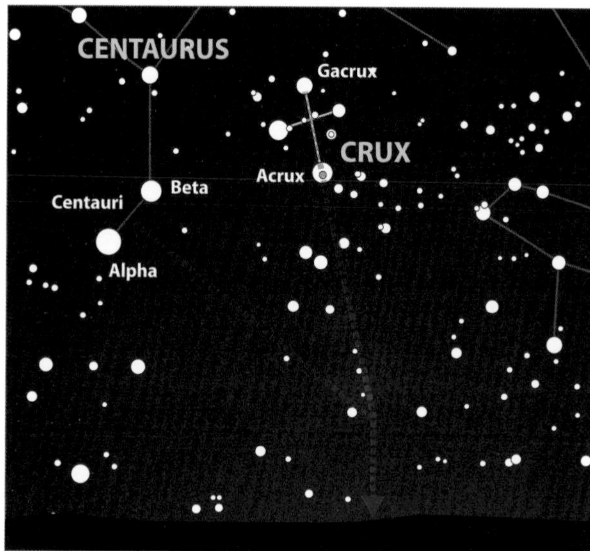

Where they meet in the sky, drop an imaginary line directly down to the horizon to give you a southerly direction. The imaginary line from the Southern Cross to where it meets the imaginary line from the pointer stars will be approximately five times the distance between the two stars of the long axis of the Southern Cross. Whatever angle the two constellations are, employ the same technique. It may be that where the imaginary lines coming from both constellations meet they are somewhat horizontal. Again, where the lines meet in the sky, just drop an imaginary line directly down to the horizon for a southerly direction.

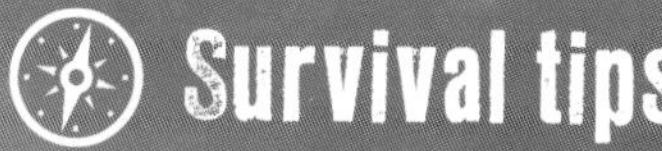

Survival tips

The moon can be an effective resource for the survivalist, providing light, direction and time. The moon itself produces no light and shines only due to reflecting the rays of the sun. Therefore the illuminated part of its surface will point towards the sun. As with the sun, the moon rises roughly in the east and sets roughly in the west. There are seasonal variations, but this is enough to provide an approximate sense of direction.

If you see a crescent moon then drop a line along the 'horns' of the crescent to a point on the horizon. This will give you an indication of south in the northern hemisphere and north in the southern hemisphere.

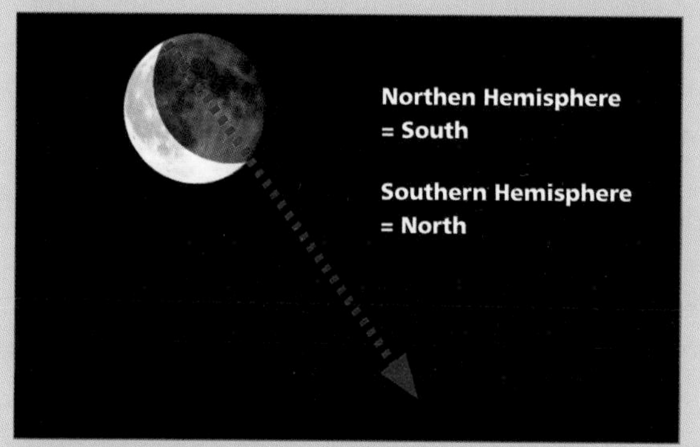

Cassiopeia

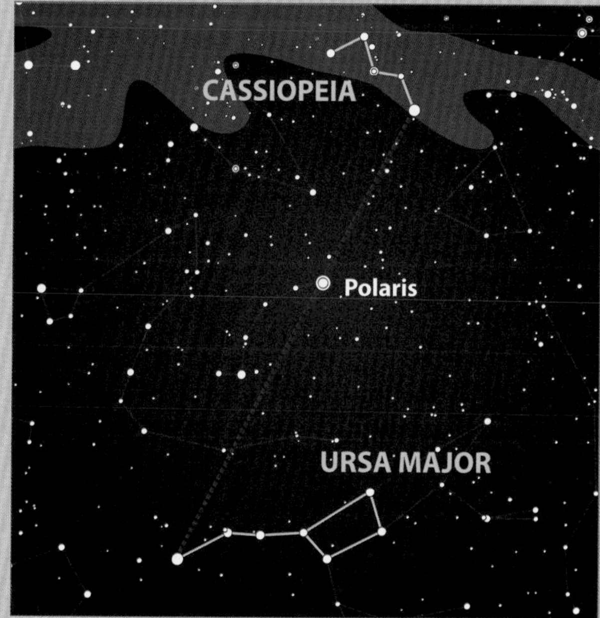

Orion

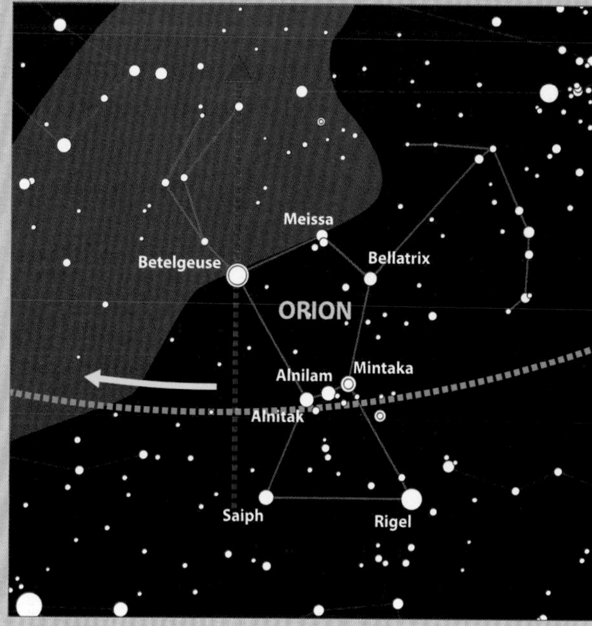

Guidance from nature

Nature provides some great direction indicators and aids when it comes to estimating the cardinal points. Getting 'in touch' with the environment will help you locate these. As you look deeper into the way that the wind shapes trees and terrain, the way animals react and travel and the effects of the sun on the environment you'll see that they offer many clues.

The effects of wind

Get to know the prevailing direction of the winds in your environment; seek local knowledge and undertake prior research. Generally, at medium latitudes the winds will prevail from the west in both hemispheres. In more tropical latitudes, for most of the year, the prevailing winds come from between the north and south-east. At the Equator they're generally from the east.

If you think there isn't any wind, just wet a finger and hold it up: you'll feel one side chill, indicating the direction of the wind.

The prevailing wind has an often visible effect on everything – trees, snow, sand and other objects. These are the most obvious indicators:

- Trees will be deformed to the direction of the prevailing wind. This is most evident with trees that are exposed or on the coast.
- Some trees will have less growth on the windward side and be bushier on the lee side.
- Flower plumes on reeds may have a heavier growth away from the prevailing wind.
- Most animals and birds will build their shelters on the leeward side of the prevailing wind. Spiders can't build webs in windy places.
- Snow and sand are affected in much the same way by the wind, for both are deserts. The prevailing wind will carry sand and snow particles along until it decelerates enough for the particles to drop. This will be on the lee side of an object or feature. Wind will accelerate up to and over an object of any size but decelerate on the non-prevailing side. This will cause an accumulation of particles on the lee side. Rocks, mountains, hills and trees will all show indications of this, particularly in exposed snow and sand environments.

- Snow in windy regions will sometimes be packed on the ground in small ridges up to a metre tall. The windward side will often be undercut, with the lee side being more barrel-shaped. These features, called sastrugi, appear in most tundra, Arctic and Antarctic regions. Sand is arranged in much the same way but these features are called barkhans. They give a good indication of prevailing wind conditions and can aid navigation. Sastrugi can be tightly packed, whereas desert barkhans are usually more widely spaced.

Prevailing winds cause cornices on ridge lines in mountainous areas. These can be huge and provide an obvious indication of prevailing winds. Because the cornice forms on the lee side of the ridge the slope below the cornice will often be loaded with snow, while the windward side will show exposed rocks. In undulating ground these signs are clear indicators of prevailing winds. Sand is affected in a similar way but without cornices.

A prevailing wind can polish and compact snow on the windward side. When the windblown snow contains a little more moisture it may stick to certain features, such as posts and some rocks. It will stick on the windward side and a build-up will occur. This is called 'rime ice'.

• WISE WORDS •

I can recall numerous occasions where I have been travelling over snow and ice in strong winds that were sometimes so strong, and the flying ice particles hitting my face so painful, that I couldn't look ahead, and was forced to look at the ground with my hood and balaclava covering most of my face. In these conditions keeping an eye on the shape of the sastrugi has enabled me to maintain reasonably accurate direction.

Rocks and terrain may also appear a little smoother on the windward side than the lee side. I vividly remember when I was serving in Afghanistan in 2001/2 seeing rocks on the windward side of dunes and slopes polished to a fine sheen by the erosive effects of the sand carried by the prevailing wind. The leeward side had larger accumulations of sand.

Survival tips

Cold-blooded insects are sensitive to changes in temperature. In more temperate climates ants will build their nests on south to south-east slopes, often with a feature protecting them from prevailing winds. During cold periods the ants may inhabit the south to south-east end of the nest. One striking example of what ants can achieve is the Australian termite, (*Amitermes meridionalis*). Their mounds – which can be up to 4m high – are shaped like a large fin with a serrated top ridge. They are found in the intense heat of the Australian deserts and all of them are orientated almost exactly north and south. The hills are made of mud and the termites can only build with wet mud, but it must dry quickly to become secure. Having the large faces of their hill exposed to the sun dries the mud quickly. The narrow width allows them to move quickly to the cooler side.

The effect of the Sun

The effect of wind is usually to retard vegetation growth, but the sun often enhances it. At times, when there's little direct sunlight available, the natural effect that it has had can help confirm approximate direction. Some indicators are:

- Moss and lichens may grow on the shady side of trees and other objects, where moister air will be retained the longest.

- Branches may be straighter and less stunted on the sunny side – although some trees in the lower latitudes, where the sun is often low on the horizon, won't always show the effects of the sun: firs and spruce grow straight and the foliage is pyramid shaped. This is to capture the diffused light on all sides.
- In the northern hemisphere, deciduous trees will be more prolific on the sunny side of slopes and evergreens on the north side of slopes.
- In the desert, barrel cactus will lean towards the sun.
- Pilot weed, or 'compass plant of the prairies', will grow with leaves on only two sides of the stem. These grow on the north and south side when growing in sunlight.
- On the cross-section of tree trunks, the rings may be more tightly packed on the sunny side than the shady side.
- The bark of some trees may be darker on the shaded side and some plants and tips of trees lean towards the sun.

Be aware that plants and trees will survive and develop in the harshest of places. Some will flourish and adapt to areas that get little sunlight, so try to acquire an understanding of the flora in your particular environment.

Improvised compass

Clues from nature will greatly help in all but one particular environment: if you get lost in dense jungle, with full cloud cover and a tree canopy that always looks the same, you can expect to stay lost unless you can fabricate some sort of compass.

Using wire or a needle

If you have your survival kit you should have a needle. If not, then try to get hold of some ferrous wire.

- Stroke the needle in one direction. Do this against a piece of silk if you have any, as this works best.
- Stroke it from the sharp end to the eye end. By doing it this way you'll magnetise the sharp end to north. Stroke the needle at least 50 times.
- If you have a magnet then stroking your needle or wire with this – again in one direction only – will be far more effective.
- Run the magnetised needle in your hair to cover it in grease. This will help it float if you place it on water.
- It's best to place the needle on stagnant water, a dish containing water, or the water-filled hollow of a dead tree trunk. Don't float the needle on anything, such as a leaf. I've tried this, and it wasn't very effective, probably because the leaf offered too much resistance to the surface of the water and was prevented from turning.
- The magnetism won't last too long so 'top up' occasionally by repeating the stroking procedure.
- Be mindful of any other ferrous materials around that may affect the needle.
- Watch carefully for the needle to move.
- If you can't float it on water suspend it by a thin thread. This won't always be as effective as placing it on water as the thread offers some resistance.

Alternative

Using a razor blade in much the same way as the needle or ferrous wire will also give you direction. Due to the metals it's made from, stroking the blade in your hair or across your palm has a similar effect – but be careful not to cut yourself!

Get your bearings as soon as you can. This helps morale and enables you to plan ahead. Time spent orientating and navigating well is seldom wasted.

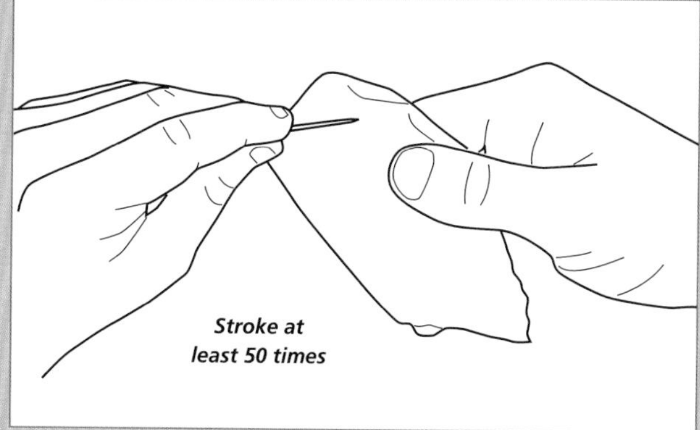

Stroke at least 50 times

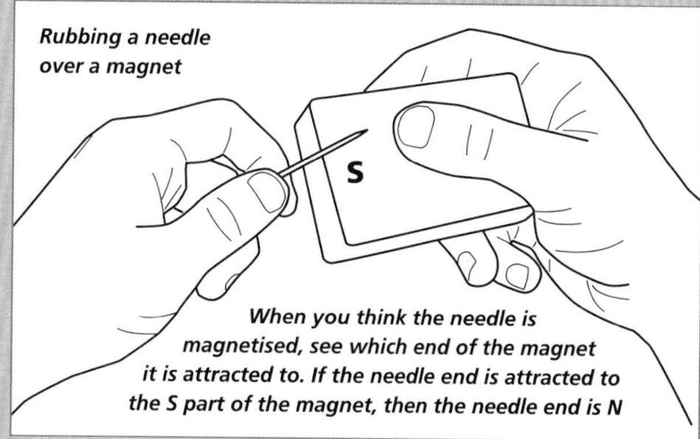

Rubbing a needle over a magnet

When you think the needle is magnetised, see which end of the magnet it is attracted to. If the needle end is attracted to the S part of the magnet, then the needle end is N

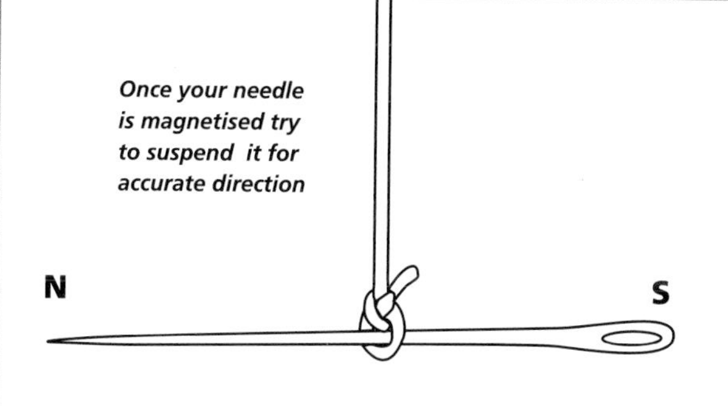

Once your needle is magnetised try to suspend it for accurate direction

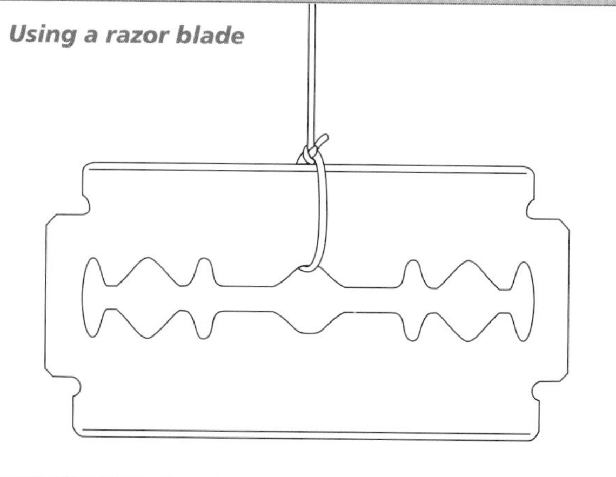

Using a razor blade

Speed and distance

When using any form of navigation, learn to estimate how far you've come and how long a distance will take you to cover.

The best way to work out the distance you've covered is to pace it. Mark out or find an exact 100m length on the flat with no obstacles. From the start, count the pace on every left foot only. I take 61 paces over 100m on the flat and it takes me approximately a minute and a half to cover the 100m at a speed of 4kph.

I've always used pacing and timing in conjunction with my map and compass navigation. It has given me added accuracy and enables good route planning. With practice the simple calculations become second nature.

The following table is based on my own pacing, speed and time. Work out your own paces and substitute them for mine:

Distance (m)	Speed (kph)	Time (minutes)	Paces on every left foot
100	3	2	61
500	3	10	305
1,000	3	20	610
100	4	1.5	61
500	4	7.5	305
1,000	4	15	610
100	5	1.2	61
500	5	6	305
1,000	5	12	610

Other speeds outside the ones shown can easily be worked out.

Pacing and speeds will change with terrain and environment. Other factors to consider when calculating speed and time are fitness and load. However, the above is a good estimate and can be used in all environments. With practice you can make your own adjustments to the time and paces as you cover the terrain.

Judging distance without aids

In a survival situation where you have to plan a route without a map, compass or any other aid it's useful to be able to estimate the distance: how long will it take

Survival tips

- **Your paces will be shorter in steep terrain, when climbing, in poor visibility and into a strong headwind. Individuals tend to lengthen their stride with a tail wind and when going gently downhill.**
- **For every contour you cross on your map, going uphill, add one minute.**
- **Adjust your paces accordingly if you have to deviate from your bearing for obstacles or features.**
- **Find a method of recording every 100m you cover. Use pebbles in your hand and add one to your pocket for every 100m covered. Use a pace counter or similar aid. Use small plastic securing ties – have a number of these on a short length of string and slide one down for every 100m covered.**

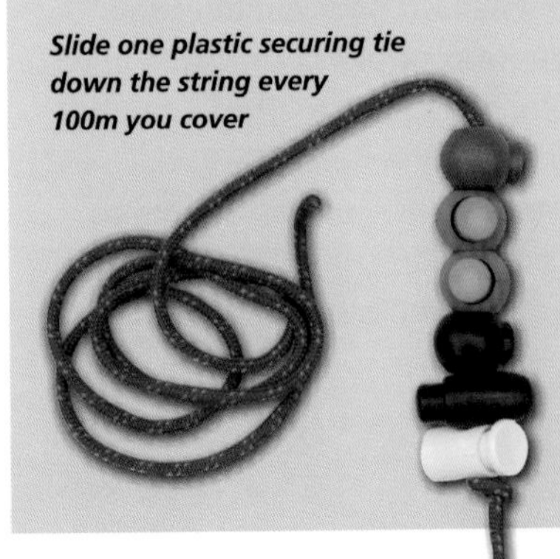

Slide one plastic securing tie down the string every 100m you cover

Cross one pebble from one pocket to another to record every 100m you cover

and what do you need to take with you? It's always worth having some indication of what distance you have to travel and what distance you've travelled – particularly should you have to retrace your route. In terms of morale too, it helps to have a clear idea of time and distance.

Factors to consider

Objects look closer than they actually are when:

- You're looking uphill.
- There's a bright light on the object.
- You're looking across snow, water or flat sand.
- When the whole object is clearly visible and has a clear outline.
- The air is clear.
- You're looking across a depression that may be partially hidden.
- When an object is bigger than its surroundings.

Objects look farther away than they are when:

- The colour of the object blends with the background.
- You're looking over undulating ground.
- The light is poor – for example at dawn or dusk, or in snow, rain or fog.
- The object is small compared to its surroundings.
- You're looking downhill.
- You're looking down a feature that creates a tunnel effect.
- Some of the object is obscured.

Methods

Dead reckoning

As the title suggests this is just a quick assessment of the distance and something all individuals will do automatically. It works surprisingly well for a skilled person who understands the factors that affect judging distance, as outlined above.

Finger method

This is based on the principle that the distance between the eyes is one-tenth the distance between the eye and an outstretched finger on your extended arm. Extend your arm with your forefinger upright. Align one eye with the top of your upright finger and one end of the feature. Without moving your finger, observe the feature with the other eye. Estimate the distance along the feature that your finger appears to have moved, and the estimated distance to the feature will be ten times the estimated distance between the two finger positions.

Group average

If you're working as a team let each individual judge the distance using any method. Once everyone has an estimate find the average.

Bracketing

Taking into account the factors and using one of the above methods, judge the halfway distance. Once you've done this, double it.

Unit of measure

Visualise what a 100m racetrack looks like, or a football pitch, or some other unit of measure with which you're familiar. Using your unit of measure increment, visualise how many units you can fit into the distance you're judging.

You can also use a person

- At 50m mouth and eyes are clearly visible.
- At 100m eyes appear as dots.
- At 200m general detail of clothing can be distinguished.
- At 250m face can be seen.
- At 450m colours can still be distinguished.
- At 750m a person looks like a post.
- At 1.5km the trunks of large trees can be seen.

Note that all of the above will be affected by the factors outlined previously.

Crossing rivers

Never underestimate any river, as by their very nature they're unpredictable. Only swim a river as a last resort. They can contain hidden dangers not visible from the bank – boulders, trees, currents and predatory animals can all lurk beneath the surface. There's the potential to get your feet, clothes or equipment snagged on something and for the current to drag you down.

Rivers in cold climates can be low-volume in the frozen winter but raging torrents in the spring after snowmelt. Lumps of broken ice are a hazard, as are the weakened thawing edges of the ice covering a river. Your weight can cause it to break and the current can very quickly drag you under an ice shelf. The shock of crossing water in cold environments and the management of clothes and equipment is extremely challenging. A common feature of rivers in such environments is large boulders brought downriver from glacial moraines: they're sometimes large enough to provide a potential crossing point, but the waters amongst large rocks are fraught with danger.

Jungle rivers will rise and fall within hours as a consequence of sudden heavy rains. Trees can be uprooted and banks destroyed. My team were working in a steep-sided valley deep in the jungles of Sumatra once, and we were trying to get down a particularly high waterfall when it started to rain. The downpour was huge. It became very unnerving as the water level could be seen rising even as we watched it. Within only an hour the river had become impossible to cross and we were forced to take refuge well away from the bank.

Although rivers in deserts aren't common, sudden heavy rain can cause flash flooding. What are usually dry riverbeds can become raging rivers sweeping everything away in their path. They can disappear almost as quickly as they appear, so it's best to wait it out by making camp well away from the banks and collecting what you can to drink, cook, wash and replenish your reserves.

Before crossing

If you come cross a river that has to be crossed then consider your options carefully. If you spot the river from high up then spend some time looking for an easy route while you have the advantage of height. Look for places where you can wade rather than swim. It's also better to hike upstream or downstream looking for a dry crossing before committing yourself to getting wet. If necessary split a team up for reconnaissance and walk upstream and downstream for a determined amount of time, then report back to the start location. Aim to cross where there's an easy wash out downstream should you be swept off your feet.

I've been forced to wade, swim or improvise river crossings in all sorts of environments. It always requires some level of preparation. We're all averse to getting wet, especially in the cold, but once everything has been accessed and is in place you should put the 'getting wet' bit to the back of your mind and just go for it. Even in freezing conditions the initial shock will quickly subside and you'll find you're able to swim.

The following guidelines should help:

- Before crossing observe the water and its movement, strength and character. The shortest crossing point may not necessarily be the safest. The centre of the river is usually the fastest.
- Looking at the surrounding rocks and foliage, determine what hazards may lie beneath the surface.
- Look for natural crossing points – rocks, boulders, choke points or shallows.

- If two waters meet then it's usually better to cross the two upper rivers individually rather than the one main flow.
- Never cross above waterfalls or obvious danger unless the crossing is easy. If you're jumping from rock to rock be mindful of wet and slippery rocks and the moss or algae that may cover them.
- There may be obstacles such as boulders in the river, where eddies have formed on their downstream side. These eddies can be areas to rest and observe.
- Always leave your boots on. In cold climates it's best to remove all clothing and socks. Waterproof your clothes but still cross with your boots on.
- If you can swim against the flow then do so at about 45° to the flow and facing upstream. Again, use eddies where you can. Use breaststroke or sidestroke and conserve energy.
- If the flow is too powerful to swim against then go with it, although there's then a risk of getting pinned on the upstream side of an obstacle. Descend feet first and float as if you were in an astronaut's seat with your legs poised ready to take the shock of hitting rocks and obstacles. Try and keep your head as high as possible as you observe ahead. Get as far into the flow as possible before swimming. Once in the flow, relax and don't fight it. Use your arms to manoeuvre yourself towards the other bank. Look for eddies on the opposite side and move yourself to the upstream end of the eddy. Just as you come towards it use all your effort to power into the eddy. Barrel rolling is sometimes a good technique at this point.
- If you're using a rope then NEVER tie it tightly around you. Make a loop that will comfortably go over your head and across a shoulder and across the chest. The person holding the rope should have it around his or her body. The holder goes upstream and works on holding and releasing the rope tension for the swimmers support. If the swimmer flounders then the holder should keep some tension when required so that the flow pushes the swimmer back to the bank.
- Baggy clothing increases surface area and drag when swimming and may enable the flow to pull you off your feet. Strip down.
- If you're jumping into water from a cliff then the depth needs to be checked. Use a stick or tie a rock to a vine as an improvised depth gauge. Lower the depth gauge in and when the vine or cord goes slack it is on the riverbed. Using a straight arm, pull up and count every metre until you see the rock. This will be the depth. You'll need a minimum depth of 7m to jump from a height of 10m.
- Try not to swallow the water; you don't know what may be in it.

River anatomy

Rivers have some of the same features wherever they are in the world:

- **Rocks will cause disturbances and rapids; vertical drops will create waterfalls. The aerated water here is less dense and therefore less able to support you.**
- **In rapids there are usually standing waves where water is forced up and over an obstacle. A standing wave may break back on itself at its tip if it's forced high enough.**
- **Water that's forced to drop sharply may cause a stopper: here water is forced back on itself and circulates back upstream for a short distance. Stoppers are often dangerous, as they can pull you under and hold you there.**
- **Fallen trees that are held static in the flow of the water can cause 'strainers'. These are potentially dangerous too, as you can get pinned to the upstream side of a strainer and tangled amongst the branches.**
- **Water will accelerate at 'choke points', and will flow faster on the outside of bends.**
- **On the downstream side of an obstacle there will be slack water or an 'eddy'.**

Crossing

Harvest or find a stick that's strong and taller than you by a metre or two. Face upstream so that your knees lock back with the force of the water. If it feels too powerful return and look elsewhere. Move horizontally across the river at the most amenable looking crossing point. Position the stick at an angle and lean into it, maintaining a stable triangle of feet and stick. Move one foot or the stick at a time and maintain the triangle for stability.

If you're in a team then huddle together with your arms on the shoulders of those either side of you and facing each other. The main support goes to the person who has the back of his legs taking the force of the water but they also create a small eddy for the supporting team members. The force will try and buckle your knees. Move in unison and with coordination.

Prepare some sort of improvised buoyancy:

- If you have a waterproof bag then fill it with your clothes to keep them dry and ensure that as much air as possible is trapped in the bag when you seal it.
- Fill your rucksack with floating material – cans and bottles, or even logs.
- Trap air in the legs of your trousers and tie off the waistband.

• WISE WORDS •

A small team and I had to go ahead to find a way across a fairly wide, fast-flowing river in the jungles of Belize. Our team at base had a lot of equipment. It took us a good few hours to 'rig the river' in order to get the team and all their equipment across. We fixed two ropes across the river at about 45° to the flow, one for the outward journey and one for the return. This allowed individuals to use the rope as a handrail and go with the flow for the outward journey and the return.

- Fill a jacket, poncho or tarp with sticks, leaves and other buoyant material. Tie it in a bundle with vines, roots or cord.
- Lashing a couple of buoyant logs together will increase buoyancy. Instead of lashing the logs completely together tie them so that there's a gap between the two logs so that you can lean your back on one and hook the back of your knees over the other. Your backside then sits in the water. In some jungle areas you may come across balsa wood, which floats exceptionally well.
- Ice floats so cut or find an appropriate sized lump of ice to float across your equipment or to use as buoyancy.

After crossing

Once you're across to the other bank get your clothing on to prevent further cooling. Cooling saps your energy. If necessary put some insulation such as twigs, brush and leaves on the ground to prevent your feet getting cold, and make a fire.

Use your experience to help your team buddies with crossing tips. If you were on a rope then walk upstream so that the flow will force following roped-up team members to the opposite bank.

Building a raft

If you intend to travel some distance by water it may be necessary to build a raft. Particularly in the jungle, travelling along a river may be your quickest form of travel compared to hacking through dense foliage. Being confident in water has a distinct advantage when making the decision to travel by river or water, but travelling by raft can be the safest, easiest and quickest way to travel: rivers provide food, water and hygiene. Even small rivers lead to larger rivers, and there are few big rivers in the world that don't have some sort of community living on or close to its banks, which increases your chance of rescue. Don't travel at night by raft unless you're forced to or have complete confidence that it's safe to do so.

You can only build a raft if you have the resources at hand and it's worth the effort. You'll need wood that floats well and is buoyant enough to support you. Spruce (in cold climates), bamboo and balsa are all excellent raft-building materials. Oil drums, sealed bottles and plastic containers all help with buoyancy whatever their size. Most rafts for a single person will have to be 3–4m long and 2m wide. Adding an outrigger to your raft is an easy way to improve its buoyancy and stability.

Constructing a paddle

Construct a paddle or punt. Soft bendy woods such as willow can be shaped into a crude paddle end. The paddle end should offer a bigger surface area for the water and thus better propulsion. The paddle end should be a 'tear drop' shape and about 30cm at it's widest. Use hide (animal skin), material (shirt) or some other available resource to cover the 'tear drop' end, secure the resource and lash the paddle end to the shaft. If the water is shallow enough to punt then harvest a straight stick. Bamboo and other hard woods are ideal.

Use the flow and force of the river to cover the distance. There should be no need to over-exert yourself.

You may have to construct overhead cover for shade in hot climates and at sea. It needs to be adequate to protect your face at least, and as much of your body as possible dependent on the effort necessary and the resources available. An improvised paddle or punting pole will also be necessary.

Build your raft close to the water, at the top of a steep bank or at the edge of the high tide mark. It's easier to carry and drag resources to the building site rather than to drag a heavy, fully constructed raft to the water.

Secure all your equipment firmly to the raft. Improvise some extra 'hand-held' buoyancy in case you're thrown from your raft and separated. This also gives you a little more confidence if you're not sure of your abilities in water.

Dragging a small log or filled water container a short way behind your raft will help you to maintain direction and to face downstream. Attach it by means of a quick release arrangement or be ready to cut it free should it get tangled.

Place containers around your raft to collect rainwater.

As you travel downstream, always listen ahead for the changing sounds of the river. The loud thunder of water dropping off an edge or over a complex of boulders signals danger and is a warning that it's time to land and reconnoitre ahead on foot. Always have the ability to get your raft to the bank efficiently.

Building a sea raft

Building a raft will depend on what resources you have at hand, what water you are rafting in and potentially how long you intend to be rafting. There is no set rule, so use common sense, good lashing and buoyancy to build an effective raft.

1 Beachcombing is vital and it's amazing what you may find.

2 Harvest enough logs or bamboos of the right length and lay them down in the configuration of the raft. About a metre in from each end of the raft logs, you can cut a notch in each log at the same point, top and bottom to help secure the 'pressure' logs in place. If you're using bamboo, then holes can be cut in each bamboo instead of notches. A further length of bamboo can then be slid through the holes to pull and secure all the bamboos together.

3 Use sledge knots (see page 63) to lash the base of the raft together. This needs to be secure and solid.

4 Harvest two strong thinner logs to sit in the notches top and bottom, one at the front and one at the rear. It may be necessary to put two more of these transverse pressure logs across the centre of your raft. This will depend on how much strength is needed to hold the raft together. The pressure logs should overlap the edge of the raft by approximately 25cm.

5 Add any extra buoyancy you may have found along the shoreline – bottles, polystyrene, buoys and fenders.

7 Test at timely intervals to check its potential.

6 Using a sledge knot, tie the pressure logs together at either end of the raft, locking all the logs together. Use cord, vine or rope to stengthen the raft, add an outrigger and lash down buoyancy aids.

8 Build an overhead cover using large leaves to give some protection.

The finished raft

CAMP CRAFT

Whether you deliberately journey or are thrust unexpectedly into a challenging environment then an early priority will be finding shelter and establishing a camp. Prolonged periods in any climate at either a base camp or on the move will require a good routine for maintaining a camp that offers all you need for protection, comfort, morale, hygiene and ultimately survival. Camp craft is a generic term for a number of important aspects that will have to be addressed to facilitate your survival. Your camp and how it is managed is essential, especially if there are a number of you. Camp craft is a team effort. Good camp craft is not a consideration – it is a must!

Making fire

The effort to create and maintain a fire is far outweighed by the benefits it delivers, and although there may be other survival priorities it will not be long before making fire becomes imperative. Fire will ensure you have:

- Warmth.
- Light.
- Protection.
- A means of signalling.
- Cooked food.
- Sterilised water.
- Preserved, smoked food.
- Dry clothes.
- Hardened wood for weapons.
- An insect-free zone.

It will also provide psychological reassurance, by giving you or your team a point of focus. Even in hot climates I've seen people put their hands close to the fire to feel the warmth or to take something else from it.

Survival tip

On too many occasions tired, wet individuals and teams have just curled up and gone to sleep after expending a considerable amount of effort in getting a fire going. In the morning it may be raining, and the precious fire has gone out! A good system of collecting fuel, maintaining the fire and protecting it through the night and day is vital.

Making and maintaining fire is tough in many environments and next to impossible in some, but you'll never make fire if you lack any of the three vital elements – air, heat and fuel. Whether you have matches, a lighter or are using an improvised method of creating fire, there are a few basic preparations to attend to first: The most important being preparation at all levels.

- Pick a location for the fire. This should be sheltered but well ventilated.

Construct a 'reflector' that is high enough to reflect heat from a fire towards you and your shelter. Make sure it's not too close to the fire!

- Prepare the area for your specific needs, whether cooking, warmth, signalling or another purpose.
- Leave room to sit close to the fire for warmth and to tend it.
- Prepare the ground where the fire is to be located. Clear away leaves and other foliage that could combust and spread. Clear overhanging foliage. Clear snow to ground level or lay logs down as a platform so the fire doesn't sink.
- Construct a windbreak if necessary, or dig a trench. Be mindful air needs to circulate.
- Build a reflector close to the fire so that the heat is directed to a certain location, perhaps your bivouac. A reflector needs to be at least the height of the fire you've nurtured. A rock face or boulder may provide a natural reflector.
- If the ground is particularly wet or swampy you'll have to construct a platform.
- Prepare other resources, such as cooking sticks, rocks for heating, water for boiling or food for cooking.
- Then collect the three important constituents needed to create combustion. Tinder, Kindling and Wood fuel.

Fuzz stick

Shave down thin strips of wood without separating them from a harvested branch. It catches flame more easily.

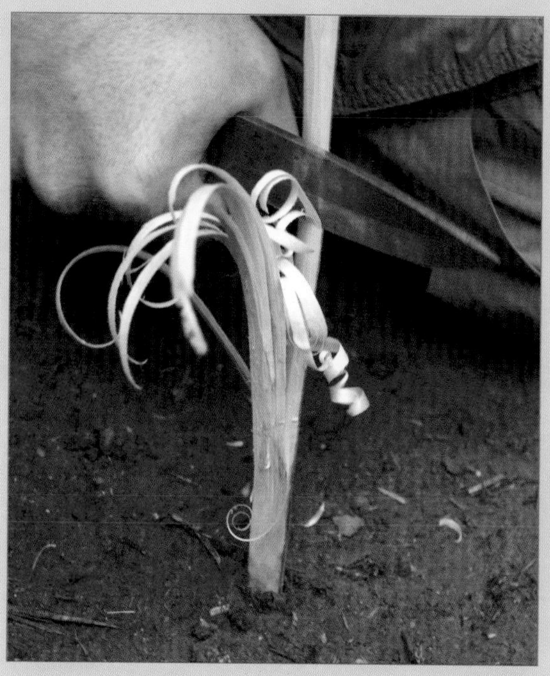

Tinder

Tinder is necessary to start the fire. It's usually a material that will take a spark or is easily combustible from a small ember or even friction alone. It should be fine and loosely compacted so that there's plenty of air amongst it: wood shavings, small dry birds' nests, certain mosses and fungi. Household examples are cotton and hemp rope fragments. Tinder needs to be dry, so gather it at the earliest opportunity and store it for later use. In wet areas tinder found in caves may provide what you need.

A number of the hardy looking fungi that grow on many trees, including birch and ash, can be easily harvested for tinder. Many of them smoulder well and have the potential to be used when you need to transport smouldering embers. Bracket/shelf fungus works well; this is the chunky, hard fungus found on some trees. Break it open and scrape the inner part down for tinder. Tinder fungus is a name applied to one of the better tree funguses that's excellent for tinder. It's found on live birch trees and is black and crumbly. Scrape some shavings off into a small bowl you've created in the fungus and use them as tinder. Cramp ball and horse hoof fungus work well as tinder when scraped into shavings. They also smoulder well so are a means of transporting embers.

Small shavings from the bark of resinous trees will often take a spark well. Conifer resin makes an excellent fire-starter. Blisters of pine resin on the tree can be burst to collect liquid resin, as liquid resin is more combustible than the lumps that have solidified due to exposure to air. Harder lumps can be used in torches for a slower burn.

Tinder or Bracket fungus.

Cramp Ball.

Other options for tinder include:

- Coconut husk, and the husk found deep in the crooks of some bushy palm trunks.
- The outer layer of a bamboo cane shaved into thin light shreds using a knife, shell or sharp stone.
- Termite nest material.
- Rodent nests (particularly those sheltered from the rain).
- Foliage found in caves. Some animals take food to caves to eat and shelter so forage well into caves, maybe using a fire torch. But make sure you can find your way out!
- Strips of rubber tyre help a fire catch. They'll burn even when wet but you'll still need good tinder to take a spark unless you can douse the strips in a man-made fuel.
- Downy parts of your sleeping bag or dry clothes will take a spark.
- Fluff from your belly button!

Kindling

This is used to 'bring the fire on'. Kindling should be small and dry but contain more substance than tinder. It won't take a match but will burn with the small amount of heat generated by tinder. Ventilation at this stage is important and a gentle blow from you may be necessary. Examples of kindling include small dry twigs, small strips of bark and dry grasses and ferns.

Wood fuel

This consists of the larger logs that will sustain the fire for longer periods and provide good heat. Start placing smaller wood on the burning kindling: continue to nurture the fire and gradually build up the size of the wood fuel to the desired amount. The initial smaller logs you place on the fire can be cut down the length to create 'feathers' of wood coming off the log: make small cuts and peel back the 'feather' without cutting it off completely.

Generally, the heavier the wood the longer and hotter it will burn. Light, soft woods burn fast. Heavy woods include oak, beech and birch. Soft woods include spruce, pine and cedar.

Damp wood fuel may be beneficial in signalling, as it produces lots of smoke.

Have everything prepared before you start your fire.

Creating fire

- Loosen up a good palmful of dry tinder to get air amongst it.
- Using a match, fire steel, optic or an ember from an improvised friction technique (see page 56), get the tinder to ignite. It will probably smoke initially, but with a gentle blow flame should appear. Have kindling at the ready before this happens.

- Place a pyramid of kindling twigs over the tinder, leaving a gap for air and for you to blow into. Don't suffocate the fire by placing too much kindling on.
- Continue to nurture the kindling fire until it's established.
- Place the smaller wood fuel logs in a pyramid style as desired and without suffocating the fire. You should continue to nurture the fire until it's clearly working well and can be left unattended.
- Maintain your fire by having a good supply of wood fuel to hand and a steady flow of air. Protect from the elements as necessary. Place your fuel reserve close to the fire so that it continues to dry, but not to burn! Consider a dry shelter for your wood fuel.

Transporting fire

After going to all the trouble of creating fire it may soon be time to move on. Transporting some element of your fire may be a practical necessity if you lack matches, a lighter or a fire-steel. As your fire is burning you should continue to dry tinder as a matter of course. Collect coals and charcoal that have cooled sufficiently, ready for another fire in your next location.

Small embers can be transported in dry, tightly packed moss or grass, animal horns or bones or the bark of some trees. As you travel, swing the receptacle, so circulating air. Check the embers regularly – they may require a few gentle puffs. If you have a small tin or some rusted metal that can be shaped and used for carrying fire then partially pack this with dry moss, grass or some semi-burnt rags. Place the embers in it and cover with the remaining packing.

Improvised torches

If you lack a battery-powered torch it may be necessary to construct an improvised torch for light, particularly if you need to go into a cave or want to go night fishing. It may also be required for protection.

If possible construct your torch from slow-burning materials. Soak material in fuel if possible. Use wire to lash it tightly to a pole. Use a freshly cut stick for the pole so that it doesn't burn well. Add pine sap nuggets or liquid within the tightly lashed material for a slower burn. Be careful not to use materials that will drip and burn, like plastics, and materials that will smoke excessively.

If you're using resources from the natural environment then construct a torch by harvesting a stick approximately 1.5m long and 6cm in diameter. Split the tip of the stick into quarters down to about 30cm from the tip. Bamboo works well for this (split down the same length of bamboo to the first node). Open up the splits and add combustible material such as nuggets of pine sap, dry dead wood, palm and coconut husk, dry bark, rendered animal fat and dry grasses packed down. Pack it all down tightly but allow some flow of air. Leave enough of a gap at the top of the splits to bind the four ends together at the top of the torch to hold everything in place – use wire if possible so it doesn't burn through. Take extra material with you to replenish your torch, or make a number of torches to keep you going.

1

2

3

Bamboo fire saw

1 Cut an approximately 1m section of bamboo about 8–10cm in diameter with your machete. Split this section into two. Thin one section down further. Use a stone on the ground as a hard surface for one end of this section and a flat piece of wood on your stomach to secure the bamboo upright when you lean on it. The sharp edge of the outer part of this section should face away from you. This is your baseboard.

2 Shred some thin and downy shaving from bamboo to make a fur ball that will take a spark.

3 Secure the fur ball on the inside of the running board using your fingers and a thin section of bamboo or vine. It must be dry. Alternatively, use cord or a thin strip of clothing.

4 Lean on the base board and, holding the running board horizontally and with the slit fixed into the sharp edge of the base board, run the running board up and down forcefully. The friction created at the slit from the vigorous up and down movement should cause the fluff ball to smoulder. Lightly tease the smoulder by gentle blowing to burn more tinder and then ignite kindling.

Survival tip

The bamboo saw may take some adjusting before that the friction is directed at the tinder. Persevere – make adjustments as you run the board up and down. Creating fire like this takes time and patience.

Friction fire

It may be necessary to create fire for signalling, cooking, purifying or for warmth at night. The simplest way is to use fuel from a vehicle, but if this isn't available you must seek an alternative. Always look for wood that's dry and fairly soft but solid throughout; dead wood works well if it's not too rotten. To make fire without matches:

1 Collect tinder and kindling. Get two sticks about 30cm long. The 'base stick' or flat piece of wood should be approximately 4–5cm thick. The 'working stick' approximately 2cm in diameter.

- Close to one end of the base stick, make the start of an indentation by cutting a small groove on one side. This is to catch the burning ember. The 'V' groove can be held over tinder so the ember falls on to it.
- Lay the base stick on a hard surface. Locate the working stick in the indentation you've made in the base stick and start rubbing between your palms.

2 Eventually the end of the working stick will round off and fit into the indentation in the base stick.

3 Rub the stick hard and aggressively and eventually an ember will be created in and around the 'V' groove. Continue until the area of friction smokes continuously.

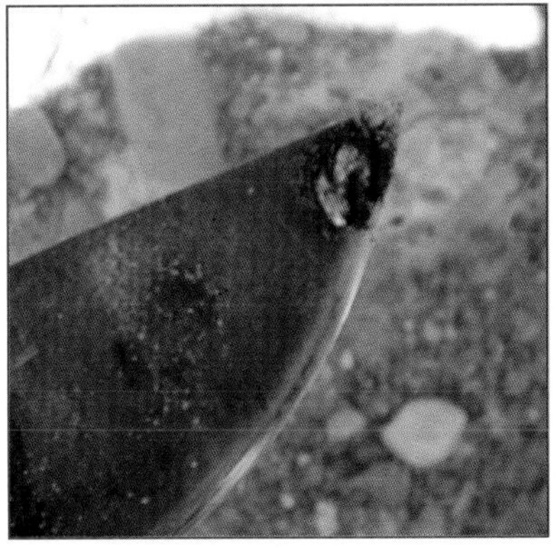

4 Gently blow the ember and add it to the tinder. Don't get too excited and blow the ember away. It will be small, so nurture it – it could be your only chance of a fire!

Make sure you take the sticks with you when you travel, and don't discard them: you may need them again.

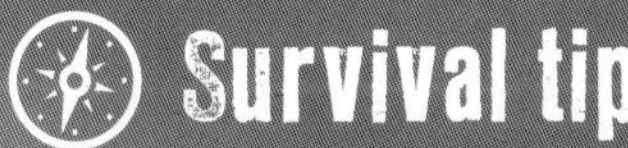

Survival tip

Whilst the sun is out start to dry tinder. Dry anything that will take a spark. Fluff all tinder up to air it and don't use too much. A thumb-size amount may be adequate.

Prepare your fire site well before creating fire. Protect it from wind and rain. Gather plenty of dry or near-dry fuel and keep it close to the fire. Cover gathered wood with leaves for future use.

Using knives

The vast majority of us aren't taught how to use a knife or machete for practical purposes. Yet both are dangerous in the hands of the untrained. On an expedition to Belize some years ago, one of our team claimed a vast amount of jungle experience. We all had machetes, but his was by far the longest. Heading into the dense jungle he very quickly wanted to take the lead, as he 'knew best'. But after only a couple of hours we heard a loud scream from the front. Swinging his machete wildly, our 'hero' had swiped at and missed a jungle branch, followed through, and hacked through his top lip to the jawbone, causing serious injury. Luckily we weren't too far into the jungle, so after some initial first aid we were able to evacuate him. It transpired that his previous use of machetes was nil!

Knife safety is mostly common sense:

- Always carve and cut away from you, and not towards others.
- Tasks that are almost impossible without a knife become possible with one, but often only after the expenditure of considerable effort, so take a good rest or swap duties if you're carving, cutting, hacking or skinning for long periods.

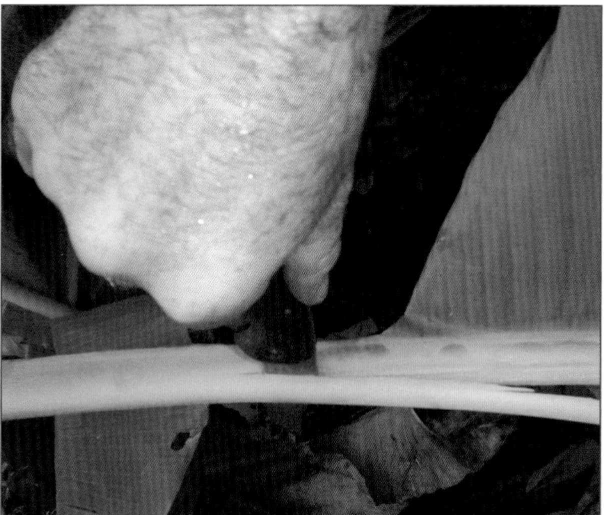

- When sitting down and using a knife, cut and carve away from your legs and especially away from your femoral artery.
- Avoid or take great care with folding blades that don't lock. As already pointed out, these can collapse and cause serious injury.
- Have some way of attaching your knife to you, either on a tether or in a sheath attached to your body.

• WISE WORDS •

I remember a guy in my team sitting down on a sleeping bag and feeling a pain high up his inner thigh close to his testicles. The guy next to him had put his knife on the sleeping bag whilst he did something else, and forgotten about it! The knife was facing up at a funny angle on a crease of the sleeping bag. If the guy sitting down had sat a few centimetres either way the result could have been far more painful!

- Don't wrap your hand around the sheath when drawing the blade, especially when drawing a machete. The cutting edge may cut through the sheath, thus slicing your fingers.
- When using a machete, make short swings in front of the body and with one foot forward. Don't swing fast, make sure others are clear, and try to cut with an outstretched arm. Don't try and keep up with the locals – they'll have been using machetes since they could walk!
- Unless you have to, don't walk or run with your blade open.
- Don't leave your knife lying around, sticking up from anything, or stuck in a log. Put it away as soon as you've finished with it.

Care and maintenance

If you take care of your knife it will take care of you. Remember the simple acronym COST: Clean, Oil, Sharpen and Tether.

After a time even the best blade will blunt. Sharpening it is one of the more important duties you must do for your knife. If you don't have a proper sharpening stone then sandstone will sharpen your blade effectively. Quartz will also work, as will some finer granite rocks: rub the rocks together to get as smooth a surface as possible. When sharpening, hold the handle with one hand and place your fingertips just above the sharp part of the blade, applying a steady pressure to the rock or sharpening stone. Have the blade facing away from you, keeping the back of it up slightly, and, maintaining a constant angle, sharpen it using a clockwise circular motion. Sharpen both sides equally – when sharpening the other side the motion should be in an anticlockwise direction. Keep the stone wet or use light grade oil.

Improvising

If you're plunged into an adverse environment unexpectedly you may have to improvise a cutting implement. Consider the following:

- **Flint (which is usually found in conjunction with chalk) can be easily chipped away to give a very sharp edge. Other suitable rock that you may come across in certain environments is obsidian (which is a dark glass-like volcanic rock), slate and other sedimentary rocks.**
- **Some seashells have sharp edges to them.**
- **Bamboo can provide a very sharp edge.**
- **If you're in a position where glass is about then this provides a sharp edge as well as being usable in other applications, such as for a spearhead.**
- **Antler and bone may be broken and worked at to provide a useful tool.**

Tying knots

It often seems as if there's a different knot, lashing or hitch for every job that requires rope or cord. It can be daunting to try to learn them all, but simply knowing how to tie a knot that won't undo at a critical moment is the crucial skill. It's also useful to be able to tie knots quickly and efficiently when time is short and the conditions are adverse.

Tying a knot that does the job is vital, but it's equally important that you're able to untie it later in order to reuse the rope or cord. The result of poor knot knowledge is often the use of too much cord and made-up knots that in the end have to be cut to retrieve the cord. This is a waste of valuable materials.

If you're deliberately taking rope or cord out to the extremes then be mindful that there are many different materials for making these and that each type has different properties, diameters, lengths, strengths and resistance to abrasion.

The knots shown below aren't exhaustive but will cover most tasks that you may face in a survival situation. Practice until tying them becomes second nature. Once you have a good understanding you can apply them to different tasks. A few are adaptations from other knots and hitches and may be known elsewhere under different names.

Overhand knot

A good stopper, very easy to knot but difficult to undo if it's been pulled hard.

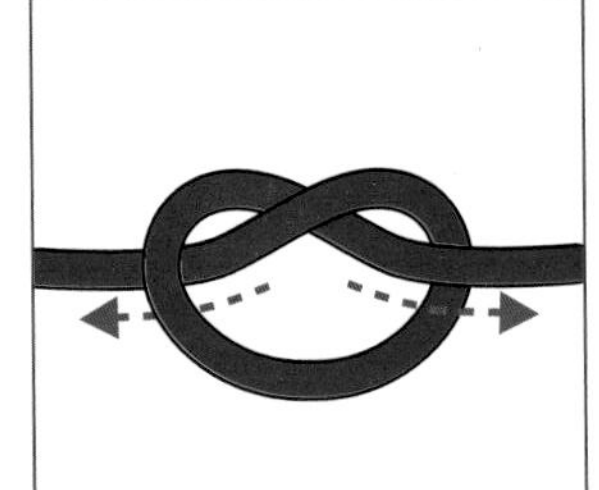

Figure of eight

This creates a secure loop in the rope. Individuals often get the figure of eight wrong, but this nearly always results in them tying an adequate overhand knot. However, though it's possible to use an overhand knot, when it's been heavily loaded it's often more difficult to undo.

The reef

A quick and useful way to tie together two ropes or pieces of cord of near equal thickness. It's a secure knot but I have seen it slip when using nylon rope or ropes of vastly different diameters. Make the tail ends long so that you can add a half-hitch; this will increase the security of the knot. After trying, pull it as tight as you can before using.

Clove hitch

This is a classic hitch, which can be applied and assembled quickly. If the strain is approximately at right angles to the hitch it will stay secure. The clove hitch can loosen when not under tension so keep an eye on it. After loading it is easy to loosen.

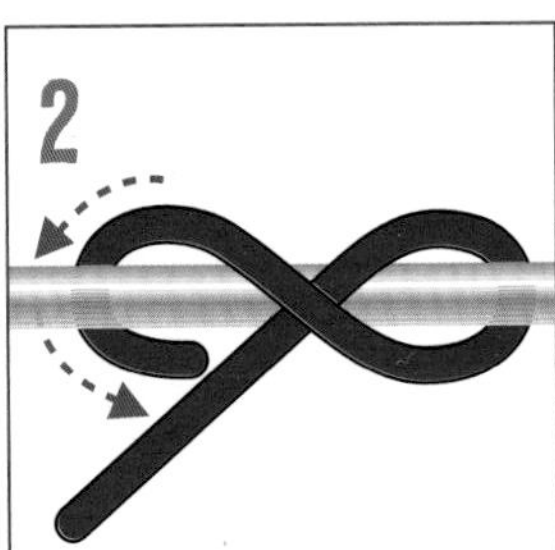

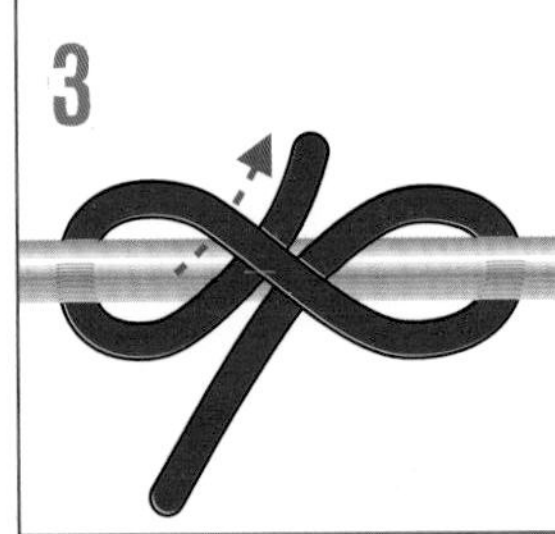

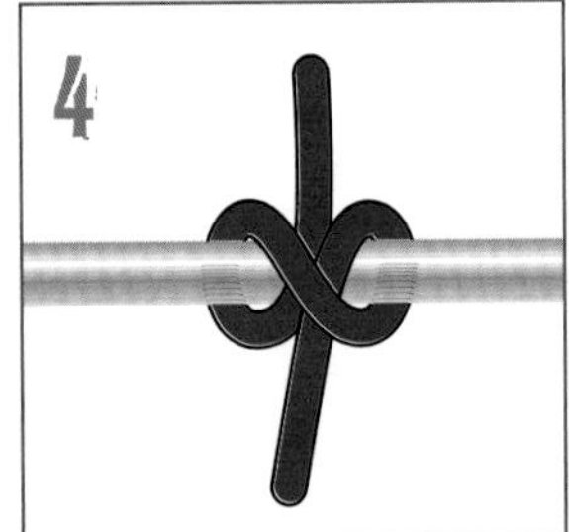

Bowline

A secure and simple way of getting a fixed loop. It's useful if you have to pass an end of the rope around something that has no access from the top, for instance a very high tree. Make sure you tie this properly and practice it well before using 'in anger'.

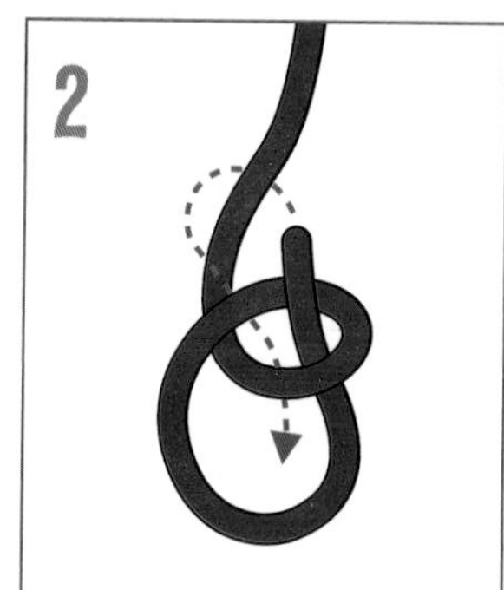

Constrictor knot

This is a great knot for tying something extremely tightly, so tightly that if you ever want to undo it you'll probably have to cut it. This is a very old knot that's probably been in use for thousands of years. It will hold wood together as tightly as a clamp.

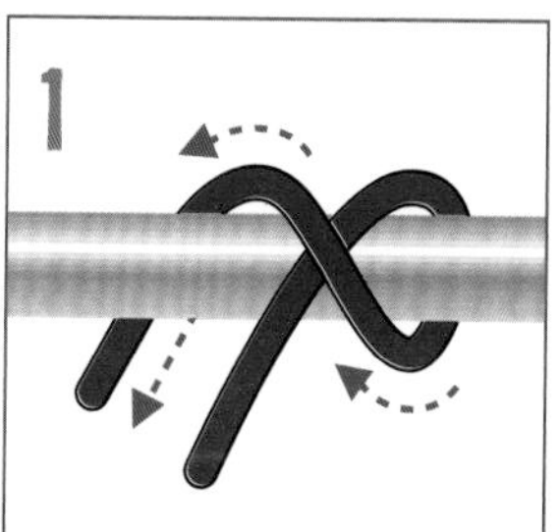

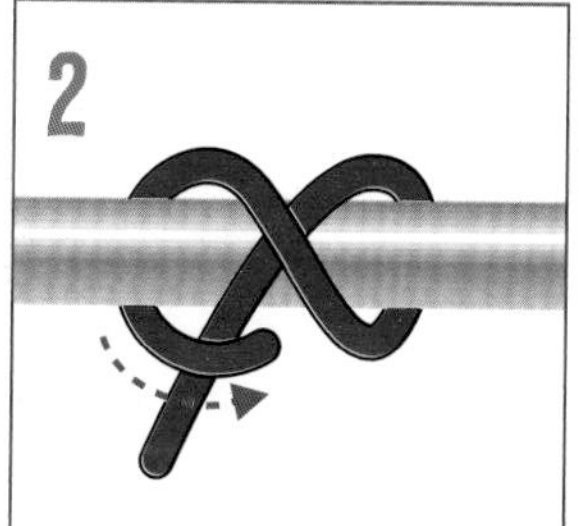

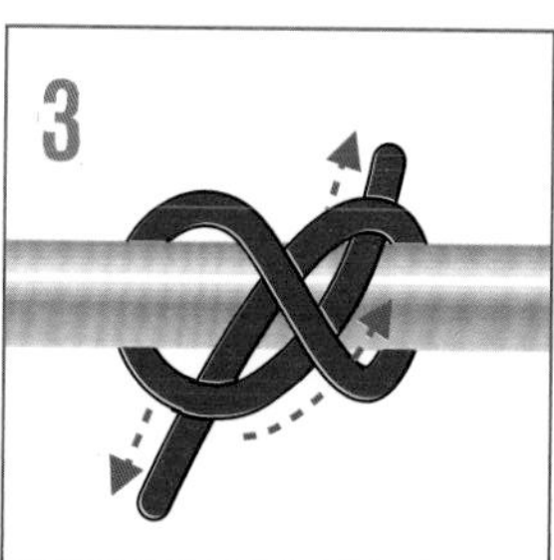

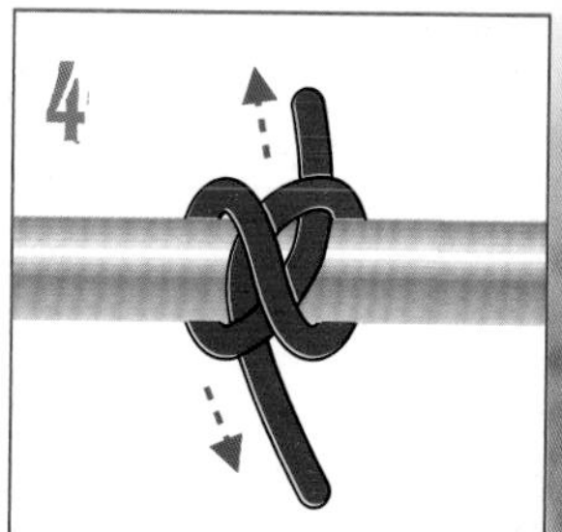

Wagner hitch

This is a simple and useful way of tensioning a rope, vine or lashing, providing a makeshift pulley system. If you're alone then it allows you to tension or lash something securely. It provides approximately a 3:1 ratio. Using a piece of wood in this hitch will help prevent the hitch from tightening when under load. Break the wood or pull it out to retrieve the rope without the pain of undoing a loaded knot.

1 Take a turn in the rope.

2 Take a 'bite' of rope in the right hand.

3 Pass the 'bite' through the left-hand loop.

4 Insert a strong piece of wood through the 'bite'.

5 Take the rope around an anchor and pass the other end through the free loop.

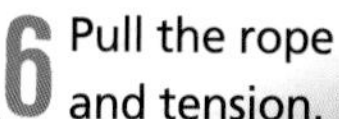

6 Pull the rope and tension.

Hammock knot or camel hitch

This is a useful hitch to know if you're 'hammock bound' for a long nervous night in the jungle. It's secure, simple to tie and easy to undo after it's borne your weight for the night.

1 Take a turn around an anchor.

2 Take 2–3 more descending turns.

3 Grab rope from the shorter length, usually in your right hand.

4 With your left hand pass the shorter end over the turns.

5 Go around the anchor with another turn and pass under the top turn.

6 Pull to tension on what will be the 'loaded' rope end.

Sledge knot

This is an excellent lashing knot. It's worth knowing as a knot for raft building, sledge repairs and lashing jobs that require a strong, reliable and almost permanent fixture. The downside is that once tied and tensioned it's almost impossible to retrieve the cord in one piece. The knot will have to be cut to salvage the cord. During the re-enactment expedition I did of Captain Scott's fateful journey to the South Pole we were completely in period clothing and had period equipment, including the sledges. We had little to no cord but instead had thin strips of leather to lash the sledge together and also use for any repairs. The sledge knot was invaluable.

1 Take a couple of turns around the anchor or whatever is to be bound together.

2 With the short end, take a turn under and over.

3 Take a further 3 turns going away from you.

4 Pass the end between the outer ropes.

5 Pass the end through the back two loops...

6 ... over the top of the 3rd loop and through the front loop.

7 Manipulate the knot to 'sit' well and 'ratchet' it taut so it bounds and bites.

Using natural foliage for cordage

Many of our strongest ropes and materials come from natural sources. There are many plants and vines, certain grasses, parts of animals and varieties of tree bark that may be useful in making cord, though it's likely that you'll have to plait natural or animal fibres together to get increased strength. Look for the following properties:

- Flexible enough to take a knot and not break or fracture.
- Strong enough to pull with all your strength in one direction.
- Doesn't dry too quickly and become brittle.
- Any plant, leaf or tree that's fibrous when pulled apart may be of some use.

Some examples of what you can use:

- In desert environments, sotol plants, century plants and especially the yucca plant are good for extracting fibre. Harvest the leaves and heat over hot coals until they blister. Pound them with a round stone and scrap any remaining pulp. Extract the thread-like fibres and manipulate. Plait them together for strong cordage. It's possible to boil then chew the leaf of the yucca to get the same result.

Survival tips

When splitting stems to break them down and harvest more cord material take care not to pull them apart in such a way that one side peels away to nothing before running the length of the stem. If the split gets thicker on one side, focus on pulling the thicker side as you separate the stem.

- In the jungle there are many vines and types of foliage that can potentially make good cord and rope. Rattan vine is particularly good. It grows long and weaves its way through the jungle using sharp, tiny hooks to attach itself. New shoots of the rattan can be eaten too, raw, boiled or cooked. It's strong and flexible.
- Parts of many palms can provide good cordage when harvested and manipulated. Leaves, trunks and stalks can sometimes be used. The husk of the coconut is particularly good.
- Thistles can make good cord. Remove leaves, needles and leaves. Choose old plants and preferably those that are dry. Lay them out and split or bend in sections to expose the pith, and scoop it out. Bashing them with a round stone will expose the pith too, but be careful not to destroy the stem too much when bashing. If necessary split larger ones into smaller sections before plaiting.
- Nettles should be soaked for a day, the pith removed and then left to dry. This should make the stems pliable. The leaves of the nettle won't sting you, but the stalks have hundreds of tiny hairs, which can irritate. Gather the desired number of stalks and plait together tightly.

- The bark of some trees can provide natural cord. Willow is particularly good. Harvest the bark from younger trees and split into strips before plaiting. Juniper can also be used but is less effective.
- Tree roots may be useful as cordage, though it will require some searching and digging to find suitable ones. Don't spend too much effort and time digging deep for them – there may be something else around that requires less effort to harvest. The roots of conifers tend to provide the best chance of usable cordage material.
- Animal hide and tendons are very good. They're parts of the animal that you wouldn't generally eat so are a useful resource that would otherwise be wasted. Larger animals are better. If possible use the tendons wet as they'll shrink and harden when drying. This will effect tighter lashing. Native Americans used tendons to lash their arrow tips to the shaft. Animal skin needs to be dried and manipulated for a good while to make usable cordage. This manipulation takes considerable effort but can be helped by adding oil to the parts you manipulate. Think of leather!

Good cordage and cord, either made from natural materials or manufactured, should have the qualities of Strength, Length, Bind and Bite.

Plaiting

Plaiting cord, rope and natural fibres well will give you a much stronger length of cord than just bundling them together. Gather three thinner strands of approximately the same length together. Tie an overhand knot in one end of the aligned strands and either anchor it to the ground, hold the knot with your teeth or get a buddy to hold it. Tie another overhand knot in the end to finish. Make the plaits tight, with no light showing between the strands.

General shelter

Constructing shelter in any environment will require a few considerations. It is better to spend time and a little effort looking for a good location that will provide the best position for your shelter. It can be false economy to lazily construct a shelter for it to fall apart during the first winds, snows or rains. It will then require double effort to rebuild and probably when you least want to. Consider these fundamentals:

- A location where the natural features offer some protection from the prevailing elements.
- Close to water.
- Construct your shelter with rescue in mind. Try to be obvious.
- Make the entrance facing away from prevailing weather conditions like wind.
- In exposed areas build a windbreak to protect you, your shelter and your fire.
- Use strong, non-rotten materials especially for the basic framework of the shelter. Less weight bearing materials can be older and more decomposed.
- Spend time on the basic, weight-bearing framework. Lash it together well with as strong a cord or natural fibre as possible.
- Be mindful of locations that can flood, are in the line of avalanches, big snow accumulations due to wind, lightning, extreme winds and rock fall.
- Try to construct your shelter so you have good observation for rescue, potential food and hazards.
- Aim to have your shelter where it is quiet. This will allow you to listen for rescue, animals and in-coming bad weather.
- In cold climates build a little way up from the valley base. Cold air sinks so the valley floor will be the coldest place at night.
- Try to get your sleeping area off the ground or insulate extremely well.
- If you are on a slope then sleep with your head higher than your feet. That said, after a long day walking it offers some relief to lie down and raise your legs higher than you head. This allows the legs to 'drain' and for me has given some reprieve after over-exercise.

1 Harvest three good, strong logs. Drive an upright into the ground. If possible the upright should have a 'V' at the top. The 'V' supports two longer logs. Lash the three together at the 'V.'

2 Lay sticks and logs along the length of the shell and across the two logs leading to the ground. Lay thinner branches and foliage along the larger sticks and cover as many gaps as possible.

3 Construct an entrance close to the end of the two main supporting logs that are in contact with the ground. Use thin spreading branches on the outside as these will hold the piled up leaves in place better. Organise the shape of the branches into the shape of your shelter.

4 Cover the whole shelter in leaves. If you have no leaves use snow or live foliage. If you have tarpaulin or something similar then use this.

Personal hygiene

Spending time at the end of each day checking over your body and those of your buddies is very important. Many health issues can be avoided by good hygiene, and to have any chance of overcoming a survival situation or coping with an extreme environment good personal hygiene is vital. Some pointers:

- Wash hands regularly.
- Carry out a full body wash at least once a week if possible. Pay particular attention to armpits, groin and feet.
- Wash your clothes when appropriate. These need to function for your own protection.
- In environments where lice, mites and chiggers are prevalent boiling your clothes will prevent infestations. Inspect hairy parts of the body for these critters.
- Keep the body well covered with clothing in all environments. This will vary depending on the environment.
- UV light kills most germs and helps keep lice, mites and chiggers at bay. Expose the body to short periods of sunlight where possible and appropriate. This goes for clothes too.
- Air out sleeping bags and clothes when you can.
- Keep feet dry and aired where possible. Be sensible in cold climates, however.
- Keep your hair short. Cut hair makes good tinder.
- Brush your teeth. If you don't have a toothbrush use bark or a twig. Use it only once. Cotton can be used as dental floss. Wash the mouth with salt water.
- Keep camp areas clean and free of decaying flesh and human waste. Human waste should be well buried away from your campsite. This goes for all environments.
- Don't keep food lying about, attracting flies and vermin.
- Keep eating utensils clean and free of food once used. Wooden utensils can crack, fill with food and rot.
- Don't let embarrassment prevent you from going to the toilet when you need to.
- Don't drink untreated stagnant water. Boil it first.

FINDING FOOD

There will come a point where you will need to eat. This can be compounded by your level of physical output. The good thing is we do not need that much to eat and there is usually something in close proximity, in most environments. Some places are harder to find food than others but keep looking and foraging and lose the squeamish thoughts that you may have. Save energy when eating by not necessarily cooking everything that can be eaten raw, such as locusts, maggots and grasshoppers. With a little knowledge you could save your life and possibly that of your team by finding food.

Living off the land

Having been thrust into a survival situation, your initial reactions will usually be fuelled by adrenalin; food is likely to be the last thing on your mind. It's true that the body can sustain itself for longer without food than without water, but there will quickly come a point where sustenance becomes necessary, if only for morale. It's important to ration what you already have, and to make plans to locate more.

The average male requires about 2,500 calories a day to maintain the involuntary functions such as breathing, blood circulation and body warmth. Females require about 2,000 calories. Once you start adding in other functions (fire lighting, foraging, shelter building, travelling) then the calorific output quickly rises, possibly to above 4,000. If your calorific output is greater than the input from food then weight loss is inevitable and, over time, body and mind functions will deteriorate. The body needs a varied diet to function effectively. Putting it simply, humans need five basic food elements. These are:

- **Carbohydrates** – these are most often found in fruit, vegetables and whole grains. Carbohydrates provide an easily digestible and good, slow-burning energy source. They help with many functions of the body.
- **Protein** – found in fish, meat, vegetables, eggs, nuts and seeds. Helps build and repair body tissue, produces enzymes, hormones and other substances the body uses. It helps the body resist diseases and helps produce stamina and energy.

Don't eat centipedes or millipedes - however tempting they may look!

- **Fats** – harder for the body to digest but provide a longer lasting energy source. Found in eggs, animal meat and fish.
- **Vitamins** – these provide no calories but help the body's functions and overall health. Found in most foods but in varying quantities.
- **Minerals** – these help build strong teeth and bones, help heal wounds and are crucial for the proper functioning of some major organs. Minerals come from most foods including water, as all minerals come from the ground.

Edibility test for plants and fungi

As omnivores there's not much in the animal and plant worlds that we can't eat and gain some level of nutritional value from. The aim here is to learn a few common edible plants from all environments, rather than expect to know them all. Wherever possible seek the knowledge of the indigenous people, who've been living off the land for generations. Don't assume that because animals, insects and birds eat a certain plant it's also good for humans – animals sometimes build a tolerance to plants that may be lethal to us. If you can identify a plant that's edible and there's a high yield about don't eat large quantities right away. Let your stomach and body adjust to the plant first.

Unless you have a good in-depth knowledge of what's good to eat and what isn't, eating something you're unfamiliar with will always be a risk. In the most extreme situations where you have little to no options left for food, the last resort is to conduct the 'Edibility Test'. Firstly, you should always avoid plants and fungi that have:

- A bitter almond, peachy or acidic smell to them.
- A mushroom or mushroom-like appearance, unless you're 100% certain it can be positively identified.
- Milky or black sap.
- Fungal infection on the plant.
- A black pea-like appearance.

Other general rules are:

- If you have strong doubts, then leave it alone.
- Ensure there's an abundant supply of the plant. It's not worth taking the risks associated with the test for the sake of just a few plants.
- Don't consume anything else whilst doing the test, or indeed for some eight hours prior.

- Only have one person in the team test the plant – this should be a willing volunteer!
- Complete the whole test – don't cut corners.
- Have plenty of water to hand (preferably hot).
- Inspect the plant thoroughly.

Avoid fungi unless you really know your facts.

- Use only live, fresh, washed vegetation.
- Consider testing the plant in the form that you intend to consume it: this may be after boiling, roasting or raw.
- Break the plant down and test only those parts you hope to eat.
- Rub the plant and sap on the skin and spend a good period of time looking for any reaction.

If all the above guidelines have been followed and there's no irritation to the skin, then proceed to the following stages:

- Place or rub a small portion on the inside of your lip. Wait five minutes for any reaction. Don't swallow any juice or saliva.
- Place a small portion on the inside of your mouth and wait five minutes.
- Place a small portion on or under the tongue and wait 15 minutes. Try not to swallow any of your saliva nor any plant juices.
- Chew a small part of the plant for a good period, hold it in your mouth then spit it out. Wait for 15 minutes for any reaction.

Wild figs – tasty and nutritious.

The berry rule

Berries can cause a severe if not fatal reaction. Take note of the following, but unless you can positively identify the berry then conduct the Edibility Test:

- **Green, yellow and white berries are highly unlikely to be edible.**
- **Approximately 50% of red berries are edible.**
- **Black, purple and blue berries are approximately 90% edible.**
- **Many small berries that make up the whole fruit, for example blackberries and raspberries are approximately 90% plus edible.**

The above is a guideline only and must be used in conjunction with the Edibility Test.

- Thoroughly chew a small portion of the plant again and swallow. Wait for between five and eight hours for any reaction. Don't eat or drink anything else during this period.
- If you have charcoal to hand and your stomach reacts to the plant, mix the charcoal with water and swallow it or else swallow some without water. Charcoal may help to absorb the poison. It may also induce vomiting. You can get charcoal from your fire.
- After the appropriate time lapse, eat a larger portion and wait for five to eight hours again.

If there's still no reaction after this test then the plant may be considered safe to eat. But eat it in moderation and prepared as it was for the test. If you've only tested one component of the plant then the test must be carried out again before any other components are eaten.

Bugs and grubs

All of us have unknowingly ingested a bug, grub or creepy crawly on some occasion. Once you've overcome the squeamishness associated with bugs they can become a vital survival food. Weight for weight they actually provide very well-balanced nutrition. Abundant the world over, they're easily caught, prepared and cooked or added to other foods.

A general guideline is that you should avoid eating hairy, brightly coloured caterpillars, spiders, mosquitoes, ticks and flies. Also avoid bugs and grubs feeding on dead or decomposing carrion. Instead, use them as bait. Avoid eating centipedes and millipedes too – these can be poisonous – and be wary of snails with brightly coloured shells.

Mostly, you should gather bugs by searching close to the ground and with the minimum of effort. Tear rotten and decomposing trees apart with your knife or hands and look carefully for termites, larvae and beetles. Look in nooks, crannies and moist areas. Check the ground and sunny slopes for ants and termite nests. Ants are loaded with formic acid, which they use as a defence. Cook or boil large quantities of ants before eating. Many crickets, grasshoppers and locusts are well camouflaged, so move slowly and carefully as you search. Moths, butterflies and other flying insects can be collected at night using a light source to attract them. This needs to be a torch rather than fire – most bugs will avoid smoke and fire. Take the hard outer shell and large mandibles off beetles before cooking and the wings and barbed legs off other insects before eating raw or cooking.

Bite the heads off large maggots and larvae before eating them raw. The larvae of ants and termites are very nutritional and particularly good to eat. Ants and termites will protect their larvae from the heat and sun. Break the nest down and put sections of it in the sun. The insects will take the larvae to the shade and make a good store ready for you to eat. Shaking these nest sections full of ants and larvae over a potential fishing spot is a pretty sure way of attracting fish.

Bite the heads off large maggots before eating them.

Avoid centipedes and millipedes as they can be poisonous.

Survival tips

I've eaten worm and seagull egg omelette with crushed nettles, raw maggots and grasshoppers. Hold the thought in your head that it's doing you good! Worms, slugs and snails are best 'purged' for a day or two before you eat them – this means not letting them eat, so that their stomachs and intestines empty. They may have eaten a plant poisonous to you. Boil or roast them to eat.

Bees, wasps and hornets

These are all edible but may be painful or difficult to catch and collect. Hives can be found in the ground, but they're more often on trees and cliffs. The honeybee and its honey are a great source of food and energy, but the bees seem to know this and guard their hives to the death. Hornets are bigger and even more aggressive, and their sting can inflict considerable pain. If you come across a nest then plan carefully how you're going to extract the insect, its larvae or the honey. Consider these points:

- Wait till it's cooler, preferably night. The cold makes such insects more docile.
- Smoke them out with a lighted torch or fire. This will confuse the insects and after a time allow you to get to the hive.
- Cover all of your skin apart from your eyes.
- If you use a naked flame close to the nest the flame will burn their wings and the insects will drop to the ground. Have a sheet on the ground to collect them. When the nest is almost clear knock it to the ground for the larvae and honey.
- Pull off the sting, legs and wings and roast or boil the insects before eating.

• WISE WORDS •

Foraging for bugs in the jungles of Panama, I climbed a short, steep mud bank to a rotten tree that I hoped would contain larvae of some kind. As I hung by the branch and started tearing the rotten bark off I was nearly knocked from my perch as a couple of searing bolts of pain hit my hand and arm. I had disturbed a bullet ant nest and had been bitten. The bites are non-lethal, but as the name suggests the pain is akin to being hit by a bullet. It was a good reminder to always be careful when you're foraging for creepy crawlies.

Be careful! Bees seem to know when they're under attack.

Eat the comb as well as the honey.

Honey will last a long time so ration yourself and find something to carry it in. Be aware that honey attracts many animals and insects so protect it well. The combs in which the honey and larvae are found can also be eaten.

Don't forget the insects and larvae that are abundant in and around lakes and rivers. Forage along the shore or use your shirt tied and stretched out between two sticks to trawl. Cook everything, as the water may be polluted.

Animal tracking

Good observation skills and an awareness of animal movement are important to the survivalist when on the hunt for food. You increase your chances of finding food, and with less effort. Most animals will see you well before you see them so you must learn to observe and interpret tracks and disturbances. A simple understanding of tracking, camouflage and stalking broadens your awareness of animals and the environment in which they live. Following animal tracks and routes may lead you to a greater number of animals, at drinking holes, in dens and around food sources.

Not all areas are rich in wildlife, so maintaining a keen eye on the landscape around you as you travel is vital. Get into the habit of looking up, down and around, as you may otherwise miss the only clue indicating that animals are about. Animals tend to move to where there's food and water, a varied amount of vegetation, and thick cover for security. Some animals will get water from sources other than rivers and lakes.

Wild animals are masters of camouflage, but it's nevertheless worth concealing yourself when possible and moving with some stealth. So:

- Don't use perfumed items to wash or clean. The smell travels, and it's better to have the odour of the environment.
- Dress in colours similar to those of the foliage around you. Dress in baggy clothes to break up your outline.
- Try to use a variety of colours rather than one. Disruptive patterns are better.
- Blacken your face with mud if necessary – not the whole face, just a few streaks across it to break up the outline.
- If you're stationary have a background behind you so that you're not silhouetted.
- Don't move along a ridge line, as you'll be silhouetted. Drop down just below it if possible.
- Use cover where you can.
- Don't make sudden moves.
- Blacken or cover items that shine.
- Break up any linear shapes and outlines.
- If possible, wear clothes that don't rustle.

If you see disturbances and/or tracks, ask yourself what happened and what it indicates. Get yourself into tracking mode. Try to think like the animal and travel as it would. Look ahead for further signs. Even ants

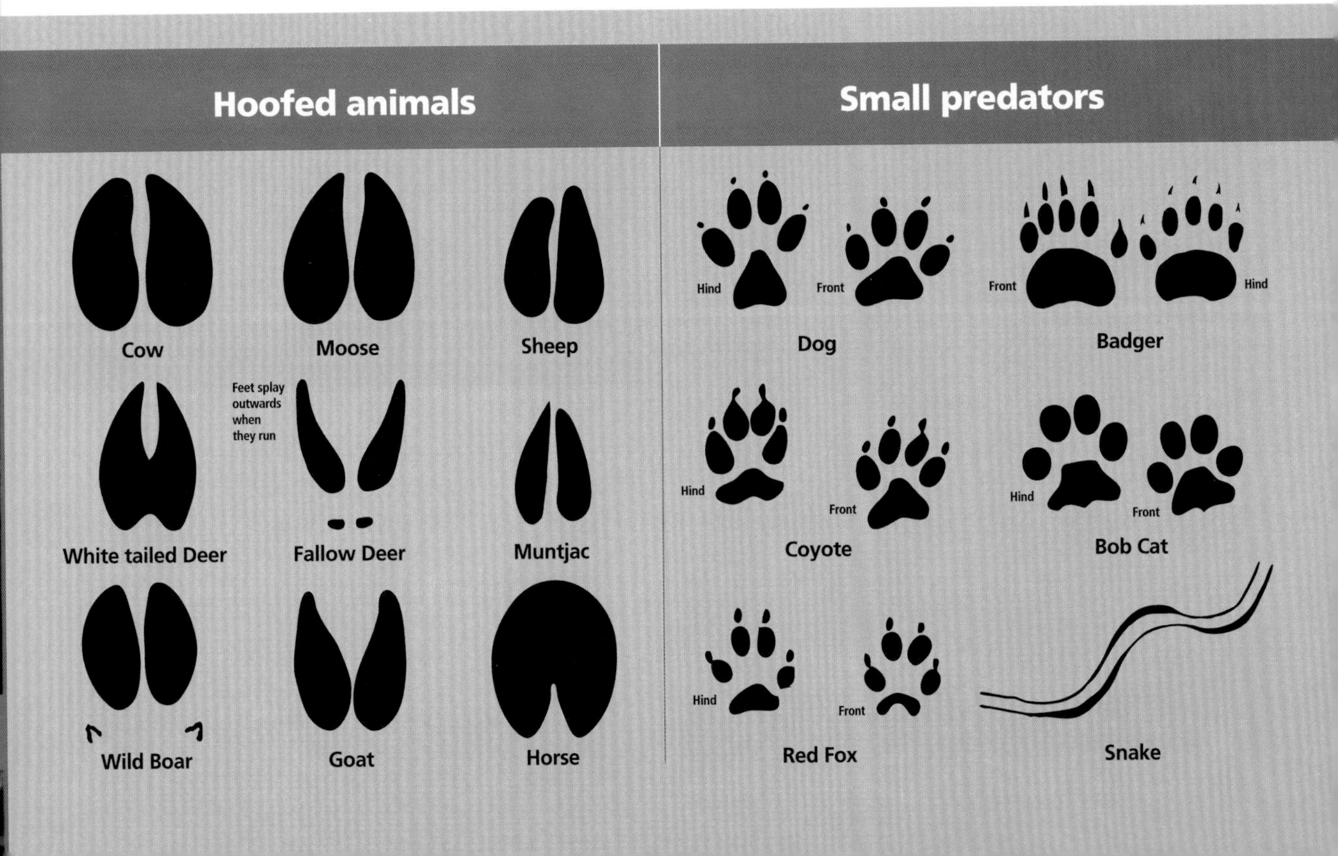

Hoofed animals

Cow

Moose

Sheep

White tailed Deer

Feet splay outwards when they run

Fallow Deer

Muntjac

Wild Boar

Goat

Horse

Small predators

Hind

Front

Dog

Front

Hind

Badger

Hind

Front

Coyote

Hind

Front

Bob Cat

Hind

Front

Red Fox

Snake

and worms make tracks. Tracking a worm trail in mud to get the worm means food or bait! Some considerations and guidelines when tracking and observing are:

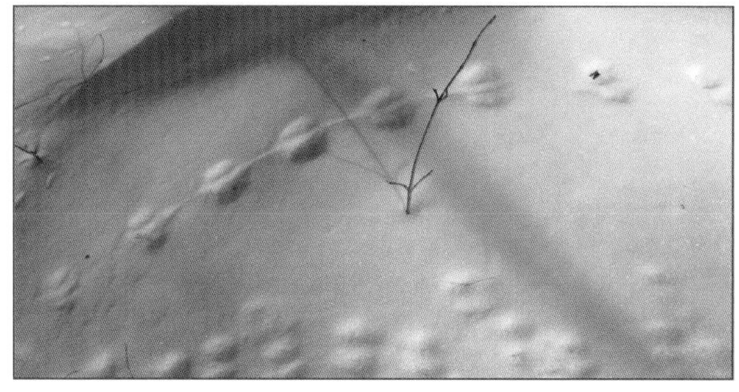

- Track early in the morning. The air is usually clearer, giving better visibility, and there's more animal movement at night so disturbances are freshest in the morning. Dew may be on the ground, which will also show disturbances.
- Take time to sit/lie, wait and observe. Do this for as long as you can. Camouflage yourself.
- Move steadily and look at all levels, and even behind you on occasion.
- Break a large area of ground up into sections and scan systematically so that nothing is missed.
- Be in the mode to observe sudden movement. Have a weapon at the ready.
- Sniff the air and listen at regular intervals.
- Look for the lines of least resistance to travel. Certain points on rivers may be a good crossing point for animals. Look for disturbances here and trap or observe as necessary.
- Look for fresh droppings, fur and hair on bushes and trees, flattened foliage.
- Animals often mark trees. Bears claw at them, deer rub their antlers on them, and squirrels hide nuts in semi-rotten trees.
- Look for signs of animal feeding. Feathers, half-eaten pine cones, circling birds or obvious ground-digging in search of grubs.
- Study the track and disturbance to determine direction of movement.
- Determine how fresh tracks are. Tracks that are partly filled in, have collapsed or have deteriorated in shape (and there has been no recent wind) will be old. Tracks that are raised and hard above the level of snow will be old. The weight of a body on snow compresses the snow and friction melts it slightly. It then re-freezes and lasts longer than the undisturbed snow around it.
- If you feel you're close to animals, stop and assess the route offering the best cover. Use natural features such as ditches, bushes and mounds. If possible get downwind so that your scent is blown away from the animals. If you're spotted, freeze: wait for a reaction – the animal may not have smelt or seen humans before, in which case it may just carry on what it was doing. Move as slowly as possible and cautiously test the next step without committing to it. Keep your weight in the heel of your foot as you place your foot and roll the foot from the outside as you bear down on it.

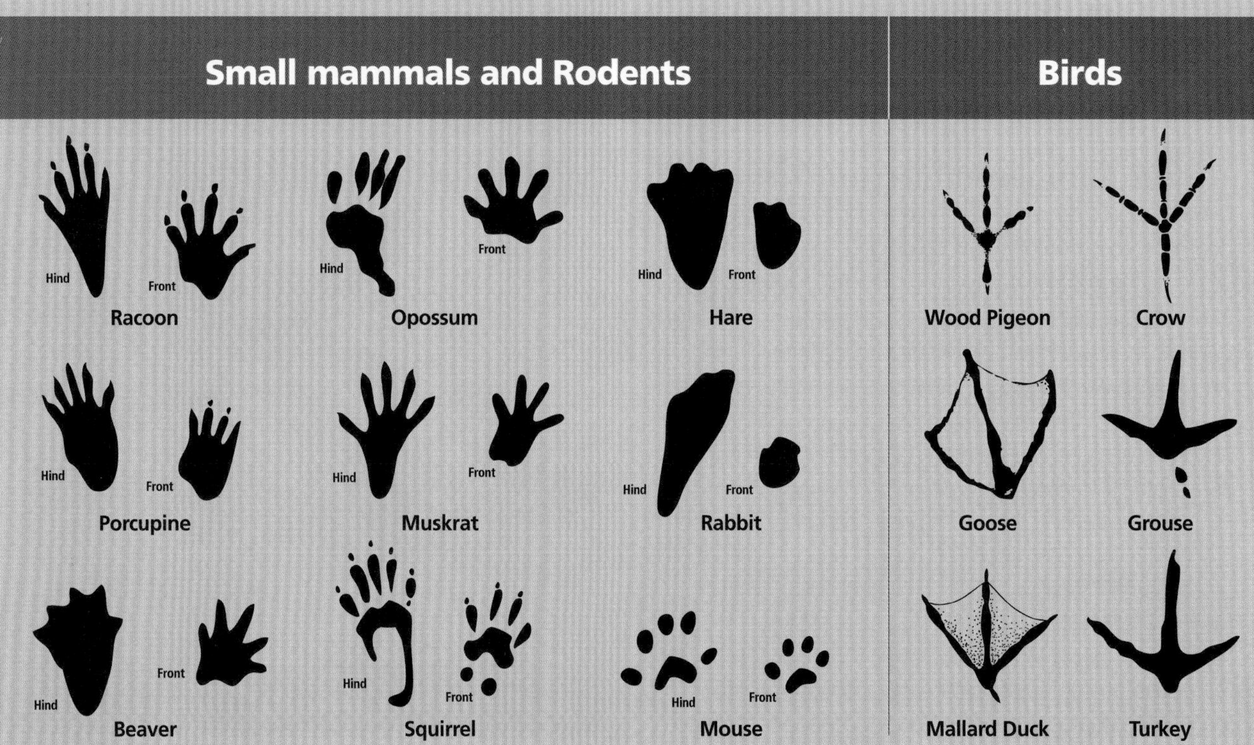

Traps and snares

Making and setting traps and snares may not be a primary requirement when you're in a survival situation, for, depending on the environment, it's often easier to forage for plant, river and coastal food. However, you should be ready from the outset to pounce on anything edible you may come across.

Traps and trapping

The following traps and snares are designed for small to medium-sized animals and birds. Larger animals can be caught using the same principles, but may not be worth the effort and danger involved. Big game takes more time to prepare, a lot of effort to transport, and although there's much more meat it will rot and decompose quickly. A big game kill may also attract dangerous animals to your location. Having said that, any kill is a success in a survival situation. Use the food wisely:

- Eat some raw if it's a fresh kill.
- Keep it safe.
- Ration yourself: preserve and store some of the meat.
- Consider using guts and entrails as bait for traps and snares.

Even the marrow from the bones shouldn't be wasted. If you have a fresh kill then break open the bones and add the marrow to water to make soup, or eat it raw. You can also extract marrow from a carcass that's a day or two old, but avoid carcasses that are very decomposed. Marrow is rich in protein.

It takes a lot of trial and error to trap and snare any animal, and success isn't guaranteed. You're in the animals' environment and they sense, see and smell changes far more acutely than humans do. But be patient and persevere. Patrol an area and look for signs of animal activity and water sources. Animals need to drink, particularly so in arid environments. Try to imagine how they would negotiate a piece of ground; most animals won't expend energy unnecessarily. Set more than one trap or snare over an area that appears to show signs of animal activity.

Areas to trap and tips on trapping

- Keep it simple.
- Rats, mice, rabbits and squirrels are often easier to trap than big game. They confine themselves to a smaller area and have regular habits.
- Look for game trails and runs to water holes and food sources; set your traps at points where such trails and runs are constricted.
- Set up improvised barriers from surrounding foliage to force animals towards your trap.
- Make traps and snares sensitive to any disturbance so that the likelihood of it being sprung is greater. To achieve this, whittle fine points on sticks you may use in the trap's construction. Aim to balance the trap with some precariousness.
- Try to camouflage the trap or snare as much as possible without compromising its efficiency.
- If you have blood and guts then spread these around the trap area to conceal your human scent and to attract animals.
- Bait your traps and snares if possible.
- It may take a day or more for the trap to lose your scent. Smoking an area can help.
- Try to smoke animals from their holes and lairs. Make sure you're well prepared to catch or kill the animal before you start to generate smoke. Block off other holes, leaving only one escape route for the animal.
- Check the traps every day and especially at first light.

A successful deadfall trap.

Snares

A snare can be made very simply from a piece of wire, rope or twine. You may only have one chance at trapping something, so pay attention to detail. Wire is best as animals can't chew through it: do you have some in your kit? Think of wire from the hood of your waterproof jacket, or as part of the construction of your rucksack. If restricted to natural materials then focus on those that are strong and springy.

Snares are simple constructions designed to trap an animal around its neck. Construct a small loop that will tighten around the neck of the animal as it travels through it. Think of a cowboy's lasso. Open the loop so it's a little larger than the head of the animal that you intend to snare: about four fingers for squirrel, fist size for rabbit, and about two clenched hands for a fox. Place the loop just above the ground or about the height of the animal's head as it travels. Use small sticks to hold the loop above the ground. If you're placing the snare at the opening to a burrow then position the snare at what you think will be head height for the animal. Attach the other end of the wire securely to a peg driven into the ground – something sturdy that the animal will be unable to drag off.

• WISE WORDS •

In the Siberian winter temperatures fall to –30° at night. Finding the signs of small mammals, we angled a narrow log from the frozen ground to a couple of metres up a tree. Small snares were set at the base of the log and where the log met the tree. The next morning we had five frozen squirrels in our snares. The raw, almost frozen meat could be eaten straight away.

A wire snare supported off the ground with a twig

Think about where you position your snare and make sure it's the right height for the type of animal.

Lift or twitch stick snares

Locate a suitable place that has signs of animal activity and preferably an animal run to water or food. Look for a suitable branch from a tree that will bend to the ground without snapping and that will have the strength to lift prey to a good height and out of the way of predators. This should be approximately 3m tall. Construct the wire into a snare in the same way as a simple snare. Harvest an approximately 2cm diameter branch and make two pegs. Whittle an interlocking latch or toggle trigger out of the two pegs and attach the snare to the upper peg whilst driving the lower one into the ground. Pull the trigger branch down and attach it to the top peg. Set the snare over the run and support the snare wire to the correct height with one small Y-shaped sticks.

If there isn't a tree with a suitable trigger branch at the snare position then improvise by using a branch that you've harvested from elsewhere as the trigger. Place the middle of the trigger branch in a good-sized Y-shaped peg and weight one end of it with a rock. Pull the other end down and attach this to the snare and toggle trigger.

Survival tips

There are many other ways to improvise traps and variations on all these shown here are possible. Other useful traps are pits and running nooses. For the former, dig a pit in an animal run or near a water hole and cover it with weak saplings and leaves. Either dig the pit deep enough so that the animal can't get out or have snares, spears or a net at the bottom to kill or capture it. The walls of the pit should be undercut to make it difficult for the animal to get out.

A running noose is useful for stalking game and birds. It resembles a fishing rod with a noose at the end of the line, which runs down a long branch through eyelets to the stalker.

Springsnares

Harvest two sticks approximately 2cm in diameter, 12–15cm long and with an angled, smaller stem to cut down. When driven into the ground about 10–12cm apart the smaller stem is angled down.

Harvest two 10–12cm sticks and a small toggle. Attach the toggle to cord and to the spring branch. Measure the length so when released the prey hangs approximately 2m high.

Work the forces so the toggle holds the two horizontally placed sticks in place. Build a small ramp to lay the snare loop on. Keep the length of cord from the toggle to the snare loop short and run it around the front of the upper horizontal stick. Place bait in the snare loop. When the ramp is weighted by the animal the lower of the two horizontally placed sticks drops and the snare is sprung.

The snare line that is attached to the tip of the spring branch should run down and attach to the base of the spring branch. Take a few turns around the branch before fixing to the base. Note the way the snare cord is set around the snare construction

Figure 4 deadfall trap

- Harvest three sticks that will support the weight and act as a securing peg, trigger and locking arm.
- Sharpen one end of the horizontal (bait) bar so that the bait can be secured.
- Sharpen the top of the upright that will be balanced on the block.
- The bait bar is notched at the opposite end to the bait, to take the locking arm.
- The locking arm should be sharpened to rest in the notch precariously. A small notch is made to it on the upright.
- Mark a pivot point approximately midway on the bait bar and whittle a small locking notch on the upright to hold the bait bar.
- Get an idea of the balance point and whittle a notch on the bait bar to sit in the notch on the upright.
- Lean the weight or deadfall on the locking arm and make sure the bait is well under the deadfall.

Make sure the weight of the box is heavy enough to secure the animal

Trigger

Daisy box trap

This is a good trap to catch prey alive. This may be useful if you intend to travel with some food, as a live animal will last longer.

- Make a bottomless box out of small logs and wood, constructed in a pyramid shape – broad at the base, tapering to a point at the top – as this requires less effort and fewer resources.
- Animals will desperately try to escape when they're trapped, so the weight of the box must be sufficient to stop the animal pushing it over from the inside.
- Attach some fine cord, horsehair, wire or thin tendon to the middle of one side of the box. Tie or skewer some bait to the cord so that it can sit in the middle of the trap.
- Measure a length of the cord that will just reach to the other side and tie it to the middle of a thin stick, which is then set to hold the box up. The cord should be taut with the bait in the middle of the trap.
- The box is balanced open and high enough so that the animal can easily get underneath it to get the bait. Useful for small prey – rats, rodents, mice etc.
- As the animal tries to pull the bait the small trigger stick is dislodged and the box falls, trapping the animal.

Deadfall traps

Deadfall traps need bait but can be effective and easy to construct. A number of deadfall traps can be constructed using natural foliage and only require the use of a knife to construct them. As the name suggests, a heavy log or rock that will kill or hold the animal has to be found. It's arguably easier to go for small prey than one big kill due to the effort of construction and materials, particularly if you're alone.

Ojibwa bird trap

This trap was used by the North American Indians and the name is Canadian. It can be used to trap almost any size of bird. Adjust the dimensions and size of the resource used to suit the size of bird you intend to catch. The description outlined below is for a medium-sized bird. All you need is a knife and some cord or wire to make a snare:

- Harvest and/or construct a spring branch that will hold your prey about 2m high and away from predators.
- Harvest two sticks approximately 1cm in diameter, 10–12cm long and with an angled, smaller stem to cut down. When driven into the ground about 10–12cm apart the smaller stem is angled down forming a small 'Y'.
- Harvest a toggle and tie cord to a third of the way down and onto the end of the spring branch. The line from the toggle should also extend to the snare and be short.
- Harvest a horizontal stick to go under the 'Y' stakes that have been driven into the ground. Place sticks to hold the snare loop in place, to keep its shape and at a height just above the bait. The bait stick prevents the toggle from releasing at one end when under load and is notched into an upright outer stick on the other end and on the outside edge of the snare loop.
- Ensure the cord from the toggle goes in front of the horizontal stick.
- As the bird tugs at the bait the toggle is released and the snare sprung.

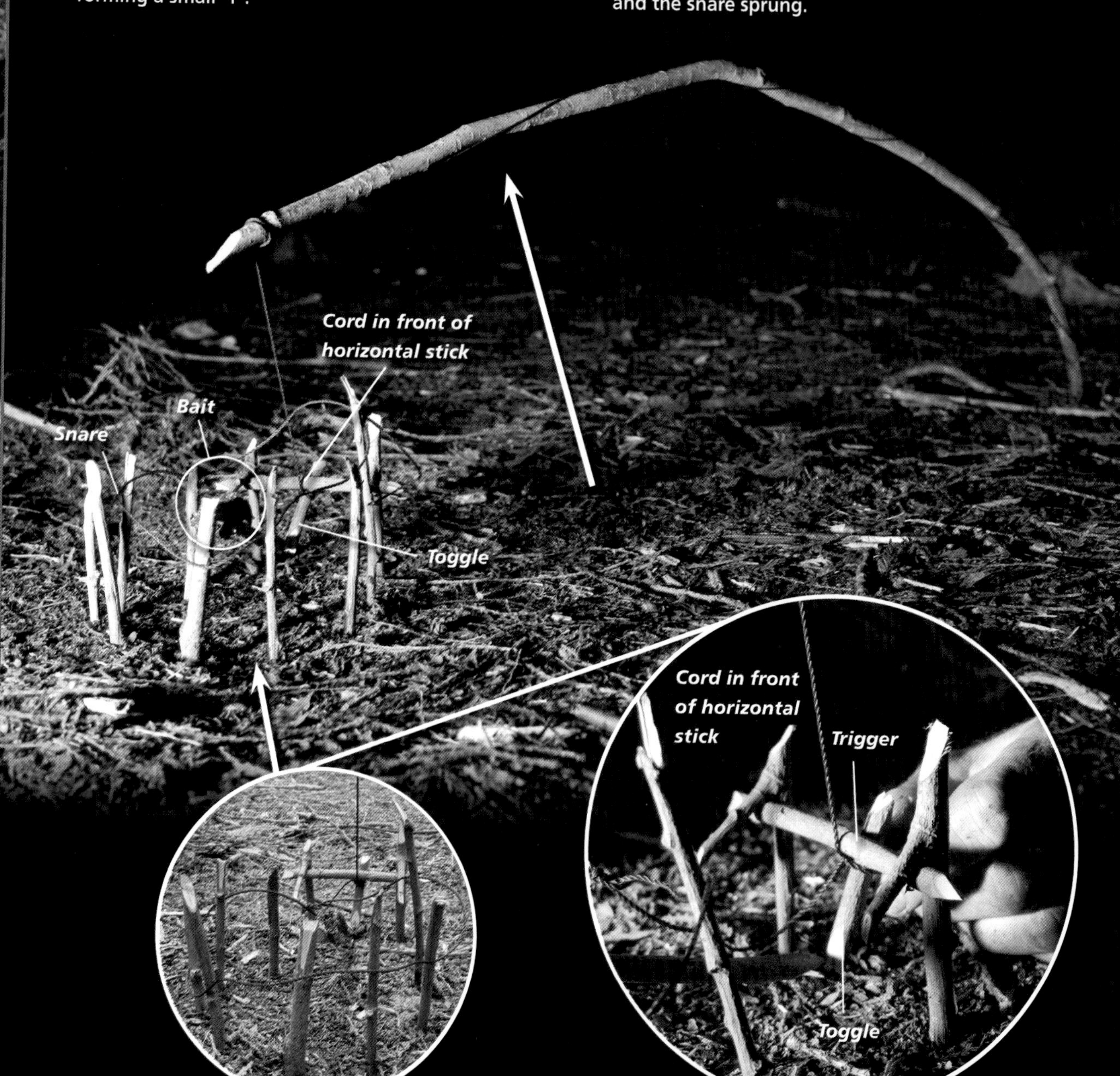

Spear construction

Simply sharpening a straight, strong stick is a good start. If you have fire then use the embers to harden the tip after sharpening. Place the spear end in embers. The aim is for it not to catch fire. Maintain a keen observation and when it is well blackened but not burnt and flaky it is ready for use and somewhat tougher.

Fire hardening the spear tip.

Construct a spear in the early stages of a survival situation. An opportunity may present itself to get food!

Other forms of construction include:

- Lashing your knife to the stick. Be mindful to lash it well, though – you can't afford to lose it.
- Striking flint with another rock to achieve a sharp edge. Knapped flint can be very sharp indeed, so be careful when shaping it.
- Bone can be sharpened and shaped to form a spearhead.
- To secure a spearhead to the shaft, split the end and secure base of the head within it by lashing. Wet animal sinew works well, as it dries hard and firm.
- A forked or trident spearhead will work better for fishing.

Arm yourself with your improvised spear or a good throwing rock. Fabricate a net, or fashion a catapult. Always be on the lookout; walk about with a degree of stealth and stop and look around at intervals to observe your environment. It's better to have found a good source of small animal food like rats, mice and squirrels than to hunt for big game.

Fishing and fish traps

Fish can be a good source of food as fishing often requires little effort. The best times to fish are early morning, dusk, at night with a full moon and at night if you have a source of light. Fish can be difficult to predict and their habits vary depending on species, time of year, salt or fresh water, temperature and the strength of water flow. The habits of fish may include:

- Resting in slack water.
- Hiding amongst debris, wrecks and boulders.
- Searching for food and oxygen-rich water where rivers meets lakes.
- Going deeper during the heat of the day.
- Seeking out the shallows of a deep lake for food and warmth.
- Resting in the shade of a tree or bush overhanging the water.

Some fish are attracted by a shine – attach tin foil, buttons, coins, a piece of bright cloth or anything that glimmers to your hook.

Consider using bait or waste animal/fish guts to 'chum' an area. Pick your spot and gently spread some bait over the area. Choose the best way of catching your prey, camouflage yourself and wait patiently. Chumming an area using ants and termites is particularly effective.

If you choose to make a fish spear it needs to be at least 2m long. Tie a long tether to the end and attach this to your wrist. Whittle or make a barbed head for the spear, with the barbs pointing back towards the butt.

Spearing fish is difficult due to the light being refracted by the water, but is easier in shallow water. To get an idea of how much to aim 'off', pick a fist-sized rock on the bottom, aim your spear at it and push the spear towards it. See how far off you are and compensate accordingly.

All freshwater fish are edible and can be eaten raw straight after being caught. Fish can also be cooked or dried. Some tropical fish are inedible. Gut the fish you catch and use the guts as further bait. Cut gutted fish into small strips to dry or smoke. The guts should be well cooked before consumption or else used as raw bait. Tiny fish of less than approximately 4cm can be eaten whole. Fish

Check out hiding places and suitable positions for traps.

Small but still nutritious.

eyes provide fluid as well as food, so don't be squeamish – swallow fresh eyes whole!

If you don't have any fish-hooks then carve and whittle them from bone or wood, or improvise them from wire, a paperclip or a hairpin. Thorns still attached to part of the stem can be used as hooks too.

Damming and netting

Damming part of a river to force the fish through a narrower, netted section may be considered, but depends on the width of the river and the resources you have at hand. Use logs, stones and deadfall to dam three-quarters of the river's width, causing a narrow yet faster flowing run to one side. Place netting or set traps across this part.

If you're able to use or make a net then a 'gill net' will provide a useful and effective way to catch fish. Ideally the mesh size should be no more than 4cm, but you may have to work with what you've made or found. Stretch the net across the river or part of it and secure it. If you can add floats across the top of the net at intervals then do so; try to improvise with whatever's to hand. Weight the base of the net at intervals so that it sits on the bottom and remains securely in place.

Woven fish trap

This is a constructed trap usually made from young, bendy branches such as hazel and bamboo. It works on the same principle as a lobster trap: the fish are lured in by bait through a small hole to a larger cavity but then can't find their way back out. Place your trap in an area of slack water with the opening facing downstream. Consider making the traps to catch small fish that can be eaten or used as bait for larger fish.

Prepare the caught fish soon after catching by removing the guts. Cut from the anus to the throat and, using two fingers, scoop the guts out and clean the inside. Hang the fish and let it bleed. Keep the guts for baiting. The fish will also last longer if the guts and blood have been removed. It's not necessary to de-scale the fish, especially if you're going to cook it.

Field preparation

Field preparing caught animals is important for both preservation and consumption. Be wary of the guts: animal stomachs may contain partly digested food and some organs may be risky to consume. Organs that are nutritious to eat include the heart – lots of muscle with little fat; the liver, but wash it and eat it as soon as possible; and the kidneys, which need to be washed and cooked.

Cover up any open wounds on your hands and arms before you start handling any animal, dead or alive. Be careful not to cut yourself with your knife or the broken bones of the animal. Avoid any contamination. Some animals can also be covered in ticks and parasites, so be mindful of this when dealing with the skin and fur.Once you've caught or trapped your prey you need to:

- Finish the kill if necessary. This is not a time to be hesitant. The animal must be quickly dispatched. With smaller animals this can be done by breaking the neck: hold the main body firmly between your legs, place one hand at the base of the neck and with the other pull the neck aggressively upwards and simultaneously twist. Cutting the neck and severing the jugular artery will quickly kill larger animals, as will severing or driving a knife into the spinal cord at the base of the neck.
- Decide if you're going to field prepare the animal at the kill site or take it back to your camp. Large animals are heavy even after gutting and it may be too much effort to drag a big carcass back.
- Field preparing the animal at the kill site may encourage more animals to the area, so re-bait and reset your traps when you've finished.

Preparing a rabbit

1 Kill the animal by breaking its neck. Grab the back legs and place your hand around the neck. Pull hard.

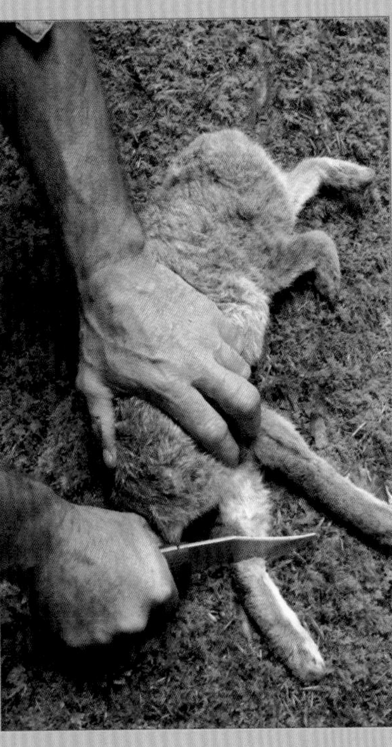

2 Cut the head off. Keep for bait. Cut the legs of at the lowest joint. Keep for bait. Watch out for sharp bones. Keep bones for fish hooks.

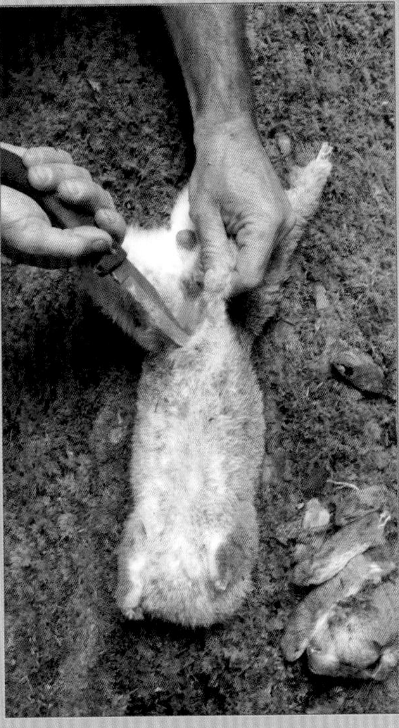

3 Cut the outer skin from the anus to the sternum. Do not puncture the intestines as this will contaminate the meat.

Here's one I caught earlier.

• WISE WORDS •

I can remember field preparing a wild pig with a buddy once. Pigs don't have to be skinned before cooking, but this one's skin was covered with large black ticks and mites. It was as if its skin was literally crawling. That made me wince somewhat! So we singed the outside of the pig with fire before field preparing it fully.

4 Pull back the skin to expose the belly and cut open to remove the guts. Be mindful to still not puncture the intestines.

5 Peel and manipulate the rest of the skin from the meat.

6 Wash the carcass if possible and prepare for cooking.

A large animal will provide plenty of food but you need to plan how you will preserve it.

- Bleed the animal by hanging it from the rear legs and cutting its throat. If the animal is large and you're on your own hanging the animal may be hard. If this is the case try to use the ground, and have the head of the animal facing downhill so that the blood will drain through gravity. Ensure you sever the jugular vein to bleed. Cut from ear to ear, or if in doubt cut the whole head off. Save the blood as this can be fried or roasted for eating, or consumed raw soon after bleeding.
- Skin the animal. There are many ways to do this. With a large animal the hide is valuable for protection and insulation. Smaller animals like rodents can be gutted and cooked/spit-roasted with the hair on, since this will be burnt off during cooking. Follow a few general rules to skin animals. Cut the legs off at the ankle or knee. Cut the head off. Cut to skin depth only from the anus to the neck. Peel back the skin from the neck or the stomach area, working your way around the animal. Use your knuckles, fist and fingers to separate the hide from the muscle. This can be hard work on a large animal. Using a sharp knife to separate hide from muscle is the most effective option, but be careful not to rupture any of the guts as this could contaminate the meat.
- Gut the animal. If the animal is still hanging, cut from the anus to the neck, using your hands to remove all the guts. The smell can be strong, so consider wearing an improvised mask across the nose and mouth. In a short time you'll get used to the smell.
- Remove the eyes from the head and eat them raw on a fresh kill. Even though there appears to be little meat on a head, boiling a whole head for a good length of time will kill any parasites and make a nutritious broth.
- Consider caching food if the carcass is too big to carry. Store food in trees by hanging or, better still, bury it – but bury it deep, as otherwise animals will smell it and try to dig it up.

Boiling is a sure way to kill anything that the animal may have been carrying that could be harmful to you. Cut medium to large animals into steaks when cooking over a fire or roasting. This ensures that it's cooked right through and free of harmful organisms. When eating smaller cooked animals and birds watch out for small bones that might get lodged in your throat.

Other methods of field preparation

Reptiles

These are prepared in much the same way as described above. Remove the guts, head and lower feet. The tails of reptiles are often large and muscular, so keep them on. Cook with the skin on.

Snakes

I've caught snakes in many parts of the world. They can be dangerous, but with some thought and agility can be dispatched quickly by means of a whack on the head with a long club. Snake makes for good eating and they're easy to prepare and cook. Cut the head off well below the poison sacs. Suspend the carcass from the neck area and peel off the skin to the tail. This should pull away easily. Remove the guts and cook. Snake steaks can be very tasty.

Birds

Birds need to be plucked. It's sometimes easier to pluck feathers when they're wet. Cut off the head and remove the guts.

There's plenty of breast meat on a pigeon

Preservation

Preserving food is important, especially if you have a big kill or are aiming to ration your food. Drying and smoking are the more common ways to preserve, but there's also freezing in extremely cold climates, and salting. You could also try to keep the animal alive.

Drying meat and fruit is the oldest known method of preserving food, preventing the onset of the biological process that causes bacteria and fungus by removing moisture. As most animals are made up of approximately 70% water once this is removed meat is also much lighter to carry.

Drying

Cut the meat or fish into thin strips and skewer to wood or cord. Make sure the portions don't overlap or fold over on themselves. Cut off the fat and eat it! Hang in the sun for a minimum of two days and turn every day. Making a small fire below will speed up the process. It will also keep the flies away. However, be careful not to cook the meat or let it drop into the fire. Once dried effectively the meat should be brittle. It won't last indefinitely but will certainly last far longer than cooked or raw meat.

Smoking

Smoking meat is an effective means of preservation. Follow the same principles as drying but aim to build an enclosed tent/tepee construction around the framework on which the meat will hang. This must have access at the base for fuel and air and a small hole at the top to allow the smoke to slowly escape. The idea is to create smoke, not fire. This takes time and nurturing. Smoking can take from ten hours to two days before the meat is dark and brittle. Smoking is especially good for fish.

Salting

At sea or near coastal areas, salting may be a useful way to preserve food. Cut the meat into strips and place in brine for at least two days. Make sure the meat stays fully covered. After this hang it in the sun or where there's good airflow to dry it out. Having a good supply of drinking water is important for the consumption of any food, but especially if it's been salted.

FIRST AID & RESCUE

Should you be inadvertently plunged into a survival situation, your first thoughts would almost be that of rescue. If there are injuries to you or others then it will also be an understandable and initial reaction to help. In many situations some form of rescue would have been initiated soon after the incident was reported. But this may take hours or days and depending on your location the rescue time could be compounded by weather, environment or terrain. Injuries do happen and when you have few medical resources with you, using what you have at hand to maintain life and prevent further injury or infection is important. Have a plan for rescue and know some basic first aid to sustain you and others until rescue and quality medical assistance is available. In a survival situation it is better to know something rather than nothing.

First aid

Prevention is clearly better than cure. All extreme environments carry their own risks, and awareness is the first step to staying healthy. Think before you act. Assess, protect yourself and minimise risks wherever possible. But when the inevitable accidents do happen, first aid should be applied judiciously and only when there's little chance of immediate expert treatment. Some injuries, however small, can be debilitating and potentially life-threatening if left untreated.

Don't move casualties who may have spinal injuries unless you absolutely have to. Any injury to the neck or back should be considered a potential spinal injury. However, Cardiopulmonary resuscitation (CPR) takes priority over a spinal injury.

Unconscious

Remember the acronym DRABC (think of Doctor, A,B,C) and follow these instructions.

D – Danger

Remove the patient from any danger eg a fire, water, avalanche, rock fall etc.

R – Response

Shout the patient's name, check for pain response by pinching the upper ear. If no response;

A – Airway

Turn the patient onto their side and gently scoop one finger through the mouth to clear any obstructions away. Turn them onto their back and gently tilt the head back to open the airway. (Do not tilt the head on babies less than 1 year old – just gently lift the point of the chin, without pushing on the soft area under it, which could block the airway.)

B – Breathing

Look, listen and feel for any signs of breathing. If the patient is breathing, check for any life-threatening injuries like severe bleeding and treat immediately. If there is no breathing begin CPR.

C – Circulation

Check the carotid pulse, which is next to the Adam's apple in the neck.

CPR

- Lie the patient completely flat on a firm surface.
- Kneel beside the patient. Position yourself midway between the chest and the head in order to move easily between compressions and breaths.

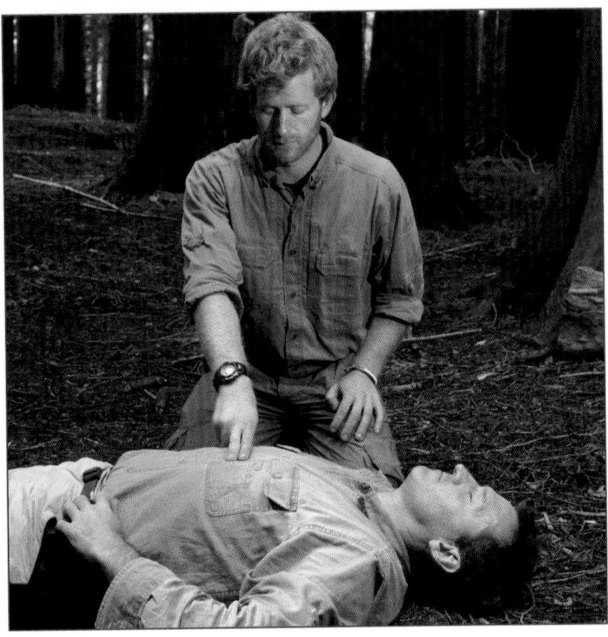

1 Find the mid point of the breastbone (sternum).

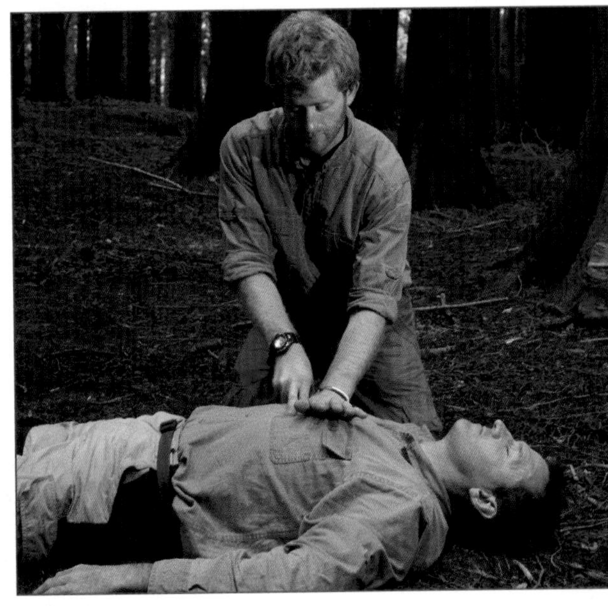

2 Place the heel of your compressing hand on the breastbone just below the mid point.

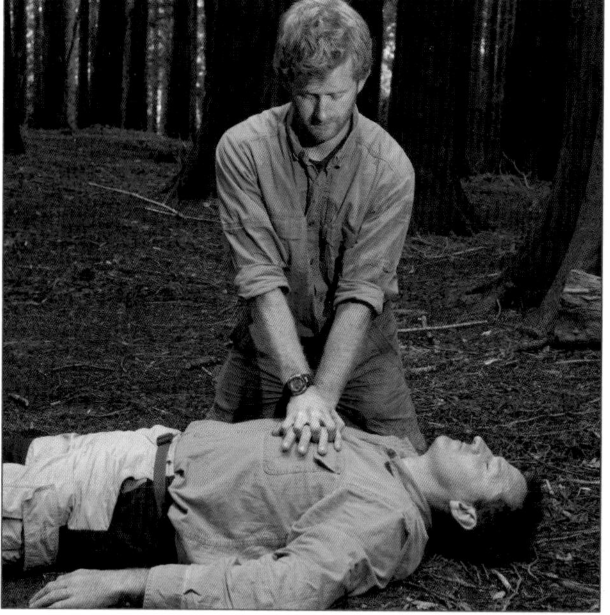

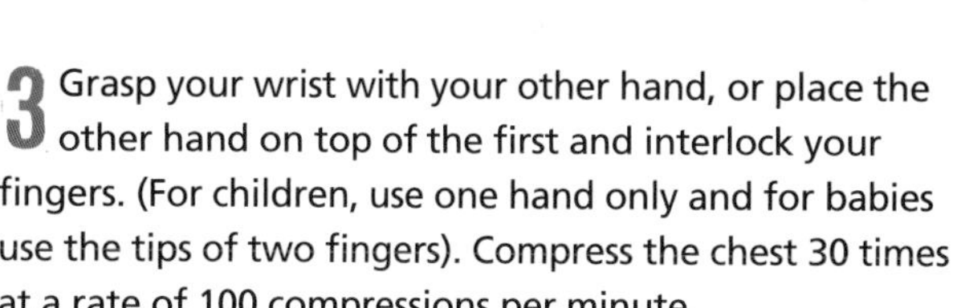

3 Grasp your wrist with your other hand, or place the other hand on top of the first and interlock your fingers. (For children, use one hand only and for babies use the tips of two fingers). Compress the chest 30 times at a rate of 100 compressions per minute.

Compression technique

- Keep your shoulders directly over your hands and keep your arms straight. Lean the weight of your upper body onto your hands to compress the chest. Keep a steady, even rhythm and do not 'jab' with your hands or punch the breastbone.
- For adults, compress about 4–5cm.
- For children, compress about 2–3cm.
- For babies, compress about 1–2cm.

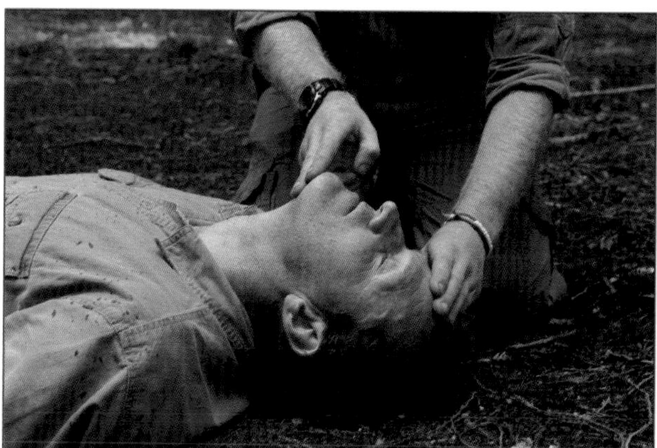

4 Then move to the head to make 2 'rescue' breaths. Check the airway is open by putting one hand on their forehead and two fingers under their chin and gently tipping the head back.

5 Use the hand that was on the forehead to gently pinch the nose closed. Allow their mouth to open and breath in and put your lips around the patient's mouth, making sure there is a good seal (For babies, make a seal over the mouth and nose). Blow into their mouth until their chest rises.

- Take your mouth away and watch to see the chest fall (if this doesn't happen, check the position of their head). Give a second breath into their mouth and then repeat 30 chest compressions. Continue this pattern of 30 compressions followed by two breaths until the patient begins to breathe.
- For children and babies or if the patient is unconscious due to drowning – give five initial rescue breaths followed by the compression and breath procedures.
- If the patient starts to breathe again normally but is still unconscious, place them in the recovery position.
- If you are in a team, share the responsibilities and take turns to avoid exhaustion.

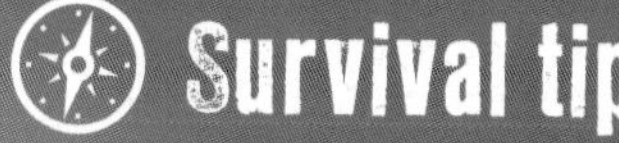

Survival tip

Information in a book cannot give you the full knowledge and experience needed in a real life emergency situation. We would recommend going on a first aid course with a recognised organisation such as St John Ambulance or the Red Cross.

Fractures and injuries

If someone has sustained a soft tissue injury such as a sprain then immediate temporary care would be to follow the acronym RICE:

- REST the injury.
- ICE it if possible for as long as possible. Don't add ice directly to skin or a cold weather injury may be sustained!
- COMPRESSION. After icing, strap the injury fairly tightly but without cutting of the blood supply.
- ELEVATION.

For lower limb fractures:

- Make the casualty as comfortable as possible.
- Try to locate the fracture. The casualty should indicate where the pain is.
- Immobilise the fracture by splinting and strapping. Use the other leg as a splint, but remember that any injury strapped below the waist becomes a stretcher case. Pad out the gaps between the legs with clothing. Strap firmly above and below the fracture. Use further clothing and belts to strap firmly.
- Rest, reassure and keep warm.

For upper limb injuries and fractures:

- Let the casualty find the most comfortable position.
- Provide support.
- Keep the injury still.
- Prevent unnecessary movement.
- Prevent further damage.
- Bandage or strap in the position that the patient finds most comfortable.

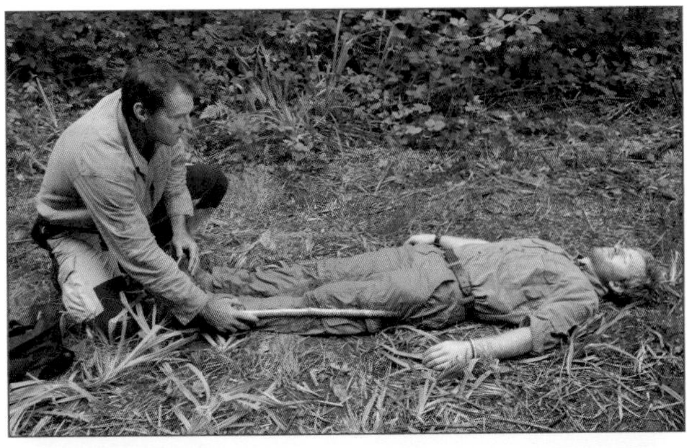

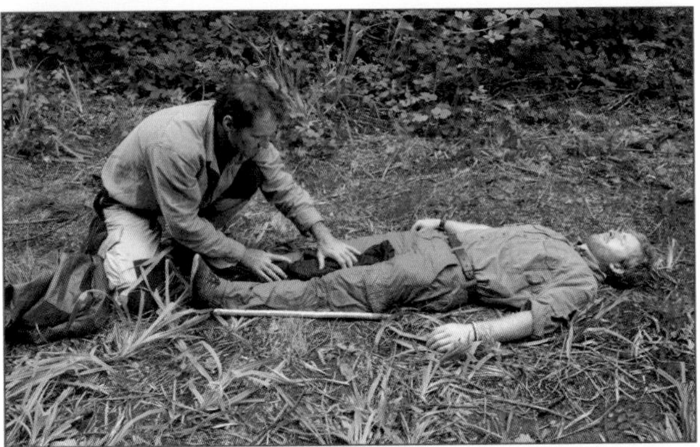

Use a belt and rolled-up clothing to keep legs and feet secure.

Recovery position

After careful assessment, if the casualty is breathing and spinal injuries are ruled out, then place them in the recovery position.

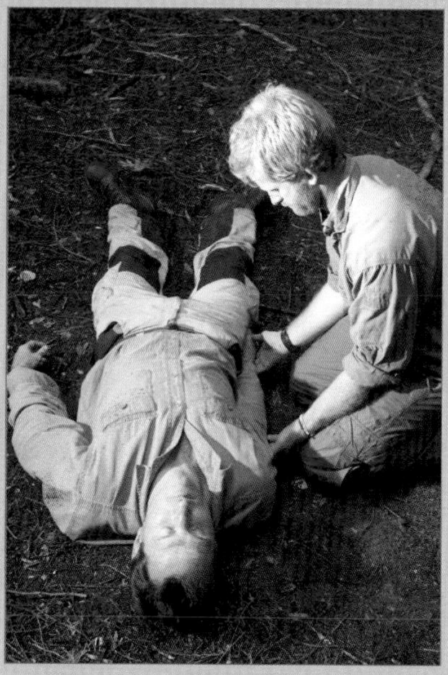

1 Kneel down next to the patient and remove glasses and any large objects from pockets. Tuck the arm that is nearest you along the length of the patient's body.

2 Bring the other arm across their chest and hold the back of the hand against the cheek nearest you.

3 Use your other hand to pull the far knee up, but keeping the foot on the ground.

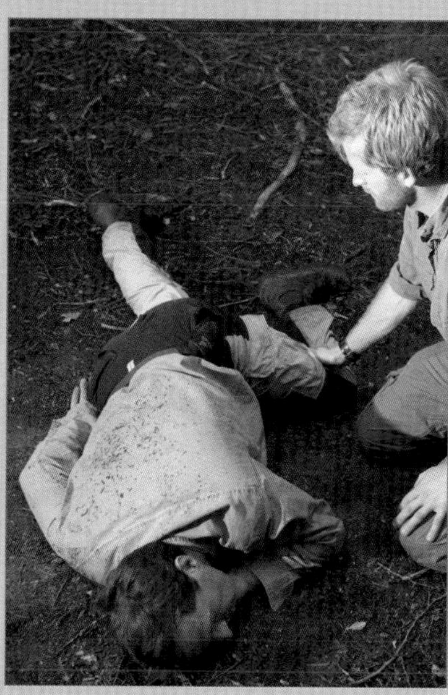

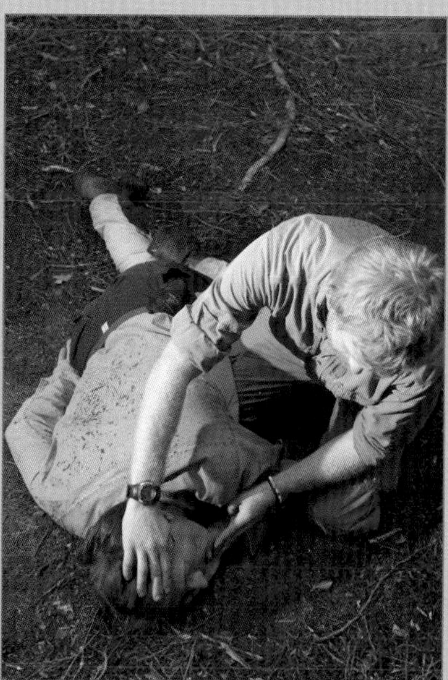

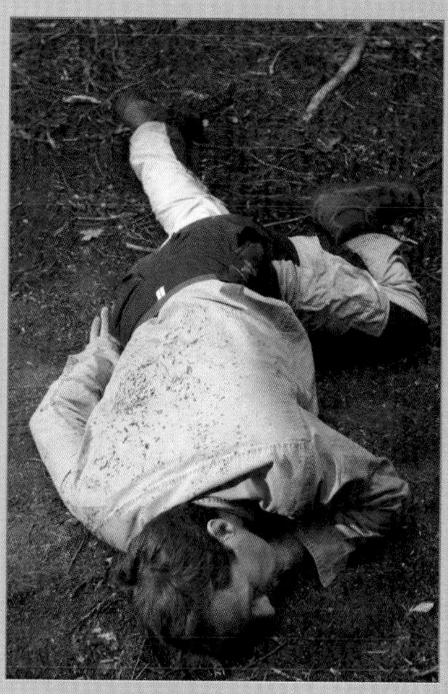

4 Hold the hand against the cheek and gently pull on the knee, rolling the patient towards you – with the knee left bent at a right angle.

5 Check and tilt the head so that the airway is open (repositioning their hand to help if necessary).

6 If you go in search of help, leave in recovery position and write an explanation for the patient or would-be rescuers.

Shock

Clinical shock is inadequate tissue perfusion – a serious loss of fluid in the system due to any of a number of reasons. Casualties will have cold, clammy and pale skin with a rising heart rate and breathing rate. You need to:

- Treat the injuries.
- Raise the legs.
- Prevent heat loss.
- Reassure constantly.
- Monitor the vital signs.

Hypothermia

Any drop in core body temperature leads to cold injury. If the patient is:

- Shivering.
- Complaining of cold.
- Looking and feeling cold.
- Alert, but perhaps a little floppy.
- Lucid but slurring his speech.

– then he's cold and needs to be warmed up before he degenerates to a hypothermic state, the symptoms of which include:

- Absence of shivering.
- Incoherence.
- Irrational behaviour.
- Reduced levels of response.
- Unconsciousness.
- Rigidity.

What to do:

- Insulate and find shelter from the elements.
- Change wet clothing or put on more, especially round the head.
- Passive re-warming.
- Keep airway open if the patient is unconscious.
- Monitor the vital signs.

I've recognised mild hypothermia in myself on occasion and acted quickly by stopping and putting on extra clothing, and eating or drinking something hot and sweet. It's important to watch team members in cold climates and act quickly and decisively if you see the symptoms of hypothermia.

Frost injury

Cooling and eventual freezing of the skin and deeper tissues will lead to frost nip and frostbite. Frost nip is the early stage of frostbite. The waxy, pale patches of skin from frost nip are very obvious and need to be treated decisively to prevent further freezing. The symptoms of frost nip are:

- Pain and numbness.
- Patches of white, waxy skin.
- Skin is hard to the touch.

What to do:

- Place a gloved hand over the affected part until the blood supply is restored.
- Protect from further damage and prevent deeper freezing.
- Do not rub.

Left unattended, frost nip will lead to frostbite. If frostbite has occurred:

- Protect the casualty from further cold. Get in shelter.
- Cover affected area and don't allow tissues to freeze again.
- Do not rub.
- Keep the casualty warm, fed and hydrated as best you can.
- Don't use excessive heat like fires to re-warm. Put the effected part in the armpit/groin/belly of an unaffected team member or place in luke warm water (drinkable, approximately 40 degrees C).
- Do not re-warm until there is no risk of freezing. Re-warming can be very painful so be prepared.
- Thawing may produce blisters and further infection is a risk. Do not burst blisters.
- Be very mindful of further infection and keep the effected part and area as sterile as possible.

Survival tip

Frost injury is hard to avoid at minus 30 with a wind, so it's important to adopt a buddy system in cold climates: make regular checks of each other's extremities, particularly if they're exposed to the elements.

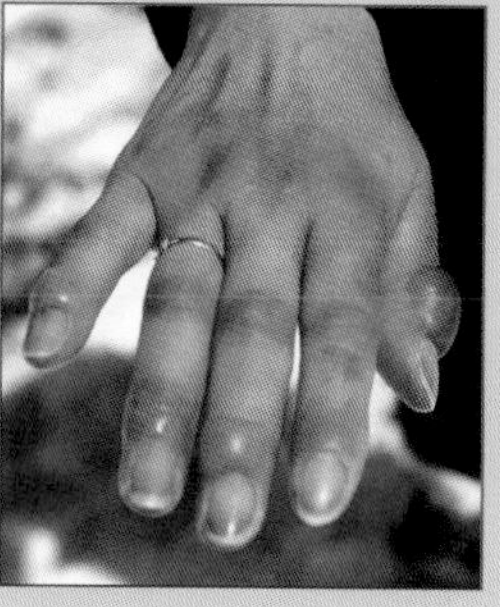

Bleeding

Severe bleeding needs immediate attention:

- **Apply direct pressure to the wound. Press hard for a minimum of ten minutes. Use thick, absorbent dressings if possible. Fleece tops, socks and hats can be pressed into service.**
- **If blood seeps through then apply more dressing.**
- **Once under control tie the dressing on to the wound.**
- **Elevate the wound, loosen clothing and reassure the casualty.**

Minor cuts should be cleaned with sterile water, dried and covered. Remove any foreign bodies such as grit and splinters. This is particularly important in jungle environments. Breaks in the skin can very quickly lead to infection.

Overheating

In hot climates particularly, the heat and effects of heat can have a potentially serious effect on the human body. If your body can't regulate its temperature then problems may occur:

Heat exhaustion

Heat exhaustion is the result of excessive loss of water and salt from the body. What you see/feel:

- Generally feel unwell.
- Headache.
- Dizziness.
- Nausea.
- Thirst.
- Fatigue.
- Muscle cramps.
- Moist skin.
- Breathing and pulse may be elevated.

What to do:

- Reduce exertion.
- Get in the shade and/or to a cool area.
- Water down the head/body if possible.
- Replace fluids and salts. Eat something if possible.

Heat stroke

This happens when the body's cooling mechanism fails. It can be a progression from heat exhaustion. What you see/feel:

- Headache and confusion.
- Intense thirst.
- Rapid pulse and breathing.
- Hot, dry skin.
- Leads to convulsions and coma.

What to do:

- Drink water and cool down. Get shelter.
- Lie flat.
- Water down with tepid water, especially the head.
- Monitor vital functions.

Trench foot

When the feet are wet for a prolonged period trench foot can occur. The onset can be more rapid in cold, wet environments, but it's important to look after your feet in any environment. What you see/feel:

- Swelling of the foot.
- Numbness.
- The foot feels cold.
- May be mottled with a blue tinge.

What to do:

- Warm and dry the foot slowly and naturally.
- Avoid walking and elevate the foot.
- As re-warming occurs the affected area may feel itchy and could blister. Keep clean to avoid infection at this point.

Bites and stings

It's highly unlikely a wild animal will attack a human unless provoked, but some animals are dangerous when defending themselves. So don't antagonise them; or if you must, then be decisive. There are nevertheless many situations in which an individual may be stung or bitten. Thankfully not all bites and stings are fatal – only a small proportion of creatures have a fatal delivery of venom, and if the casualty goes to a hospital as soon as possible then anti-venom will be administered successfully. This will be helped if the creature is recognised or caught. Mammals such as bats, cats, dogs and apes can also carry rabies.

Signs and symptoms of a poisonous bite may not be immediately obvious and can take anything from 15 minutes to two hours to appear. In order to stop the spread of the venom or poison through the body:

- Stop, rest and relax.
- Try to keep the bitten area lower than the heart.
- For animal bites, wash the bitten area with running water for five minutes. Wash any residue venom away with water. However, if you're able to get to a hospital leaving venom on the skin may help identification.
- Apply pressure and immobilise the affected area. Apply a compressing bandage but not a tourniquet. For a bite to the hand, bandage from the armpit down to the fingers. For the foot, start from the upper leg and proceed to the toes. Bandage as much of the limb as possible.
- Splint the limb.

Never:

- Cut or massage the affected area.
- Attempt to suck the venom out.
- Use a tourniquet.
- Try to catch the animal or snake unless you know what you're doing.

Ticks

Remove ticks with tweezers by gently pulling up. The aim is to not break the body leaving half the tick still lodged in the skin. Use heat or submerge the body part in hot water. Check clothing daily to clear it of ticks and lice.

Leeches

Leeches are generally found in moist, tropical jungle areas and can sometimes carry infection. Don't pull them off: apply salt or insect repellent or burn them off by touching them with a hot ember.

Other problems

Blisters

Don't burst them but try to cover and protect them. If they do break treat them as an open wound and air them where possible. If you do have to burst a blister because of its size then make a small pinprick puncture at the base with a sterilised implement and gently squeeze out the fluid. Cover and protect the blister. To sterilise a needle, boil or burn it.

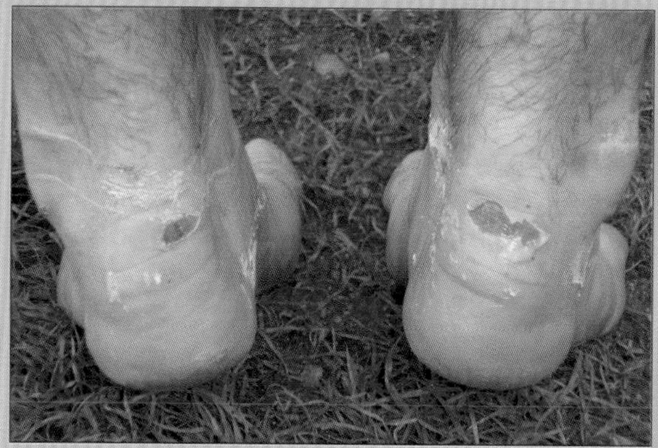

Fungal infections

UV light is an antiseptic, so air the affected area when you can and keep it dry. Avoid scratching.

Burns

Run as much water over the wound as possible. Keep doing this for as long as possible and until the burning stops. If the burnt area is large the major concern is subsequent infection. Cover the wound but allow for swelling. Drink to counter fluid loss.

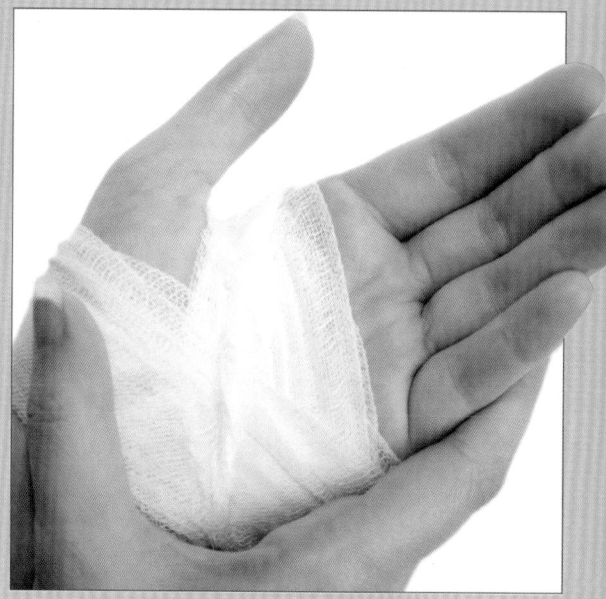

Rescue helicopters

Though you may have been located by a plane or boat, it's usual practice to send in a helicopter to effect a rescue. Helicopters have the ability to hover, assess difficult locations and lower a line to recover equipment and individuals. But they have their limitations. They can't land on undulating, mountainous, wet or very rocky ground. Visibility, wind strength and distance also play a part. Altitude can have an impact as the air gets thinner the higher you go, which reduces the payload that the helicopter can lift. At extreme altitudes helicopters can't fly, though I've seen casualties taken out by helicopter at 5,500m. The helicopter was stripped of everything it didn't need and seemed to be just a shell with rotors. It screamed as it tried to take off and then literally dropped off an edge to get forward air speed. Very scary!

If you're awaiting rescue and are convinced that you've been spotted, don't immediately discard any food, water, protection or shelter you have. It may be days before a helicopter can fly in. You may also need to move to a more accessible location or cut and clear a landing zone yourself. If you move you'll have to signal or leave markers along the route to your new location and the landing zone. But don't be too quick to move just because the helicopter has flown away. It may be safer to stay put, or the helicopter may return with a winch and line. Base any decision on the situation and the terrain you're in.

Selecting a landing zone (LZ)

If you've been spotted from an aeroplane or helicopter it's likely you're already in a place that's open and may therefore be a natural LZ. If not, and you have to locate or clear an area, then follow these general rules:

- Don't attempt to clear a dense wooded or jungle area: it's too much effort and almost impossible. Look for natural features. In jungles there are often clearings on riverbanks. Mud-slides may have cleared an area of trees as they flattened out. If necessary trample down an area in snow; but be wary of frozen lakes, as they may not be strong enough and the pilot is unlikely to take the risk of landing on them.
- You're looking for an open flat area that's approximately 30m in diameter. A helicopter will land on a slight gradient but not more than approximately 7–10°.
- If possible mark the LZ with material, rocks or clothing of contrasting colours. Whatever you use needn't be too big, but ensure the helicopter's downdraught can't blow it away or suck it up into the rotors.

- Clear the area of stakes, upright sticks and small trees – it's often difficult to see these from above. Fill in any large potholes.
- Assess the direction of approach. This needs to be free of obstacles and have good all-round visibility.
- Cliffs and steep ground can cause updraughts and downdraughts: avoid.
- Assess wind direction and mark a 'T' on the ground, with the top of the 'T' upwind. If you can't make a 'T', stand on the edge of the LZ with your back to the wind and your arms outstretched above your head and just over shoulder-width apart.
- At night use small fires in appropriate places to mark the LZ and wind direction. If you have torches then use these, but be careful not to dazzle the pilots. If the helicopter has night-flying capability then it will be equipped with good searchlights.

When the helicopter arrives:

- Move off to the edge of the LZ and face the approaching helicopter so that the pilot can see you. Secure any loose clothing or equipment and huddle down. If you're part of a team, huddle down together. Cover your face and eyes, as the downdraught will scatter debris. Wait to get the 'thumbs up' from someone on the helicopter before you move.
- Move towards the helicopter at about 45° from the pilot or co-pilot's vision. Don't approach from the rear of the helicopter, always from the front. Keep your head down.
- If the helicopter has landed on a slight incline be aware that the rotors on the uphill side will be closer to the ground than the downhill side.
- Sit where you're told and put your seat belt on. Don't disembark until you're instructed.
- Many pilots can hover with only a light touch of the skid on the ground. This is particularly useful in wet and mountainous locations. If he does, don't pile on to the helicopter all at once – wait for instructions. Too much weight in one go and the helicopter will drop. You, the pilot and the crewmen should use hand signals to communicate. If the pilot shuts down the helicopter then wait until the rotors have stopped turning before you approach.

Rescue boats

If you're at sea or on the coast, your rescue is likely to be by boat. Note the following key points:

- **Embark small boats one at a time, from the sides and towards the stern.**
- **Look for boat ladders that may be lowered. Climb ladders one at a time. The weight of others below could trap the fingers of those above between ladder and vessel.**
- **If ascending a scramble net on the side of the vessel then pull with your hands on the vertical lines of the scramble net. This stops those who are above standing on your hands. Push with your feet from the horizontals.**
- **Don't embark on the vessel from the stern: this houses the propellers.**
- **In heavy swells and out at sea wait for the waterline to be at its highest alongside the boat before you try and pull yourself aboard.**
- **Vessels won't beach in heavy swell or if they're not designed to do so. You'll either have to swim out to the vessel or find a sheltered cove or beach.**
- **If crossing from one vessel to another be aware of the swell and the irregular up and down motions of each vessel. Be very aware of vessels smashing together and fingers being crushed or severed!**
- **Be careful of barnacles on the hull of the boat that can be exposed as it rises in swell. These can be very sharp.**
- **Make sure the helmsman and other crew can see you at all times as you approach the boat and as it approaches you. In heavy swells and at night a boat can very quickly lose sight of you.**
- **Help others into the boat by pulling on the clothes around the shoulders or under the armpits.**

SURVIVING THE COLD

Cold and extreme cold climates almost seem impossible to survive in. However, people have and they do. These environments can appear incredibly tough and uncompromising but with a little knowledge and thought it is possible to be somewhat comfortable and to overcome the harshest of cold conditions. Even with snow and ice all around, it may only be just below zero and with no wind this can be almost pleasant. Learn some basics, adapt to the environment and your chances of survival and hopefully that of your team are increased. Surviving the cold is possible.

Cold environments

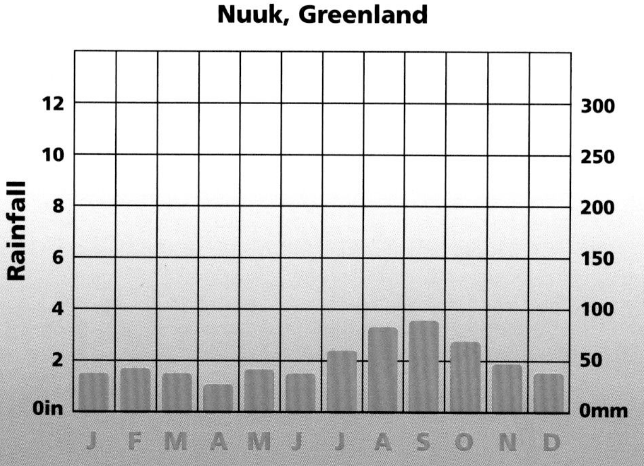

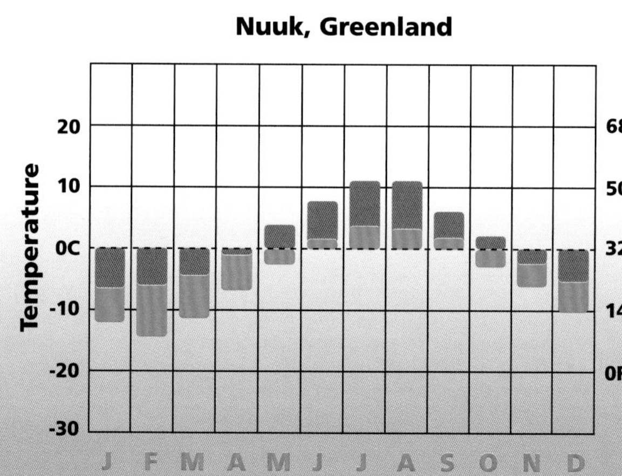

With little life and foliage, covering vast areas of sea as well as mountainous land, Arctic and Polar regions are frozen deserts. In the summertime temperatures can climb above freezing, but during the winter can drop well below –40°C. Remember also that the higher you go the colder it will get.

In these extreme winter temperatures a cup of water thrown into the air will freeze before it hits the ground! Winds of over 100mph can lower the overall temperature to –60° and these raging winds can both whip up snowstorms that stop you in your tracks and pound the snow so hard that it becomes solid. You may encounter glaciers, crevasses, cliffs and seracs in the long darkness of the polar winter. The low angle of the sun during the long summer also has a considerable effect on the environment: warmer temperatures can cause huge rivers of melting snow near coastlines.

Polar regions are a tough environment and to be thrust into such areas without preparation is extremely dangerous. There's next to no chance of survival unless rescue is swift. If you're able to remain near your mode of travel then your chances are somewhat improved, but exposure to the elements here will cause the body to deteriorate faster than lack of food and water.

A very small population of people do live, hunt and travel in these hostile environments. Unlike most of us, their bodies and metabolism have adapted to cope with these extreme conditions, and they have also adapted their clothing, shelter and eating habits in order to sustain themselves.

• WISE WORDS •

Filming an expedition in Greenland, our film crew lost a snow skidoo in attempting to cross a glacial river. We had to travel at night (although it never got quite dark) because, even in a Polar region, the rivers on glaciers were too dangerous during the daytime temperatures.

Building a shelter

If you have neither a good Arctic tent nor shelter from your mode of transport, using the snow and ice around you is one alternative. You must find protection from the wind. Precipitation is low in the frozen deserts, but the wind may be a friend here by providing drifting snow; on the other hand, the winds may have packed the snow so hard that cutting into it without saws and shovels will be tough. Building a snow hole – as described on page 155 – is the best option. Snow coffins, igloos and windbreaks may all provide temporary shelter.

Snow coffins

- Dig a coffin-sized pit in soft snow and if possible in natural shelter.
- Make a quarry to one side and cut slabs to lie on top of the coffin. Lean the slabs against each other like a regular gable roof. This gives you some height.
- Cover up one end.
- Place blocks at the other end to make a small entrance.
- Dig a 'cold trench' at either end of the coffin, lower than your lying area. As it's a trench, cold air will sink.
- Construct an additional windbreak on the side of the prevailing wind.
- Cover up the gaps in the roof with snow.
- Insulate the lying area as best you can.

Igloos

Igloos are a little more challenging to construct but they do provide shelter without having to dig down. Constructing a decent igloo will require a good saw for hard-packed snow, although a shovel might be adequate depending on the density of the packed snow.

- Mark out a circle in the snow about 4m in diameter.
- Start a quarry pit for your blocks close to the shelter site.
- Lay the blocks down on the marked area. The blocks should be about 50cm–1m square.
- Taper the top of the first layer inwards slightly ready to receive the next layer.
- Keep the taper going layer by layer until you construct a dome. Fill in the gaps with snow.
- Cut an entrance and use additional slabs to make a tunnel leading to the entrance.
- Build a further windbreak to protect the entrance.

The inhabitants of these regions build igloos with considerable speed and skill. With good insulation, a candle burning and body heat they're surprisingly comfortable. Although they're not at all easy to build, I've found that by taking time and thinking practically something close to what the locals build can be achieved.

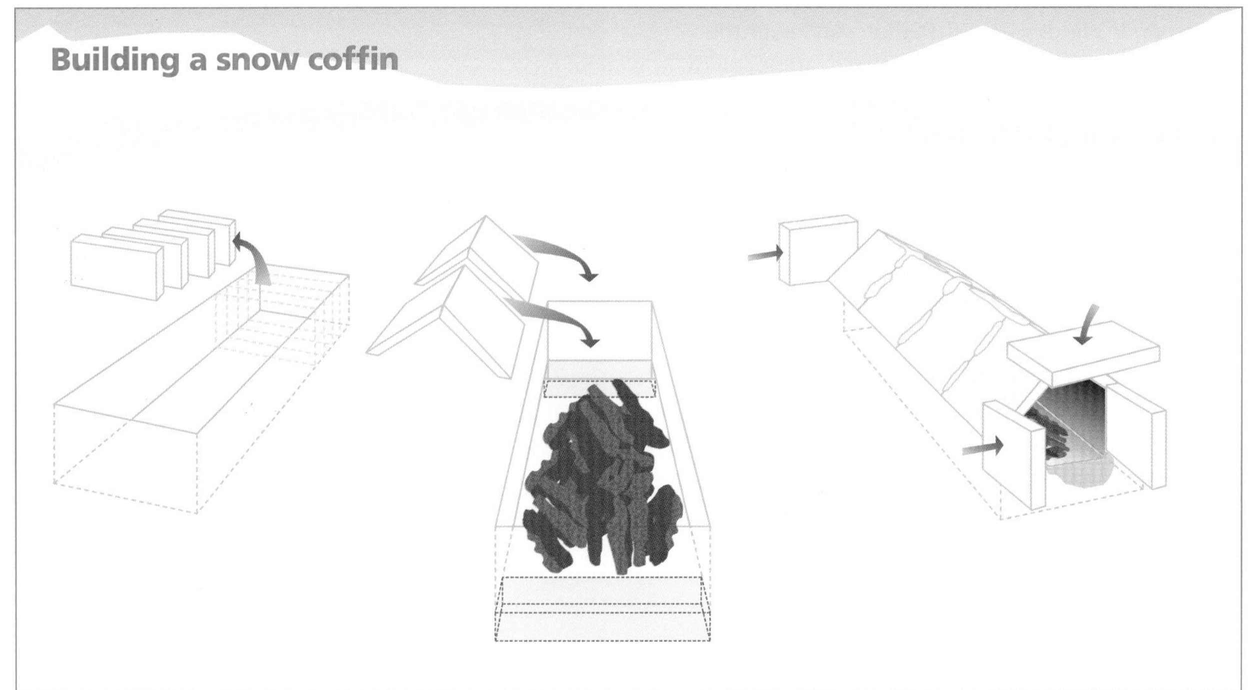

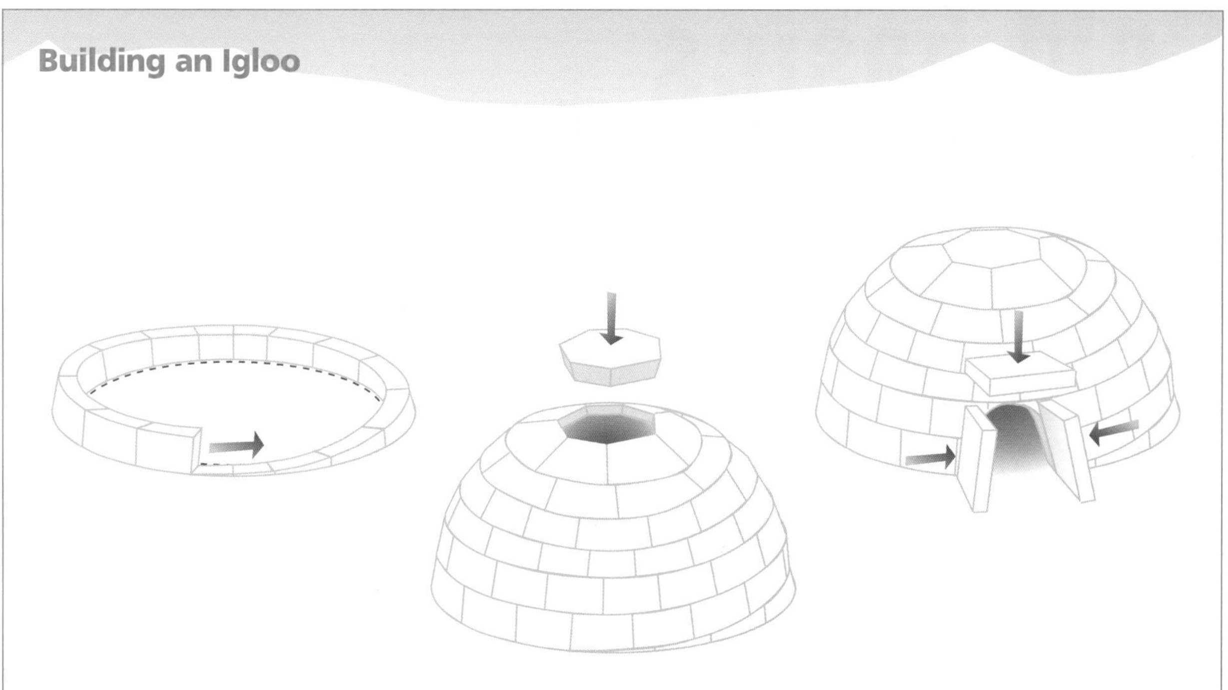

Improvising with overhead cover

- Mark a circle or square on the snow to indicate the perimeter of your shelter. This should be slightly smaller than the size of your overhead cover. A piece of tarpaulin, parachute or canvas – intact and about 4m diameter or square – is useful for the overhead cover.
- Build a wall from snow blocks to about a metre high.
- Lay the overhead cover on top and put blocks on the edge to anchor it down to the snow wall.
- Cut a small entrance and build a tunnel and windbreak if necessary to protect the entrance.
- Use a pole, a shovel or a ski to push the overhead cover up in the middle from the inside. This will prevent snow accumulating and give you more headroom.
- Insulate the floor as much as possible.
- Dig a 'cold trench' at the entrance.

Don't block every hole in a shelter. Ventilation is important.

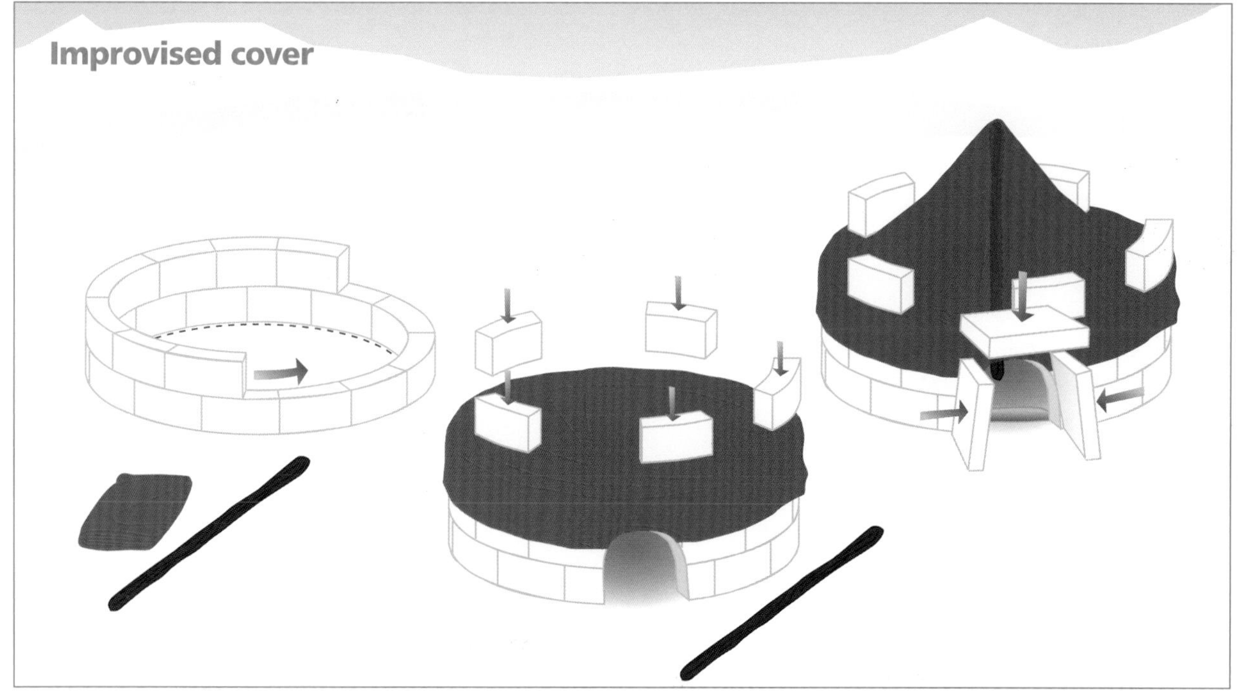

Cold basics

Water

Water isn't an issue in these environments if you have the means to melt snow and ice. If you can collect melting water then do so. Glaciers close to the coast in summer will melt in the day. It's as important to drink in cold climates as in any other region.

Choose an area away from the shelter for human waste and make sure everyone in the team knows its location and uses it.

Food

There's little to no food in the interiors of Polar regions. Most food will be found in the sea and around the coast. Exposed rocks may have some lichens and mosses, but trees are unlikely except for the firs of lower latitudes. Animals in remote areas are not often startled by humans so catching them is sometimes not too difficult. They principally comprise:

- Penguins – these are found only in Antarctica and have supplemented the diets of many early explorers.
- Rabbits and lemmings.
- Foxes and wolves.
- Reindeer, musk ox, caribou, elk and moose.
- Seals – rich in blubber but large and sometimes aggressive.
- Polar bears are best avoided – they're very large and usually aggressive.

Most of the vegetation in Polar regions is edible. Generally it can be stripped, dried and boiled. It can be added to boiling water for herbal teas, and some can be eaten raw. However, a few mushrooms may be poisonous. The plants most likely to be encountered are:

- Arctic willows – the bark, shoots and young roots are edible. Good vitamin C.
- Reindeer moss – boil and soak.
- Mosses and lichens growing on rocks are mostly edible but boil or roast before consumption. Don't eat too much in one go. Rock tripe is the best of the bunch and can be eaten raw.
- Spruce and pine needles when found. Young shoots and bark can be boiled and eaten.
- Lingonberries – red berries that are rich in nutrients. The leaves can be boiled or roasted.
- Cloudberries – golden berries high in vitamin C. Leaves can be used to make tea.

Fire can be made for cooking if you have resources like wood and foliage about – animal fat can make an effective fuel. Prepare fires as outlined in Chapter 3.

Mosses and lichens – good food source – but not too much!

Signalling and rescue

These drills are much the same as for rescue in the mountains: bright colours and linear shapes are easily spotted from the air. Even a square piece of black cloth laid out on a featureless snow plateau is easily visible from a distance. Burning animal fat will create smoke; and you can use scattered ash and burnt debris to etch a signal on the snow and ice.

Search and rescue flights will only operate when they're assured good weather so be prepared for that eventuality. Helicopters are unlikely to rescue you; most rescues involve aeroplanes that may have snow skids, so you'll have to find a location that has potential as a landing strip. The area doesn't have to be totally flat but needs to be free of obvious features that could damage the aircraft. Large, hard and windblown waves of snow called 'Sastrugi' make landing impossible. A few hundred metres of level ground with a thin covering of snow is ideal.

Cold travel

If you're forced to travel then do so after careful consideration of the risks involved. Travelling at night is often possible as it may not be completely dark, but temperatures will be lower. In the daytime, the sun can be literally blinding. Protecting the eyes and face from the sun is as important as protection from the cold and wind. As you get a base tan the risk of serious sunburn is reduced, but don't become complacent; even your tongue can burn as you pant while working hard.

If you don't have GPS, navigation by means of celestial objects is the most reliable – compasses don't work too well near the poles. Plan your route with a distinct aim in mind, as walking aimlessly in these environments is foolhardy. Gaining altitude will only make the temperature colder so head downwards if possible.

Once you've established a heading try to pick a feature as far off as practical and move to it before establishing another heading. As Polar environments are huge and almost featureless, be aware that spotting a feature on the horizon doesn't mean you'll get there soon: it could be over 100km away. For instance, when we were on the Greenland ice cap we spotted a small black tip on the horizon. We hadn't seen any features in weeks of travel, but had been heading for the mountains on the coast and knew that this black tip was our first glimpse of them. It was very exciting to see something different and we made camp and chatted enthusiastically about reaching the mountains in the morning. Two days later and

Hygiene

Although these environments are almost sterile, and I've never fallen ill in Polar regions, maintaining a good level of hygiene is important:

- **Build your toilet area away from the shelter and make sure everyone uses it and knows where it is.**
- **Quarry an area for snow and ice to melt for water. This must be well away from the toilet area and other potential contaminants such as dogs and fuel.**
- **Air your clothing when you can and lay it out in the UV light on warm sunny days.**
- **Clean your teeth regularly.**
- **Cook food well and always hydrate.**

Dave 'enjoying' a snow bath!

- **Clean hands, knives and other tools well after dispatching and gutting animals.**
- **When weather and temperature allow, strip down and have a 'snow bath' and then bask in the sun. The UV light and clean air on the skin does wonders for body and mind.**

we still weren't there! It was a stark reminder of how vast these regions are.

In Northern latitudes where the sea is frozen, lines and patches of water known as 'leads' may appear as the tides move the sea ice. Avoid these by travelling to a solid point where you can safely cross. Submersion in a Polar environment without proper protection will almost certainly lead to death. As there's little chance of getting wet in other ways, garments that keep you warm by protecting you against the wind are generally the best option. But don't overexert yourself. You can sweat even when the temperature is below freezing, and damp layers will only freeze when you stop. Be disciplined and stop regularly for breaks and checks. Keep an eye on other team members and employ the 'buddy-buddy' system of looking out for each other. Watch out especially for signs of frost nip on the face (see page 97).

If you're travelling and the weather starts to turn then make camp early and don't struggle on – if the weather gets too bad it may become difficult to make camp. Ferocious winds and freezing temperatures can make the simplest of tasks impossible.

Dave demonstrating that submersion in water, in cold climates, is possible – but not recommended!

• WISE WORDS •

Eager to push on and make up some ground, we broke camp one morning with a light breeze blowing and a temperature of approximately –25°C. The conditions seemed a little unusual: the sky looked threatening and the atmosphere haunting, but we loaded up the sledges and harnessed the dogs and set off. After only a few hours the weather seemed to be turning against us so we went straight into the arduous task of making camp, having only broken camp two hours earlier. A ferocious storm ensued that pinned us down for nearly three days. We could hardly leave the tent and only did so by holding on to the line of dog traces in order to dig the dogs out so that they didn't suffocate. Going to the toilet outside the tent was impossible so we had to coordinate our needs so we all went together in the tent. We did this by pulling the ground sheet up, each digging a hole in the snow and passing around the toilet paper……grim!

COASTAL SURVIVAL

Being immersed in sea water, far from land, with no vessel and in certain seas then survival will potentially be short lived if rescue is not swift. Sea survival is difficult without adequate resources. However, if you are to reach the coast or travel from inland to the coast then your survival chances increase. Many people live on the coast, animal and sea life can be abundant and ships may pass. I have been amazed as to what gets washed up on very remote coastlines that I have been to around the world. Understanding what the coastline and seas can provide you to endure your plight will only increase your chances of survival.

Coastal environments

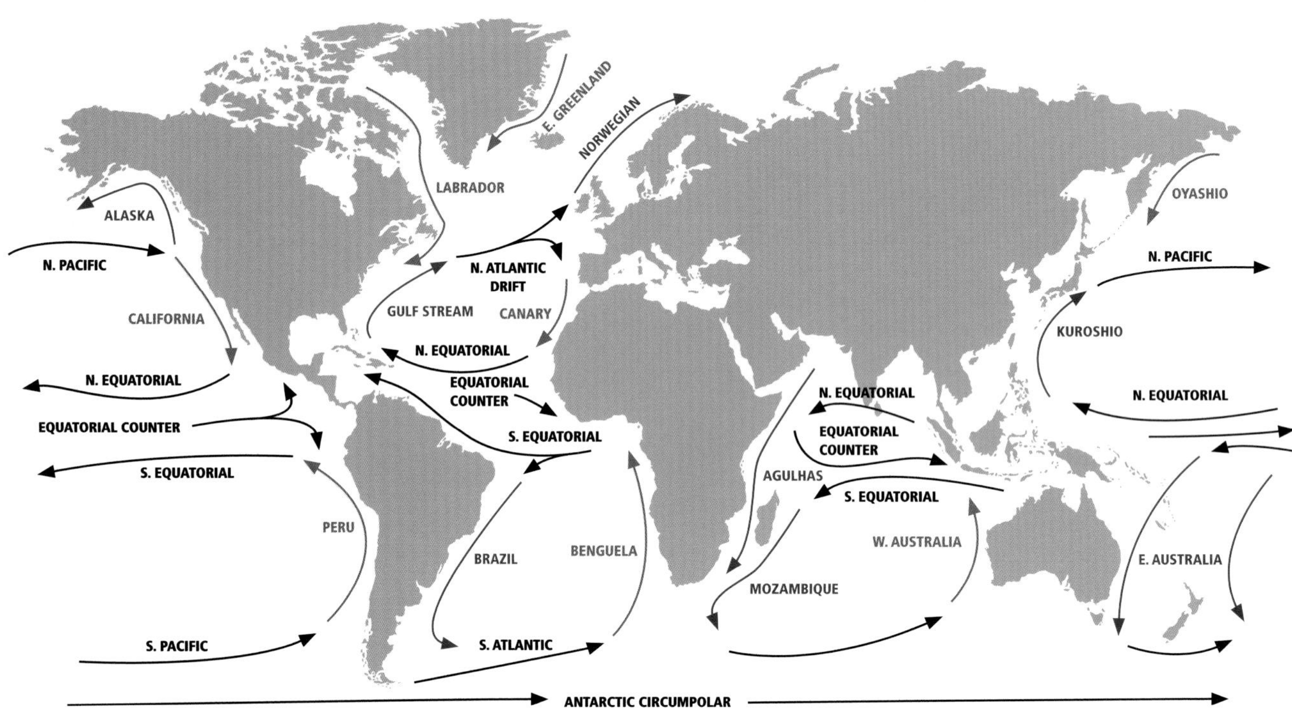

Four-fifths of the Earth's surface is made up of water, and a large part of the human population lives beside the sea. Many communities use water as their roadway for trade, and it's likely that most of us at some point in our lives will travel over huge expanses of open ocean by boat or aircraft. Almost every day there is an incident at sea, and though many people are quickly rescued others are not so fortunate.

Arguably, the sea is the most challenging environment in which to survive. Being stranded on a raft or vessel is in itself a major challenge, but immersion in the sea without any sort of craft at all means survival is extremely difficult unless you're rescued quickly. Add to this the tides, currents, weather, sea state and dangerous sea life, and survival time in water is dramatically reduced. The effects of hypothermia, frostbite, sunburn, blindness (as a result of UV light from the sun), seasickness, dehydration, constipation, sunstroke, heatstroke and sunburn are further hazards.

The sea can turn on you quickly and when least expected, even when skies are blue and the wind is in your favour. I recall being on a sailing trip with a good friend. We were five miles from land following the coastline, and the weather was favourable. I took the helm while my friend went below. Suddenly I heard loud shouts of 'We're taking on water, lots of it!' I looked down to see seawater sloshing around the cabin – not good! After a battle we limped into a cove to work the problem out and slowly made it back to port. Even though we had land in sight, the thought of being in the sea without a boat made us very anxious.

Even with modern technology such as EPIRBs (Emergency Position Indicating Radio Beacons), GPS, VHF radio, survival suits and equipment, remaining alive at sea will always be a challenge. Even so, there are many stories of tenacious survival in this harsh, unforgiving environment. With the right mindset, resolve and fortitude, you can give yourself a fighting chance.

At sea as on land, the basic principles of survival remain:

- Protection.
- Water.
- Food.
- Rescue.

You should establish as accurate an idea of your location as soon as you can (refer to Chapter 2), since knowing approximately where you are can obviously aid and affect your decision-making and boost your morale.

Protection

Whatever the situation, you'll have to find almost immediate protection from the elements. The effects of the wind on a wet-clothed body can be dramatic, reducing the core body temperature and inducing hypothermia. Too much sun and salt water on the body are not conducive to physical well-being and deplete the body in time.

If your vessel has capsized, then aim to get it the right way up. Work as a team if you're not alone. This is usually achieved by pulling on lines that are secured from one side of the capsized craft and run over the hull to the opposite side. You then brace your feet against the hull of the vessel and pull on the ropes, walking your feet over the hull as the boat tries to right itself. If you can't right your vessel then stay with it and get out of the water as best you can. Staying with the vessel gives you a bigger 'footprint' on the sea, so making it easier to be spotted. Retrieve what you can from the water should anything be floating nearby, but don't risk getting separated from the vessel by trying to get things that are beyond reach. You can very quickly find yourself drifting away from your vessel, and, if the tides and winds are against you, you may not be able to get back.

Many modern survival rafts come with built-in protection, but if you don't have this you'll have to improvise. Construct overhead cover to protect you from the elements, but be mindful of maintaining good visibility in order to search for food, watch the weather and look out for rescue. If possible secure the protection in such a way as to make it as waterproof as possible during rough seas and storms.

As soon as you're in your raft or have established a survival situation in your vessel, secure everything to it as best you can. Everything becomes vital for protection and survival, so even if the sea state seems calm and the weather is good, lash, lash and lash again!

Other protection considerations:

- Cover your body with clothes, for warmth or protection from the sun.
- Improvise a hat for warmth and protection from the sun.
- Improvise or wear sunglasses to reduce glare and damage to the eyes.
- Dry all wet clothing, or at least wring water out of it as best you can.
- In cold climates, keep as warm as you can with some light exercise. It can take more effort to warm up when you're cold than when you're reasonably warm.
- In cold climates huddle together for body heat.
- If you're in a team then work out a watch system covering water collection, food/fishing, lookout, helm and sleep.
- Have a container or two dedicated to baling out.
- Where available and necessary, inflate any bags and secure them for extra buoyancy.
- Maintain good hygiene in your vessel. Body waste goes overboard, and if this seems undignified then get over it! Everyone else can turn the other way. After a while you'll start to get sores, cracked lips and maybe some cuts from work done, and maintaining the best level of hygiene is important in order to limit infection. Illness will dehydrate you more. Keep saltwater ulcers at bay for as long as possible by moving about a little and not sitting for too long. Avoid cuts and abrasions, brush off accumulating salt crystals, wash skin in the rain if possible, keep skin as dry as possible, and keep your body aired by means of the odd dose of sunlight.

Protecting your vessel from rough sea states and from capsizing will be a high priority in most seas. If you're at sea for long enough there's a strong possibility of bad weather and rough sea conditions. In rough seas and strong winds the aim is to keep your vessel pointing into the wind and for the breaking waves to break over the bow. Large waves and especially breaking waves hitting the port or starboard side may capsize the vessel, especially if it's a raft or inflatable. Circular survival rafts are built to withstand breaking waves from all angles and are rarely provided with any form of oar or means of manoeuvring them.

If your vessel has a sea anchor then deploy it to keep you close to the accident or crash site and to assist you in keeping the vessel facing into wind and rough seas. A sea anchor is best described as a large bag that has three to four attachments, with each attachment having rope coming from it which after a metre or so converge into one rope that leads to your vessel. The aim is for the 'bag' to fill with water and create drag and some stability, thus potentially swinging your vessel into wind and waves. Sea currents have an obvious effect on the sea anchor and performance of the vessel, so be aware of what's going on. If possible, improvise a sea anchor if there isn't one on board. In rough seas extend the sea anchor line to your vessel by anything over 5m, so that the anchor is in the troughs while you're on the breaking wave.

In the water

If you're in the water, then evidence shows that keeping your clothes on will protect you far more than removing them. This goes for all climates. If you do need to remove clothing then this will probably be in order to make improvised buoyancy.

You can improvise buoyancy by removing trousers and tying a small knot as close to the end of each trouser leg as possible. After taking them off, position the trousers to the back of your head and, holding the waistband, aggressively sweep them over your head, capturing as much air in them as possible. Hold on to the waistband below the waterline. The trousers will need to be reinflated from time to time by repeating the process.

If you're not alone, huddle together. Should you be on your own then aim to bring your knees to your chest and fold your arms, to conserve warmth. Floating on your back uses the least energy. Spread your arms and legs out and arch your back. Breath steadily in and out and your face should always be out of the water (you can even sleep in this position for short periods). If you cannot float on your back float facedown in the water as shown below.

Swim slowly and steadily, and if you have a buoyancy aid on then let that do the work. If you're swimming to land then continue to swim slowly and steadily. Conserve energy for when you really may need it, and remember that although you may see land it could be a long, long way off.

Falling into or entering the water in extremely cold climates can lead to cold shock, but if you remain calm and relaxed this can be overcome. The next challenge is getting out and getting dry and warm! The chances of survival in very cold water are dramatically reduced the longer you're there. I have been thrust into very cold water in extremely cold climates on a number of occasions, sometimes clothed sometimes not. The effects are the same, and the initial shock is always there. I have also swum under ice for approximately eight to ten metres. After relaxing and calming myself I was able to hold my breath to swim under the ice for a reasonable distance.

Staying afloat

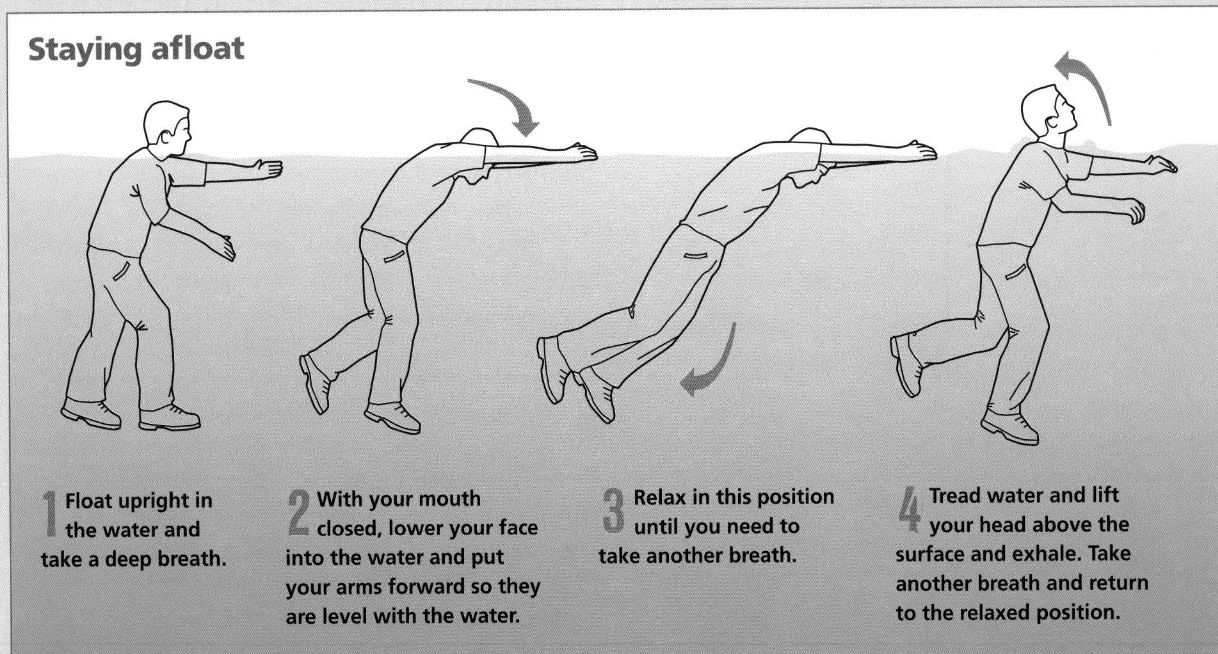

1 Float upright in the water and take a deep breath.

2 With your mouth closed, lower your face into the water and put your arms forward so they are level with the water.

3 Relax in this position until you need to take another breath.

4 Tread water and lift your head above the surface and exhale. Take another breath and return to the relaxed position.

Finding water

Our bodies need water, and after even a few days without it, and with the body enduring exposure to a sea environment, the effects will take hold. Lack of water will affect performance. The body needs water to help break down food, so eating without water isn't always a good idea. Being surrounded by water and air that's saturated with water vapour means that the body will take in some fluid simply through breathing. This is in contrast to dry, arid conditions on land, and it appears that the body can last longer without drinking at sea than in a dry and arid environment. However, loss of body fluid is constant, even at rest, so getting fresh, uncontaminated water is a priority. Death from dehydration can occur after between six and ten days, depending on the environment and other factors. There is a story of a man surviving 15 days without water, but it isn't known if it rained during that time.

If you have water, then guard it well from contamination, secure it, and ration it. As a general rule ration water as follows:

Fish eyes will provide a certain amount of fluid.

Day 1	No water
Days 2–4	Approximately 110ml per day
Days 4–8	Approximately 110–200ml per day
Days 8–?	Approximately 220ml per day

It would be somewhat foolish to be drinking lots and then urinating unless supplies are very plentiful and replenishment obvious. Urinating, even daily, becomes a waste of valuable fluid. Measure your fluid intake somewhat by the amount you urinate. Obviously, the rations suggested above depend on supply and availability.

When you drink from your ration do so on calm days, or when there's little risk of dropping and losing it or contaminating it with seawater or engine oil.

If water isn't immediately available there's still a chance of getting some, and it's no reason to give up.

In hot climates, use wet clothes in the heat of the day to cool your body (to limit sweating). This will leave salt crystals on the clothes. Clothes are also protection, so be mindful about conserving them too.

Fresh water

A fundamental rule of survival at sea is do not drink seawater! Nor should you drink water contaminated by engine oil or human waste.

Preparing to collect and obtain water should start on day one.

Collecting water

- Strategically place and secure around your vessel anything that can collect rainwater – use shoes, bags and plastic to shape and improvise containers. Also try to improvise a gutter and drainpipe system on the vessel to collect more water. If available, keep a storage container to decant what you collect, and do this at regular intervals. Make sure your main storage container is well secured!
- Check that larger collection areas such as the canopy or stretched overhead cover are clear and free of salt crystals, particularly after a heavy sea. If a storm is coming then it may rain, but you'll have to protect your containers from seawater contamination as waves break over your vessel.
- If possible keep a sponge at hand, and free from salt contamination, to collect morning dew from canopies on the vessel.
- Icebergs can provide water, but only old ice will be free of salt (ice loses its salt after a year). 'Old' ice tends to be more rounded at the corners and darker blue. Taste it carefully and in small amounts before consuming lots. There may also be pools of melted water on the iceberg. This will require less effort to harvest.

• WISE WORDS •

I have eaten fish eyes and other eyes on a number of occasions. It's not difficult to swallow fish eyes and if swallowed whole they're hardly noticeable. The watery and somewhat slimy texture and rounded shape seem to make them 'slip down' with little effort.

- Don't fill containers to the top but leave an air gap in the sealed container. This will help the container to float should it go overboard and may help as buoyancy. Use dark containers if possible or store them out of the light, to reduce algae growth.

Other water sources

- Fish eyes provide some relief when you're very dehydrated, and the bigger the fish the bigger the eyes and the greater the amount of fluid. As in many survival situations, catching big and challenging animals and fish requires effort, and sometimes the effort expended in battling and hauling aboard a large fish can outweigh the nourishment it may give you. If you catch a fish, carefully priSe the eye out

Old icebergs should be free of salt, but check a small amount first.

using a knife. Push the knife tip to the rear of the eye, being careful not to burst it and lose the fluid. Eat the eye raw and whole. You may want to chew it to get that feeling of fluid in the mouth for some psychological relief.

- You can obtain small amounts of spinal fluid from fish, and once again, obviously, the bigger the fish the more fluid it will provide. Skin the area around the tail and base of the spine. Make a small cut just above the tail and into the spine. Keep the fish's head held down when you do this so that the fluid doesn't drain out. Then tilt the head up and collect the fluid in a container or suck it from the spine. Leaving the fish skin on to suck the fluid may contaminate you with a little seawater, taking away the full benefit of what little fluid you would get from this source.
- Turtle blood can be drunk to provide fluid if you can catch one. They move fast, so netting is usually the easiest way. Once caught, suspend the turtle from its rear, and when the head eventually appears from its shell cut it off and let the blood drain into a container. Drink it immediately before it congeals. There's a similar concentration of salt in turtle blood to that of human blood so the benefits are positive.
- A solar still may be part of your boat's onboard survival equipment. These are usually spherical or conical in shape. Solar radiation passes through the clear outer material and heats the darker inner material. There's an air gap between the clear outer and darker inner layers. The darker inner is saturated in seawater. Water vapour pressure is increased between the two layers and non-saline water forms as droplets on the inner part of the clear outer and runs down to a collecting container. However, it can be difficult to keep the collecting container free from contamination and the water provided is potentially only a supplement to what you can get from other sources.
- Reverse osmosis provides a reliable source of water should there be such a kit on board as part of your stowed survival equipment. Reverse osmosis produces drinking water from seawater by pumping the latter at high pressure through a membrane, which is impermeable to the saline particles. However, it does require effort to pump one, and in hot climates this could be a challenge, though more modern kits should require less effort. Again, treat this source of water as a supplement to other supplies.
- There is little evidence to prove the effectiveness of salt-water enemas. However, administering an enema of water contaminated by, say, engine oil has some possible benefits. The rationale is that the lining of the rectum will absorb the fluid, and as the process bypasses the stomach vomiting and diarrhoea will be avoided. Find a thin tube long enough to attach to a container that will hold the contaminated water above your head. Lie down, relax and insert the tube at least 10–14cm. Pour at least a half a litre of the contaminated water into the above head-height container and sing merrily!

Finding food

Food becomes important long after water, since dehydration can kill in just six to ten days whereas death from starvation can be between 40 and 60 days.

Fish and other seafood will provide nourishment and a limited amount of fluid. As has already been said, the body needs fluid to process food, and too much food without water may make your survival situation worse. Also, more fluid is needed to process protein than to process fat. Fish are high in protein while turtles have a high concentration of fat on the underbelly. Note too that the body may crave food more in cold climates.

Food at sea

- Improvise fish hooks and lures to attract fish. Hooks can be made from pins, wire, wood, small penknives, metal and bone. Line can be obtained by unravelling material from a piece of clothing, canvas or shoelaces. Ideally you should attach something shiny to the top of the hook as a lure. Sharpen the hook and if possible cut a barb close to the tip. Improvise a spear to harpoon any marine life should the opportunity arise.
- Marine animals may be attracted to the underside of your vessel, where they shelter from the heat of the sun, so keep a look out.
- If you have a light source available use it to attract fish and marine life at night. Fishing under a full moon may be more productive.
- If your boat is stationary 'chum' the area close to the vessel with blood and guts.
- Gut fish and other marine life, eat the eyes and use the guts as bait for further fishing. Fresh fish can be eaten raw – the heart, blood and liver are all edible raw. Small fish of approximately 5cm can be eaten whole. In cooler and less humid environments fish strips can be dried and so preserved for future consumption. Cut strips thinly and turn them regularly.
- In order to keep your vessel clean, gut caught fish over the side or on a surface that can be cleaned overboard.
- Seabirds can also be a good source of food. If birds are about then you may be close to land, as most birds won't stray more than a hundred miles offshore (though there are exceptions). Birds may use your vessel to rest and perch, so with the added lure of bait catching them becomes possible. Use snares, the overhead cover to smother an unsuspecting or feeding bird, or simply sneak up and dive on it!
- Seaweed can be a good source of food too. Improvise a grappling hook to trail behind your vessel or collect it as you see it. Seaweed is salty and should not be eaten in large quantities without a good supply of water. Small crustaceans may attach themselves to seaweed. These are edible raw. Seaweed is often found in the shallows so it may be that if you're finding seaweed you may be close to land.
- Be careful when handling fish and other marine life. They can bite, sting, thrash about and have sharp, pointy appendages that may be poisonous or at least painful! Use gloves or material to restrain the fish.
- Some tropical fish may be toxic but fish caught in the deep oceans are likely to be OK.
- Do not risk capsizing your vessel if large marine fish are caught. Avoid this by not attaching the line to the vessel – wrap it around your body instead, and always have a knife at hand to cut the line immediately in an emergency.

Food on the shoreline

Foraging along the shore at low tide will provide food and bait as well as other useful flotsam and jetsam. A coastline with a good tide revealing lots of rock pools will often provide enough food to mean that you don't have to venture out to sea.

Don't get cut off by the tide and treat coastal areas with great respect, as hazards are often hidden. Be careful of rogue waves hitting the shore at unexpected intervals – spend some time observing areas exposed to the swell before you approach.

Forage by looking under rocks in rock pools and on land: disturb too much silt and you won't see anything, so lift the rocks slowly. Use a knife or rock to prise off limpets and have something in which to collect molluscs, crabs, mussels and other foraged food. Never forage barefoot on the shore: if not treated, infection from a coral or rock cut can set in rapidly. Also, something may bite your big toe!

If you're unsure whether a fish might be toxic to eat then place it in or close to ants and termites. If it is toxic, it's possible they won't eat it. Observe them closely.

Bivalves are hinged shells that open to filter water through their digestive system; they include molluscs, mussels, oysters and clams, and are found in both seawater and freshwater. In polluted or stagnant areas toxins can build up in their bodies, so if you have any reason to suspect the presence of toxins 'purge' bivalves for a day or two and cook them.

Dave searching for seafood.

Gastropods such as winkles, whelks, abalones and limpets are good to eat after boiling. They also make good bait. They can be eaten raw, but this increases the risk of illness. If you do opt to eat them raw make sure they're fresh when you find them, and wash them in fresh water.

Barnacles, sea snails and sea slugs are also edible and should be boiled before eating.

Use a pair of tights or another tightly woven, small-gauge, improvised net to trawl through murky water. Stretch the net between two sticks. You never know what you may catch – shrimp, small fish or even plankton. It all makes for good, nutritional survival food!

Crabs, lobsters and sea urchins are all good to eat once boiled or roasted. Watch out for the spikes of sea urchins: they're easily broken off with rocks or sticks, but a barb will quickly infect your foot. Once the spikes

Sea Urchin guts

• WISE WORDS •

I learnt the lesson of not foraging barefoot on the coast the hard way, on a remote island off the coast of Asia. Diving for squid and fish with an improvised spear, I needed to cross some rocks. I trod carefully, but a wave pushed me backwards and my bare foot ran over some barnacles, giving me a number of deep and bloody lacerations. I had to work hard to keep infection at bay.

Hermit crab – good eating!

are off either put the whole shell in embers to roast or scrape the guts out to eat raw or boil. Crabs and lobster are easily caught with bait and make good eating. Crabs have a poisonous section that should be removed: break off the legs and claws (but don't throw these away, as they're good meat), break open the shell and look for the lungs, resembling 'dead men's fingers'. These should be discarded or used as bait.

Octopus and squid are good to eat, usually when boiled, although coastal octopuses are smaller than their deep-sea cousins. If you have clear views of the seabed then bait the area and be ready to pounce with a spear! They can be hard to catch and will often require diving or the use of a hook, line and bait, but using light at night may attract them. Some Octopuses can be poisonous so avoid handling if possible by using a spear or stick. Remove the guts and boil or roast. The meat is tough but very nutritious. Eat everything apart from the beak and guts.

Turtles are highly nutritious and easy to catch – at least, out of water! If you're lucky enough to come across turtles and eggs then good eating is on the menu. Roast or boil the meat after breaking the shell. You can put the whole thing directly on to the fire or into the boiling pot.

Seabirds that nest on the coast can be a readily available source of food. Bait a fish-hook and place it in the open, close to nests and cliff tops. Have the hook on a long line to a point from which you can observe whilst remaining hidden.

Be careful if you have to scale cliffs to get to nests. Seabirds will attack to save their young and eggs and can easily knock you off balance. On the other hand, on a remote Central American island I once found that the seabirds weren't used to humans at all and we could easily stalk them. And their nests were on the ground, so finding eggs wasn't much of a problem either. But everything tasted very fishy!

Seaweed

It may look less than appetising but most seaweed is edible and very nutritious. All the seaweeds found around the coasts of Britain are edible. Eaten raw seaweed is salty and draws water from the body, so ensure you have a good freshwater supply available. Seaweed can be boiled down to make soup or added to other foods and cooked. If possible wash seaweed in freshwater before eating. Only harvest living seaweed and not what's been washed up. Seaweed will decay rapidly once out of sea water so either cook soon after harvesting or dry it properly. Dehydrate using fire at a high enough temperature to evaporate water quickly to avoid mould growth, but low enough temperature to avoid the seaweed being 'cooked' instead of dried. Seaweed should dry in six to 16 hours, and should be leathery when done. If using the sun, temperature and humidity are going to be important to your ability to dehydrate. Typically you need three to four days of temperatures higher than 100 degrees F (38 degrees C) to dehydrate successfully, and very low humidity. This is also true when using a drying rack, with the added need for adequate ventilation for the seaweed on all sides, in order to dehydrate evenly and completely.

Rescue

If you have flares, smoke grenades, sea dye, torches, whistles or other signalling equipment on your vessel, familiarise yourself with its use so that you're ready to deploy it quickly. Keep it secure but have it ready to hand. Use signalling equipment when you assess that deploying it will give you the best possible chance of being sighted.

If you have no signalling equipment then improvise as best you can to in order to make yourself an obvious target and to create as big a 'footprint' of colour as possible. Get into the habit of observing all 360° of the horizon. If there's more than one of you get a watch system going. Not seeing a ship's light at night or a fast, low-flying aircraft on the horizon may be a missed opportunity if good observation isn't maintained around the clock or at regular intervals.

Finding land

Watching out for signs and indications of land can be used to aid survival. Not only will it boost morale, but since many people live by the sea shipping and human activity may also be more regular. However, even though there may be signs of land the land itself could still be far away, so continue to look for water and to ration yourself. Don't abandon any of your survival routines.

Clouds can be a good indicator, especially if you're in the open sea where there are no clouds. This is because land forces air up and it condenses into cloud. You may see isolated clouds on the skyline but no sign of land – this is because the land itself could be hidden below the horizon. Clouds over land tend to be stationary whilst other clouds pass them by.

Lightning in the far distance may indicate storms over mountainous areas or land. This is especially so in the tropics.

An increased number of birds may also indicate land. As had already been mentioned, birds don't usually travel too far from land but can still be up to a hundred miles from shore, and in some cases more, especially along migration trails. Many seabirds will fly out to sea in the morning to find food and return to land in the evening, so look for land in the direction that returning seabirds head later in the day.

Increased amounts of floating garbage, such as bottles, wood and plastic, may also indicate that land is close.

Maritime survival tips

- If you have improvised a sail, don't lash it securely at both the bottom corners. Allow one side to be manipulated by hand or released quickly. If it's secured at both corners and a large gust hits it, it could capsize your vessel or tear the sail, possibly destroying valuable resources.
- Once you see land, observe the coast for landing points, especially if there's heavy surf. Getting trashed and tumbled in surf is dangerous, especially if there are coral reefs – all the effort to survive may be wasted just as you get to land! There will be areas of less hectic or big surf to land. Surf viewed from out at sea appears smaller than it actually is, so approach with caution. Look to breaking waves on cliffs and on the beach to get some sense of scale.
- Rip tides can occur as the water from waves returns. They can suck you out to sea and conversely mean you can't get inshore to land. Indications of rip tides are:

1 A channel of smaller surf than in the surrounding waves.
2 Churning or choppy water.
3 A difference in colour, or 'lines' of foam and debris at the edges.

- If you're caught in a rip then don't try to fight it. Relax and let it take you – it will dissipate, usually out beyond the breakers. Swim parallel to the coast for a distance and then swim to shore, probably through the bigger surf. Try to keep hold of your raft if you're capsized in surf, but ensure you have your back to the open ocean and the raft in front of you. Never tie yourself to your vessel! Always watch out for freak waves that can catch you unawares, and keep perpendicular to the waves.
- Even if you think you've been seen from a ship, a plane or land, don't give up your routines. Keep looking, preparing and working until you're shaking the hand of your rescuer.

There's a mixture of physical and psychological stresses when you're faced with survival at sea. The trauma and psychological recoil from that first impact into what seems a desperate situation, the effects of the environment on your body and the possible loss of life among people around you may initially make the situation seem hopeless. However, your determination to survive will increase if you're mentally and physically prepared and respond to the situation calmly, deliberately, effectively and where possible as a team. Don't give up, but take action as soon as possible and get others to take action too. No action leads to no result.

DESERT SURVIVAL

If you are not acclimatised or have not adjusted to some level in any environment, then it will initially be tough going and the desert is no exception. Deserts can be difficult and relentless, but people do live, journey and adapt to the desert environments. Unlike other environments, I personally find the climate and heat of most deserts particularly hard to cope with initially. However, after a reasonably short period of time I come to terms with the conditions and am able to function fairly effectively. On the face of it some deserts seem devoid of anything and too harsh for individuals to function; but there are ways to tease and sustain your survival time until possible rescue arrives. If you are in the desert then a little knowledge aids hope, boosts morale and gives you time.

Desert environments

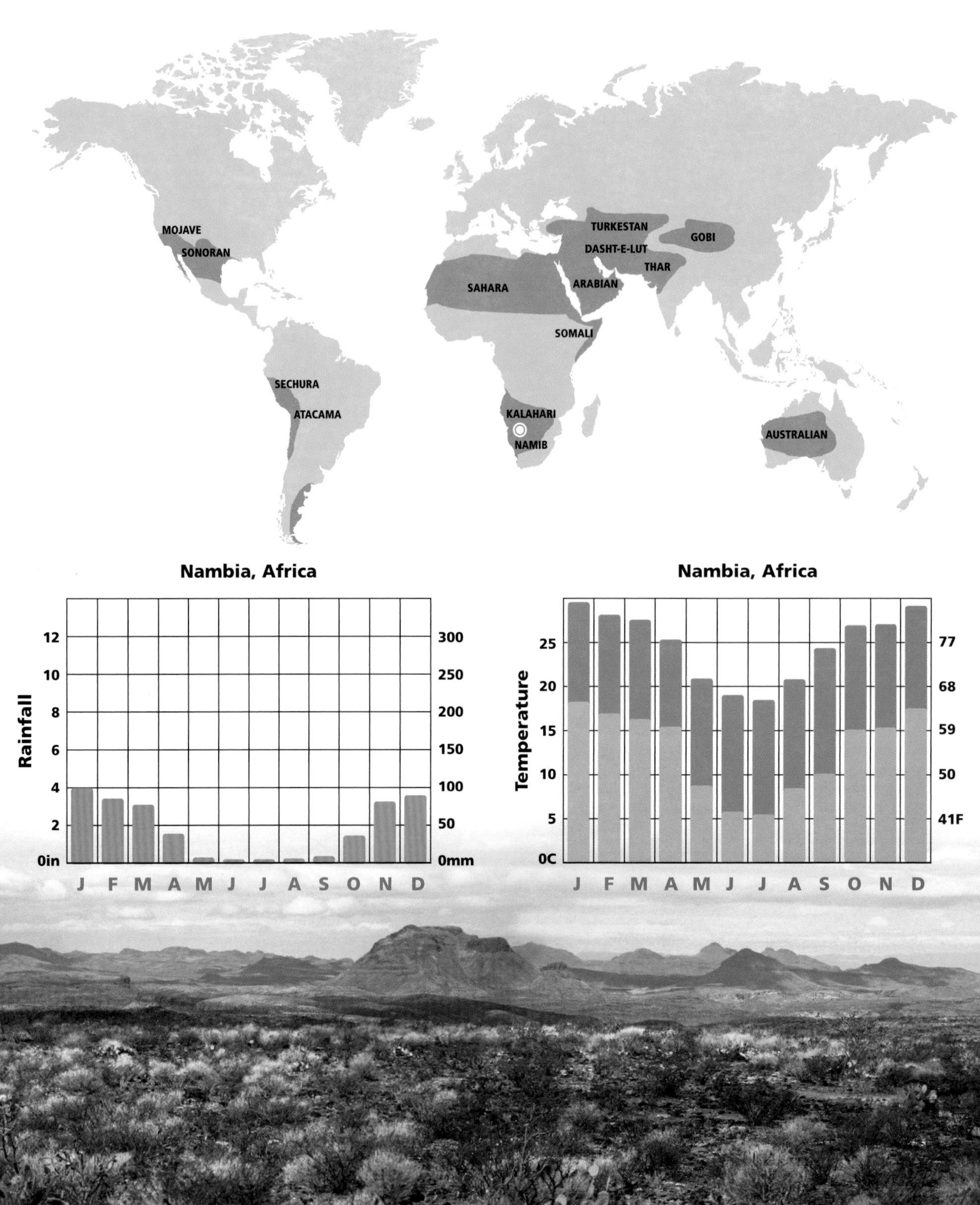

From high cliffs and rocky canyons to featureless stretches of sand, deserts cover approximately 15% of the earth's surface. Receiving minimal rainfall, desert air is dry, the land parched and the sun fierce. Exposure to the elements can cause death well before lack of water and food, for temperatures can fluctuate from below zero at night to over 50°C during the day. In high mountain deserts the risk of hypothermia and other cold-weather injuries is real.

Dust and sandstorms can hit with little warning, forcing sand into every corner of your body, clothes and equipment. After months of no rain, flash floods can also occur, washing away everything in their path. But precipitation is always evaporated quickly, whatever the amount.

Life is tough, but animals, reptiles and insects do live in these inhospitable places. Having adapted to function on very little water and food, they tend to avoid the heat of the day. Many live in burrows, and some will lie dormant during rainless periods. Plants, bushes and trees survive and grow by reproducing when rains arrive, often storing the water in their cells.

As humans we have a long history of existing in extreme arid environments, but never by conquering the desert, only by coming to terms with it.

• WISE WORDS •

Teaching us the skills of desert life in Mexico one local warden, who had known the desert since he was a boy, said to the team 'Why struggle and waste energy fighting against something you'll never change?'

Protection

Primary protection is available from clothing that you take, salvage or improvise: ideally it needs to be effective against sandstorms and cold as well as the heat of the sun. Protection from heat and sun will reduce water loss, preserve energy and prevent injury. Protect your face as best you can and don't strip off clothes and expose bare skin.

- **Cover as much of your face as you can: wear a wide-brimmed hat or cover your head with a headscarf.**
- **Protect your eyes with sunglasses or improvise by using a resource that allows you to cut two small slits for the eyes. Some plant leaves will allow you to improvise eye protection: the challenge is securing them to your head.**
- **Cover your neck, arms and legs.**
- **Wear loose-fitting clothing. This will allow air to circulate.**
- **Wear underclothes to prevent rashes.**
- **Wear high leg boots to stop sand and dust getting into boots and socks. Tighten the end of your trouser leg around the boot and cover any holes in the boot as best you can: sand and grit will rub, causing blisters. Tyres can be cut up to provide further protection and repair material for boots.**
- **If you can salvage clothes then take enough layers of clothing to keep you warm at night.**

Finding shelter

It's inevitable that at some point you'll have to find or build shelter. You may initially make the decision to travel in the cool of the night and lie up during the heat of the day, but remember that shade provides a significant reduction in temperature (up to 8°C), so finding natural shade or improvising it will almost certainly be necessary. It's unlikely that you'll be feverishly constructing shelter from rain, as your priority will be to collect it, preserve it and enjoy being wet!

Abandoned transportation will provide your first resources for constructing a shelter, but don't waste effort, energy and vital fluid constructing a plush shelter when something simpler is close at hand: this could be a natural feature or a simple lean-to against the transport. Also examine the potential of any cliffs, bushes, trees and undulations in the ground.

The basic requirement of your shelter should be to minimise fluid loss by creating shade and to let air flow freely around you.

- Locate immediate shelter and wait until the cooler hours before constructing anything more robust.
- Utilise the landscape: caves, rocks, trees, vegetation and creek beds. Be mindful that rocks radiate heat, especially in the evening.
- Rocky outcrops are the preferred places for scorpions. Use sticks and boots to turn stones and clear the area well before choosing it for a shelter site.
- Draping overhead cover over rocks or bushes provides immediate shelter. Securing the cover to the shady side of your transport as an awning is adequate. Don't seek shelter in a vehicle: it can heat up like an oven. Use cord to anchor the edges of overhead cover to bushes, sand, rocks or pegs made from sticks. Try to get the cover high enough so that you can sit or even stand. This helps with airflow; if you can get off the ground then do this too.
- If you have the resources then double the layers of overhead cover with about 20–30cm between each layer. This allows air to cool and circulate and provides greater protection.
- Your shelter should be in a position to offer protection and shade throughout the day. It's a waste of energy to have to abandon a shelter due to the sun shifting.
- Sand behaves in much the same way as snow. In windy conditions it will accumulate on the lee side of slopes. Avoid these areas if caught in a sandstorm.

- Cold air sinks: bear this in mind whether constructing a day shelter or a night shelter.
- Digging into the ground provides shelter, and burying yourself in the sand will also help as a last resort. Digging is an effort, but aim to get down at least 80cm. Cover the 'grave' with overhead cover, brush or other protection. Dappled light is better than full exposure to the sun, so if you can only cover your sand coffin with brush then do so.
- Either place your shelter with its entrance away from the prevailing wind or block the windward end. Mud, rocks and other resources could make a windbreak, but don't restrict airflow unnecessarily.
- Lightning storms are possible in the desert so be mindful if your shelter is on a ridgeline or peak.

• WISE WORDS •

I recall making a hasty shelter in the desert with a small team whilst on active service. We constructed a simple lean-to by some large boulders. It offered us camouflage, protection and a good position to observe movement in the distance. As the sun went down the four of us wriggled uncomfortably as the heat radiating from the rock cooked us alive! It was several uncomfortable hours before the rock cooled. An early desert survival lesson!

Desert basics

Food

Food won't be your primary concern in the desert. Initially it's more important to concentrate on rescue, water and shelter. However, there is food to be had in the desert environment, and finding a supply is certainly a boost to morale. Be mindful that the body needs water to digest food, so eat in very small amounts, and with water if possible.

Plant food

- All grasses are edible but provide little nourishment.
- The new shoots of most plants are edible and many of the leaves can be added to water and boiled.
- Palm – new palm shoots and the hearts can be eaten. Date palm yields edible fruit.
- Acacias – these scrubby, thorny medium-sized trees have seeds that can be roasted and flowers and leaves that can be boiled. Most parts of this tree can be eaten and the roots can contain water.
- Prickly pear cactus – the fruits that grow around the pads are edible. Remove the prickles and split the fruit. Eat the flesh raw. The inner part of the pads can be eaten; it's sticky, and you shouldn't eat too much in one go. Young, small leaves of the cactus can also be eaten.
- Most cactus fruits can be eaten and provide moisture. The pitahaya fruit is particularly good. It's small and the inner seeds are edible.
- Cattails and reeds – these are found around water. The young shoots can be boiled and eaten raw. Because they often grow around stagnant water cattail shoots should be harvested and cooked on open coals for a few minutes. Peel open the charred outer layer and eat the flesh.
- Sotol and century plant – the hearts of these are at the base and difficult to harvest, as it takes effort to pry up the heart. Peel off what you can and roast on coals for at least 12 hours depending on the size. The outer leaves are peeled off and it's eaten like an artichoke. Don't eat if it's bitter.
- Mesquite bush – the ripe pods can be roasted and dried for food. High in protein and sugar.
- Yucca – the flowers, fruits and young shoots are edible either raw or roasted.
- Creosote bush – this tight bush with small leaves smells of creosote. It can be boiled and drunk as a herbal tea.
- Baobab trees – large edible fruits.

It's always best to forage for food; the effort of making traps or tracking and chasing larger animals often isn't worth the nutritional gain.

Animal food

Forage for rodents and reptiles in cool sheltered areas such as caves and the base of cliffs. Rotten trees and stumps should be explored in the search for grubs but, as always, forage with care. Lift stones and boulders slowly and use a stick if you can. Animals that are relatively easy to find may include:

- Scorpions – use a stick or other implement to pin the scorpion to the ground. Cut off the tip of the tail and the pincers. Roast or eat the small ones raw.
- Snakes – use a stick to hold the head down, then kill quickly. Cut off the head and tail and strip out the gut. Roast or eat raw.
- Lizards can be caught with some stealth and a quick hand. Move up slowly and from behind. Kill and cook.
- Larger spiders can be cooked and eaten.
- Grubs, locusts, grasshoppers and ants all make good raw eating.

Circling carrion birds are an indication of a dead animal. It may have been there for some time so cook strips of it thoroughly. Don't forget that the eyes of many animals provide fluid as well as nourishment: swallow them whole.

Pitahaya fruit from the pitahaya cactus.

Finding water

The importance of water is obvious in such a hot, harsh climate. You must try and conserve, preserve and locate water whenever you can. It's little use drinking water if you can't retain it, and lying in the shade will obviously conserve body fluid whilst any effort will use more. The amount of fluid you require will depend on your physical work rate, but as a basic rule you will need approximately four to five litres per day when working physically. Depending on factors such as temperature, physical condition, injury and mindset, individuals lying in the shade may survive for between two and five days in the desert with no water. To conserve water:

- Keep fully clothed. Baggy clothes help control perspiration by not letting it evaporate so fast. Clothes prevent sunburn too.
- If you need to urinate then do so on to a cloth or, better still, something absorbent like a tampon or baby's nappy. It sounds unhygienic, but human urine is actually fairly sterile. Wrapping the wet cloth around your head or dabbing your body and face will aid cooling.
- Avoid eating until you really need to. Digesting food uses body fluid. The body can last longer without food than water.

- Don't rush. Move slowly and steadily to avoid sweating.
- Don't use water for washing, cleaning or cooking unless your water supply is unlimited or you can be absolutely certain of rescue.
- Don't gulp water: take small sips.
- Breathe through the nose whenever you can: this reduces water loss from the body.
- Keeping a small amount of fluid in the mouth helps reduce dehydration, not only by making you breathe through the nose but also by moistening inhaled air and providing liquid for your body to absorb gradually.
- Don't talk unless you need to and don't get excited or agitated.
- Avoid salt.
- No alcohol, coffee, tea or sugary drinks unless that's all you have. Pure water is best.
- Sleep as much as possible.
- Make sure water containers are secure and there's no way the water can evaporate from them. Everyone must know the location of water tanks: it's not unknown for someone to get up in the night and accidentally kick over the water tank.

Locating water

Finding water in the desert will always be a challenge, but it is possible. There are some desert indicators that give away water sources, and there are methods for improvising water collection. There's always a need to weigh up the need to find water with the loss of fluid caused by the search.

- Search at the bases of mountains and high hills. Clouds and precipitation may have occurred high up and on the windward side. Water might then seep down underground above an impervious layer. Limestone rock is more likely to yield seepages of water. Water may pool at the base of the mountain, where there may be vegetation too.
- Digging into the concave sides of dry river creeks may yield water. Don't dig far if damp soil isn't found. The effort won't be worth it. Generally speaking there's more chance of finding water 'downriver'.
- Water may be present below the surface in deep, tight sunless gorges, especially if vegetation is growing.

- In an arid area a concentration of vegetation indicates water. You may have to dig down, but trees, palms and vegetation will grow where the water is closest to the surface.
- Dew or snow may be present on some desert nights. Spend the night sponging dew and collecting snow. There may be only a little snow but it's better than nothing. I recall operating in a desert in the western United States when the nights were freezing cold and a light frost covered our equipment.
- Deserted settlements and workings such as mines often would have had a source of water.
- A concentration of animal trails may lead to a watering hole, possibly the only one in a large area. The 'V' of converging tracks may indicate the direction of the water source.
- Birds may well flock as they fly to waterholes. Carnivores get much of their fluid from the meat they eat, but other birds need to drink: watch for a regular pattern of behaviour.
- Bees, wasps and flies are never too far from a water source.

If you do find a source of water then dam it, conserve it and preserve it by covering it to limit evaporation.

Gathering water

Water can be extracted and pooled using a variety of techniques. These often require you to be stationary for a period of time so your first requirement may be to construct a shelter.

Plant sources

- **Prickly pear cactus – as with most cacti, these have vicious spikes, are tough and don't harvest easily. You'll need to cut with care and remove the spikes. The pulp can be mashed down for fluid but it's sticky and unappealing. The young leaves can be eaten, providing both moisture and food.**
- **Barrel cactus – these can be large barrel-shaped cacti with a concentration of sharp hook-like spikes. Cut the top off as you would a boiled egg and mash up the inner pulp. You may be able to suck fluid from this or squeeze it to extract moisture. The sap is often milky or opaque, which goes against the general rule of only consuming clear fluid!**
- **The fruits of cacti are often juicy and provide fluid as well as food. Most are edible, but do eat them with caution: ration yourself and take some with you.**
- **Other plants, such as the agave, have a thick cluster of tough leaves that grow from a central point. Water can linger deep in this central concentration of leaves.**
- **Bagging vegetation – this method involves putting a plastic bag over the green, living foliage of a tree or bush. You'll need a location that has direct sunlight. If necessary, pull the stem of the tree down to head level and secure it using cord, cloth and a rock or wooden peg. Put as large a bag as you've got over the most prolific greenery and make as airtight a seal as possible. Pull the bag down and arrange it in such a way that the water can pool. It may take up to five hours to get results. The water produced is normally bitter and isn't necessarily totally free from plant toxins.**

Prickly pear cactus.

Solar still

Gathering water from stills requires effort and the payback of water is often limited: you may lose more water by sweating during preparation than the solar still will provide. The gains depend upon the moisture level in the soil and/or what you can put in the still to provide fluid.

Direct sun is required on the still. At night or during the 'cool' periods dig a pit, in moist soil, at least 90cm deep and slightly smaller than the diameter of the plastic sheet you have. Ideally, the sheet should be approximately 90–100cm in diameter:

- Place an open container in the centre of the pit.
- Around the container, place either cactus parts, bushes, contaminated water, or even the guts of animals.
- Using sand and stone, secure a plastic sheet over the pit. Ensure the perimeter of the sheet is airtight.
- Place a tennis ball-sized stone in the centre of the sheet. There should be enough slack in the sheet so that the weight of the stone makes the sheet sag over the water catcher. Make sure the plastic isn't in contact with the sides of the pit and the gap between the sagging plastic, where the stone is, and the container is small so drips can run to the apex and into the container.
- Add further moisture-providing material after a time. If you need to urinate then do so into the sand under the still or into another container which you should then place in the still. It all helps, but only urinate if you really need to.

Heat generated under the plastic creates a greenhouse effect and humidity increases, evaporating as moisture. Touching the cooler plastic, it condenses and runs down to the container.

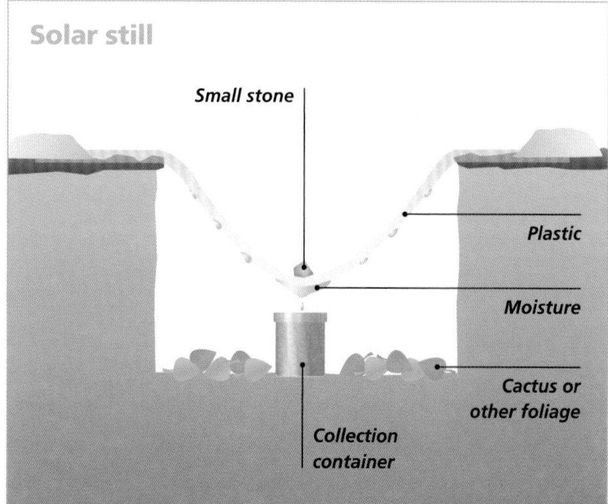

Reverse still

This works in much the same way as the solar still but requires less effort. It works best when you've located an area of stagnant water:

- Drive a stick into the ground in the centre of the moist soil, stagnant water or plant cuttings. It may be best to collect the water in containers and make the still away from the source if it's too big a pool.
- The stick should be about 60cm high.
- Drape the plastic sheet over the stick and roll the plastic edges inward, making one edge lower than the rest (which will help to identify where the moisture will collect, so you don't waste any when dismantling the plastic). Seal the outside edges with dirt and create an airtight seal.

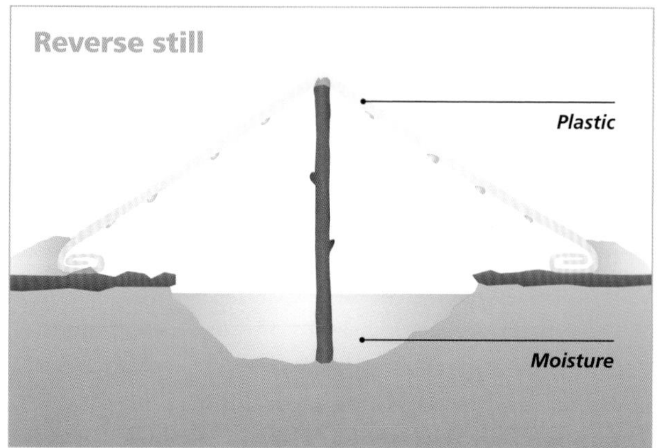

Dew pit

Place your plastic sheet around the inside of the pit and secure the outer edges. Lay stones in the bottom and keep the top open. At night the moisture condenses on the rocks as the air cools, and trickles on to the plastic sheet. Suck the water up well before first light.

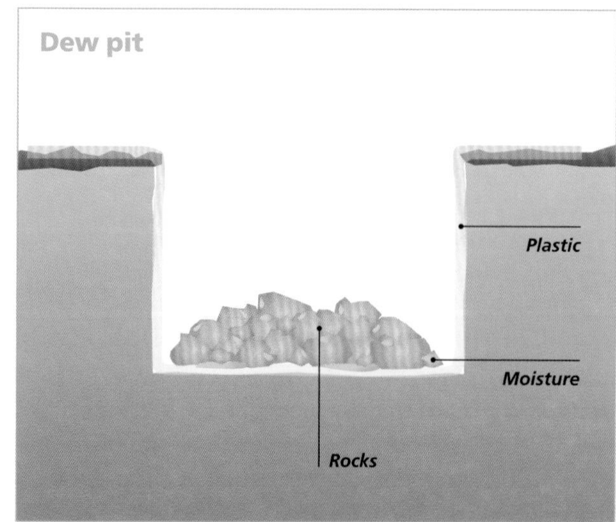

Trickling water

You may locate or stumble on small seepages or water from amongst rocks or moss. You can simply suck and lick it up, but if you have string, a shoelace, cotton or thread and a container then:

- Tie a small knot in the string and lock it into the seepage by wedging it in a crack or stuffing it in the moss.
- Let the string dangle down into the container.
- The moisture wicks down the string into the container. The longer you leave it the more water you'll get. Check that the container is secure and able to hold a gradually increasing weight of water.

I tried this with a couple of friends and the results far exceeded our expectations. The moss on the cliff face, although not dripping with water, was damp, giving a clear indication that there was some seepage. We extracted a good couple of bottles.

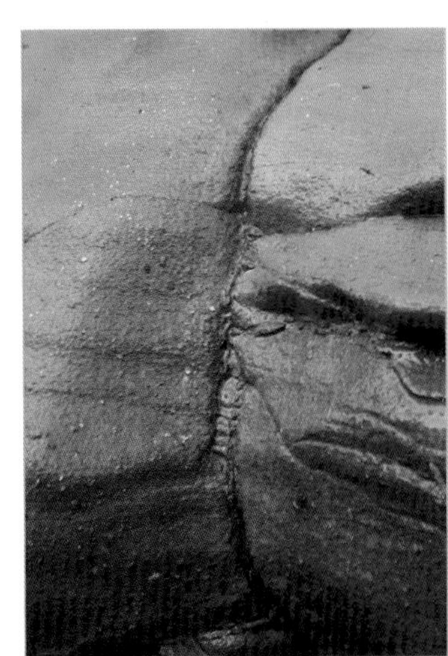

Purification

It will be necessary to purify water that's stagnant or contaminated. One way is to use the solar still as described above, but chemical means are more convenient, using purifying tablets or crystals. A small amount of potassium permanganate per half-litre will sterilise contaminated water: it will go slightly pink, reminiscent of dentist's mouthwash.

Boiling is the most effective way to sterilise water. Bring the water to the boil and let it boil for five to ten minutes.

If you're at your lowest ebb beside a source of stagnant water then purify it as best you can. It may be better to take the risk in order to extend your chance of rescue. A simple filter will get rid of the larger lumps. Pouring the water progressively through your shirt, sock, moss, fine gravel, sand and charcoal will help, but won't eliminate all bacteria.

Desert travel

Make the decision to travel only once you've exhausted every other option of rescue. Desert travel is tough. The terrain can vary considerably and it may change radically over the course of your journey. You may encounter steep-sided gorges, marshy areas, mountains, boulders and sand.

If you have water at your start point then you need to take as much with you as you can. Clearly, the more you take the better, but this has to be balanced against the considerable effort it takes to carry heavy loads in such a difficult climate. Estimate how many days of water you have: with this in mind plan long-range reconnaissance based on your supply. You may have three days of water: if after two days' travel there are no signs of rescue or other signs of human activity it may be worth returning to your water supply and planning for a further long range reconnaissance in a different direction. Once you decide to travel:

- Use water carriers that are robust. Protect them well.
- Protect yourself and your water from the elements: create a makeshift rucksack for supplies and something that will hang on the shaded side of your body.
- Wandering aimlessly can be disastrous. If you have a compass then trust it. Note landmarks: this will help you maintain direction and judge your distance and speed. Aim to walk at about 3kph. Distances can be deceptive in the desert as landmarks are often limited. When you travel, walk steadily, don't feel rushed and don't overestimate your abilities. Stop for five to ten minutes every hour. Look to the horizon for natural shelter – cliffs, caves, foliage and rugged hills.
- Plan to travel in the cooler parts of the day and at night. Be under the protection of shelter before the full heat of the day.
- Desert nights can be dark. Before nightfall, pick silhouetted landmarks and features to travel to. Use celestial markers to maintain direction.
- At night stop at regular intervals and just listen. Sound travels well on desert nights and you may just hear human activity.
- If you can, head for the coast. Coastlines can be cooler and are more likely to be inhabited. There's also the possibility of signalling to boats.
- When possible get to high ground during cool periods, make shelter and then at sunrise observe the terrain ahead. There's more chance of the visibility being better at sunrise than in the scorching heat of the day.
- Travel uphill using wide zigzags and not at too steep an angle. Never go straight up as it takes more effort.
- Don't travel in sandstorms. If you sense an approaching sandstorm them make shelter in good time and protect your face and eyes by wearing a face scarf or bandana.
- Follow the line of least resistance even if it's not the most direct route. Avoid loose sand if possible and look for hard ground to travel on.
- Build cairns, mark the route or use landmarks as you travel. If you have to return then your route back is marked, and if your start location is found by rescuers they'll have a good idea of your direction. Try and make your trail easy to follow.
- When you lie up, try and remove socks and clothing in order to dry and air them. Under shelter let your body air, with limited clothing. Take time to look after your body and treat, nurse and protect any cuts, blisters or injuries. Body administration is very important.

Signalling and rescue

As always, this should be the top priority from the commencement of your survival situation. Search and rescue planes will have good visibility and wide arcs of observation over open arid environments. Be prepared. Be ready to signal as soon as you hear or see any approaching plane or vehicle: a systematic search pattern means that it'll probably search an area only once.

- Make sure the aircraft is coming towards you. It may turn away from you and your fire signal will have been wasted.
- Only leave the mode of transport you have if absolutely necessary. Use fuel for signal fires: diesel will create more smoke than most other fuels, and it's smoke you need rather than flames. Petrol explodes rather than burns, so soak material in petrol before lighting it. Tyres and upholstery create good smoke. Check your transport for flares.
- Consider creating your signal fire at the base of a tree or bush so that this will also ignite.
- Make a signal fire that will ignite rapidly. Have a large, dry stash of fire material to add as the fire smokes and burns. Don't add too much too early, as the fire may be smothered.
- If you don't have the resources for fire then linear shapes on the ground may be an alternative. Make them as big as you can and in open ground if possible. Consider using letters that spell HELP, SOS or MAYDAY. Colours that contrast with the ambient natural shades work best.
- Use anything shiny to reflect light towards the aircraft. Use the horn and lights of your transport to signal. If you have a torch then repeated flashes during both day and night help you to be noticed. If you have a light don't waste power by needlessly giving yourself light at night: save the power for signalling.
- Movement may catch the eye of a would-be rescuer. Aim to use high ground and ridgelines to create silhouettes.
- If you think you've been spotted don't give up on your survival plan. You may not have been seen or it may still be some days before your rescue is executed.
- If you decide to leave your location then create a large sign or indicate that you were there and in which direction you're now travelling.
- Prepare a helicopter landing site if necessary. Smoke will give a pilot wind direction. If you don't have fire, try and indicate the wind direction with an improvised flag. If a helicopter is going to land then hunker down in a ball away from the landing site and with your back to the helicopter. Protect your eyes.

JUNGLE SURVIVAL

Jungles are complex ecosystems, rich in plant and animal life. Something seems to lurk under every leaf and stone, and everything thrives – including bugs and bacteria. To the uninitiated the jungle can feel threatening, chaotic and oppressive, but with a little time, acclimatisation and knowledge you can learn to exploit its abundance of water, food and resources. Nevertheless, it's undeniably one of the tougher environments to operate in. It's relentless and energy sapping in so many ways. Trying to beat it is pointless: you have to work with it.

Jungle environments

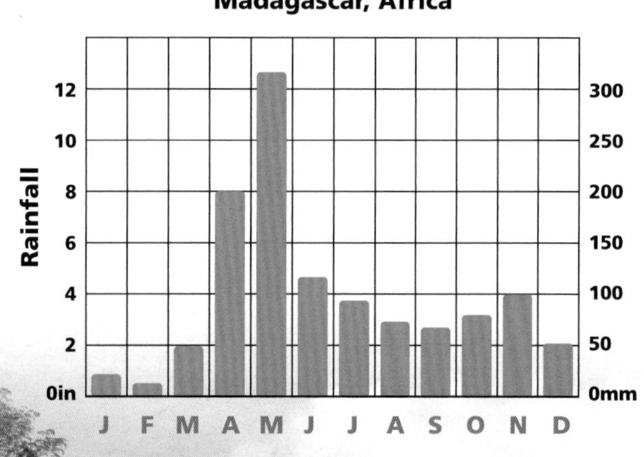

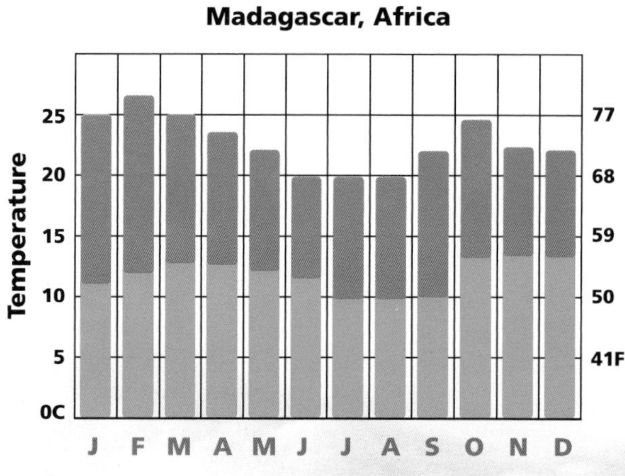

Watch out for howler monkies who pee on you from a great height.

I still recall the first night I ever spent in the jungle: I hardly slept a wink. The whole place seemed to come alive. With the absolute black of night came relentless noise and the luminous eyes of animals that seemed to be staring only at me. It was an experience I shall never forget, and I've loved going back ever since!

'Primary' jungle is distinguished by the abundance of giant trees – some over 40m – creating a thick canopy. Below this canopy there's little light and the foliage is less dense. Travel is relatively easy but it's hard to be spotted from above. Where primary jungle has been cut down for cultivation the result is a dense undergrowth of creepers and low plants, as there's no canopy to block the light. This is 'secondary' jungle and is far more difficult to travel through.

Some jungle is at high elevations where you may find pine trees and night-time temperatures are chilly. This 'high jungle' is difficult to survive in as it's often consumed by cloud and everything is constantly wet. It's sometimes referred to as 'cloud forest'. Here it's better to head down as soon as possible to the lower altitudes; but before travelling down, take some pine sap with you for fire-lighting and some pine needles (rich in vitamins) for tea.

Rainfall in jungle areas is often heavy and the humidity oppressive. Heavy rainfall usually occurs in the afternoon and can be associated with thunder and lightning. Rivers swell by the minute, lightning strikes prominent trees and mudslides can occur without warning. The onset of darkness is rapid and travel at night impossible, so leave time at the end of the day to build a shelter. Jungles can have vast areas of swamp or mangrove where they meet the coast.

There are myriad animals, insects, bugs, reptiles and fish in the jungle. Some are docile, some poisonous and others aggressive: many eyes will be on you but your unfamiliar scent will persuade most animals to leave you alone.

Protection

The onset of infection can be very quick in the jungle, where protection from scratches and bites is as important as protection from the elements. Although indigenous people of the jungle tend to wear very little, for those not used to bites, stings and scratches clothes should be the first line of defence. Wear long-sleeved tops that button at the wrist and neck. Boots should be high and if you can tie in the bottom of the trousers to block leeches and crawling bugs then do so. Failing that, gather the bottom of the trouser leg and stuff it into your boot. Hats and improvised head protection are useful for stopping bugs dropping down your neck.

If possible have two sets of clothing. One is kept dry and worn only at night while the other is for daily use. This is good for hygiene and comfort. Store your 'night rig' in something waterproof. Everything will get wet in the jungle and rots quickly even when well maintained. The humidity makes drying anything difficult unless you have direct sunlight or fire.

Dave in the Sumatran jungle – water to the waist and dense jungle above – very tough going!

Building a shelter

The aim of jungle shelter is to get yourself off the ground and to have overhead cover. Happily there are unlimited resources in the jungle to make shelter, but you should also salvage what you can from your mode of transport: straps, cord, tarpaulin and knives.

- Select an area away from swamp or stagnant water in which mosquitoes thrive.
- Remember that heavy rain makes many slopes potential mudslides and causes rivers to rise rapidly.
- Check above you for large logs that have broken off from high trees and are lodged in vines and foliage. They may fall in high winds or in very heavy rain.

- Check the area for snakes, ants and other animals. Make noise and beat the area with a stick.
- Have an abundance of large-leaved trees and palms close at hand.
- Angle your overhead cover steeply to deflect rain.
- Dig a gutter around the base of your shelter so that the location doesn't become a quagmire.
- Build your bed off the ground or use an improvised hammock.
- If you have a mosquito net then use it. If not, create smoke or improvise something to at least protect the face.

A simple A-frame

- Sink strong branches that will support your weight to construct a rectangle of four uprights that are body-length and body-width apart. The branches should be long enough to sink deep in the ground (for a foundation) and high enough to get your sleeping bench at least hip height. If you can improvise with what's growing, saving you the time and effort of harvesting, then do so. Harvest branches that can be cut to a 'V' at the top; this will support the horizontal bed frame.
- Construct a bed frame using strong branches. Lash the ends of the branches to the 'V' cut in the uprights with cord or a strong vine such as rattan. The bed frame doesn't have to be too high. Make it easy to get in and out of.
- Use strong vine or branches to weave or lash the space within the bed frame. This must be strong enough to support your weight.
- Lay a thick bed of palm leaves and branches on the bed frame for comfort.
- Lash a ridgepole horizontally at least 2m above your bed and at least as long as the bed frame.
- Lay branches down from this ridgepole to the bed edges or to the ground and lay more branches to the ground and cover your overhead frame with broad palm leaves.

Harvest the largest palm stems you can. Make an inclined cut at the base of the stem and hook the palm over the horizontal branch so the palm lays flat with the stem end/inclined cut end hooked on the ridgepole. It may be necessary to lash some cross-branches down and across from the ridgepole on the overhead frame to support the palms that make the roof. Layer the palm leaves so water runs off.

Bamboo hammock

Bamboo grass is strong, flexible and easy to harvest. It's an excellent resource for shelter material, but splitting and cutting bamboo creates extremely sharp edges, so take care. The bamboo hammock is a useful bed should you be amongst large bamboos.

In jungle storms large bamboo canes can snap in fierce winds with a piercing crack. Splinters can be cast all over from the break and are very dangerous.

- Cut down a bamboo stem that's about 3m long and a good 15cm in diameter.
- Split the bamboo between the last two knuckles at each end.
- Take out one half diameter of the split section.
- Split the attached section into strips of about 2–3cm.
- Open up the splits and weave strips of bamboo across to open up the section into a hammock base.
- Cut holes at the ends and use rattan, strong vine or cord to hang the bamboo hammock between two trees.
- Lay lots of palm and soft foliage on the hammock for comfort.
- Construct an A-frame overhead cover if necessary.

Always arrange any other overhead cover you may have (like a tarpaulin, parachute or poncho) so that it's as taut as possible. Some jungle storms can be quick and violent: construct your camp to cope with dramatic changes in weather.

Jungle basics

Water

Although it's an environment that will make you sweat, replacing the lost fluid is never too difficult. Water is not usually far away in the jungle, but drinking from rivers can have its risks: there may be dead and decomposing animals just upstream and out of sight. Rats and other rodents often live near rivers and burrow in the banks, and when rivers flood the burrows are washed away along with their urine. This urine may cause leptospirosis or Weils disease, which can lead to death.

Swamp and stagnant water should be avoided. Don't drink milky-looking or coloured liquids out of plants. Boil all water if possible. Rainwater is your best option.

I once asked an indigenous tribesman why he carried a 20cm-long bamboo straw. He showed me by sucking up fresh water from the crooks of trees, plants and rocks. He would suck the water from just below the surface, thus not sucking up the debris from the surface nor from the bottom.

Some options for obtaining water:

- Angle your overhead cover so that the rainwater drains to a gutter for collection. Bamboo makes excellent guttering – split a section down the middle and smooth out the inner knuckle areas if necessary.
- Use secured hats, cans, material and other resources you may have to collect rainwater.
- The sections between the knuckles of bamboo often hold clean water. Tap the lower part of a section with your knife: the sections that don't sound hollow may contain water.
- Coconuts can provide liquid, especially when still green. Remove the husk by forcing it off using a robust sharp stick secured in the ground. Split the nut or drill a couple of holes in the base. Use the husk as good fire-lighting material or plait it for excellent cord.

Survival tips

Indigenous people often wait 10–15 minutes once the rains have started before collecting rainwater. This is to wash down all the small bugs and beasts that are in the forest canopy, along with their bodily waste. This makes the water even more pure. A good tip.

Harvesting water from Bromeliads.

- Some plants – such as the pitcher plant and bromeliads – are natural water catchers. They collect water in and around their leaves. The water will be a little discoloured and may have small dead insects in it, but drink the lot as the insects are good protein.
- Banana trees draw up water rapidly. Cut the tree near the base and scoop out a bowl in the trunk. This is easy as the tree is soft. The bowl will fill with water in a short time.
- Water vine is a wrinkly, woody-looking vine that contains water. Cut a section and keep it horizontal. Tilt it towards your mouth when ready to drink.

A bucket-sized hole can be dug above the waterline of some swamps and stagnant pools that may be fed by a spring. The hole will fill with discoloured water. Boil this or filter it. Filter water by:

- Running the dirty water through a sock, shirt, tights or some material with a tight weave. Do this several times or construct a tripod with a number of filter layers. Add water to the top and let it drip through all the layers before catching it at the base.
- Add a layer of dry sand or fine gravel to the filter material. Live moss makes a reasonable filter.
- Use a good handful of charcoal from your fire and place it in the filter. Charcoal is an excellent filter. Although the water will be discoloured you can still drink it.

Food

The jungle can provide an abundance of food, both plant and animal. Track, catch, snare and prepare animals using the techniques outlined in Chapter 4. In some jungle environments it may be less effort to harvest plants rather than constructing traps and hunting for animals. Even so, always be on the lookout for snakes, scorpions and animals when out foraging; have a weapon to hand and be ready to pounce.

- Just about all jungle animals, insects, bugs, birds and reptiles are edible. Some can be eaten raw but it's best to cook them if possible. It's best to skin reptiles, as some secrete poison, so wash your hands in water after skinning. Don't skin reptiles if you have exposed open wounds.
- Larvae and grubs from decomposing wood are a good source of live food and easy to forage for. Grubs can be eaten raw: pop them in your mouth and swallow whole. It might sound challenging but they're very nutritious.
- Termites can be eaten raw or, better still, roasted.
- Fish are abundant in jungle rivers and lakes. Standard and improvised fishing techniques are likely to be successful. Throwing a section of a termite mound into the water will attract fish quickly. Crustaceans, snails and shrimp may be found around rivers.
- Date, sago and nipa palms – most hearts of palms can be eaten, as can new shoots. They taste better if roasted or boiled. Good source of carbohydrate.
- Bamboo – the new shoots of bamboo can be eaten raw and are a good source of starch and carbohydrate. Peel back a few layers of a new shoot, expose the white flesh and eat. Watch out for little brown hairs on new shoots as these can pierce the skin and irritate.

Bats should be cooked thoroughly before eating.

• WISE WORDS •

I've eaten some pretty grim-looking things in the jungle, both raw and cooked, and I've watched a good buddy of mine eat some even grimmer looking bugs, beasts and insects. I've watched the guts of a bug shoot from his mouth and the last of the long, thin black legs of an insect disappear down his gullet. We've never had any adverse reaction to such food, but that doesn't mean you should be complacent about what you eat in the jungle.

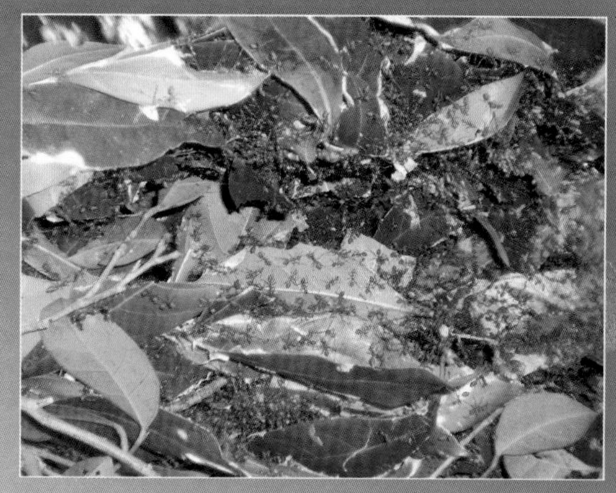

- The young inner flesh of the banana tree fruit can be eaten. Break off the outer leaves to expose the soft flesh. Don't eat young, green bananas as this will lead to dehydration problems through diarrhoea.
- The new shoots of the rattan vine can be eaten raw or roasted.
- Other edible plants include mango, breadfruits, figs, yams, papaya and coconut. New shoots and the fruits can be eaten.
- Bats can be smoked out of caves and beaten using a makeshift racquet. Locate a bat cave and reduce the aperture of the opening as much as possible: do this by blocking the entrance with natural foliage. Block any other obvious exits. Make a fire torch or light a small fire just inside the entrance to the cave and close to the bats. The bats will react almost immediately to the smoke so be ready to knock them down as they're forced through the small aperture you've created. Cook well before eating and be mindful that bats can carry rabies.
- Eggs are always good nutrition if you can get them. Crocodiles make their nests on the ground and an obvious white band around the egg means it hasn't been fertilised and is thus edible.
- Avoid jungle fungi unless you're sure they're edible.

Jungle travel

If rescue seems unlikely or danger is imminent and your only option is to move, then have a plan. Avoid moving until you're well acclimatised to the humidity and weather. Take into account your fitness, physical state, mental state, resources and direction before moving. If you're leaving transport, then take what you can. Know the time of sunset so that you have an idea of daily travel hours. Don't feel oppressed by the thought of travelling in the jungle; as we've seen, water and food are generally plentiful. Don't follow a bearing rigidly and attempt to fight the jungle; it won't work. Go with the line of least resistance and make regular assessments of your location.

- Consider getting to some high ground before you depart to get an idea of the ground and direction. Pick out a large feature to walk to, such as huge trees and cliffs. Some trees are quite obviously bigger than surrounding ones. Even though you won't see it when you're below the canopy, if you have a system of maintaining direction and the tree isn't too far it should be obvious from ground level.
- Break camp just before first light and use the maximum amount of daylight hours to travel. Be mindful of the time and make camp well before dark.
- Construct a makeshift rucksack and take what you can with you. For example, wrap food, full water containers and dry clothing in a shirt or blanket and wear it like a bandolier.
- Try not to travel across numerous ridgelines. The military call this 'cross graining': it's tough work and slow. Trees are often more spaced on ridgelines and drainage is better so there's less chance of difficult, muddy surfaces.
- Following rivers and river valleys may be a good option but rivers can swell extremely quickly and the vegetation along the bank is often thick. Rivers may also present waterfalls, huge rapids and extremely steep and muddy banks, as well as possibly swamp.

Survival tips

The rattan palm makes great cord but it has very sharp and prickly thorns that grow out of it for some considerable distance. It's often referred to as the 'wait-o-while' within the military, because fighting against it will just increase its grip on you and your clothes, eventually tearing material and skin to shreds. If caught by a rattan, slowly back off, unpicking the rattan as you go. Don't forget that the young tips of rattan can be roasted and eaten.

Dave looking for a way down steep, unknown jungle slopes and cliffs.

- Move slowly and in certain types of vegetation don't expect to move much faster than 2–3kph, in some cases less. Travelling over 5km in a day through difficult jungle is extremely good going. Initially you should plan on less.
- Use high points and open areas to rest and observe the ground ahead.
- Stop regularly for rest, water and a little food. Also check for leeches and parasites at these stops – it's better to sort them early before they get embedded in the skin as the day wears on.

Following the lines of least resistance will give you more chance of stumbling across local and animal trails. Always be on the lookout for human indicators.

• WISE WORDS •

Either leading a team or as a team member in the jungle it's always important to STOP and orientate. Some people will tend to simply follow the team leader/navigator, but as it's so easy to become disorientated everyone should have a good awareness of their location, direction and escape route options.

Signalling and rescue

Search teams are highly unlikely to operate at night in the jungle, either from the air or on foot. Weather conditions are also a consideration as pilots won't put themselves at risk: the humidity of the jungle often creates clouds followed by heavy precipitation later in the day as the heat builds. Therefore be prepared to attract attention during the first half of the day and especially early morning, when weather conditions are more stable. Rescue teams will try to narrow the search down to as small an area as possible, but being seen from the air is challenging due to the thickness of the jungle canopy. If a mode of transport has failed, then stay with it for as long as possible and use its resources to attract attention. Your transport may have opened up some of the canopy on impact, creating an open area to signal from and to get a helicopter in.

- You may be able to get access to the top of the canopy by using vines to climb trees. Drape contrasting colours above the canopy if possible. Be mindful of the increased risks involved.
- Any open area is better than nothing. Rivers will generally have carved an open area through the jungle. If you have to travel then follow a river until it opens up the canopy.
- If you have the means to clear an area, then do so only to the size needed for a helicopter to land or get down to below the canopy. Some helicopters will have a rescue winch. The approximate area and considerations for helicopter landing sites are outlined in Chapter 5.
- High ground is better wherever practical. Plan your signal location well, cut a good trail to the site and have to hand everything you need to attract attention by colour, movement, recognisable shapes, noise, reflective surfaces, camera flashes and flares, plus embers ready for immediate use to light the fire.
- Use dry foliage and resources that will produce the most smoke – dead, dry palm, dry grass, some greenery, rubber and other man-made materials.
- Smoke is dissipated by the trees so locate your fire at the base of the least dense area of high canopy, find an open area, or consider floating a signal fire on or close to a river where the canopy is less dense. Beware of flooding. Many rivers will have open areas of mud or rocks where they meander.

Jungle hazards

Leeches

You'll find these on the ground and in damp places waiting to attach themselves to you or an animal. They are not painful and you are unlikely to notice them, but the anti-coagulant they secrete keeps the blood flowing. They will eventually drop off after their fill. Do not pull them off as you can leave behind the head. Dab them with an ember, salt, sun cream or repellent.

Mosquitoes

These little things can be the bane of jungle life. They're most prevalent at evening, night-time and early dawn. They often carry malaria in some parts of the world, so cover yourself well. If you're in a mosquito-infested area with no spray or net then cover your head as much as possible with a spare garment. Covering your face in mud will keep them at bay too. Bivouac away from swamps and water, particularly if it's still and stagnant. Smoke is another sure way to repel mosquitoes. Don't scratch bites as this can cause infection. Instead, soothe the irritation with warm water or mud.

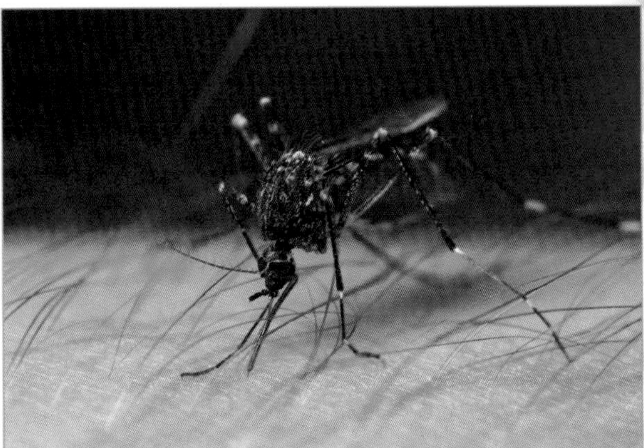

Mangrove swamps

There are different species of mangrove but they all present a significant obstacle. Associated with soft mud and complex inlets, mangroves are generally found in coastal areas where there's tidal influence; and tidal range can be huge. Although the mangrove isn't always extensive, due to the tide it still presents a considerable challenge. Visibility is minimal and the roots hamper movement but are nevertheless often the only surface to travel on. It can take a full day to cover a single kilometre.

Getting your bearings is important. You either travel towards the sea or inland. If you wander aimlessly then food and particularly fresh water will run out. You may harvest molluscs and catch the odd frog, fish or crab, but ideally you should enter only when you have good supply of water and food.

Camps will be uncomfortable and you'll be plagued by insects, but improvise your shelter above the high water mark and never sleep at ground level. Mangrove swamps can have aggressive saltwater crocodiles as well as freshwater crocodiles!

Rivers

It's inevitable that you'll have to cross rivers at some point on your journey through the jungle. Their width, depth, speed, rocks and sub-surface threats can all present risks when crossing. Look for a manageable crossing point. Rivers swell and ebb very quickly in the jungle, so if it's been raining hard for a good period of time it may be worth waiting for the rain to stop and for the river to ease.

Many jungle rivers will have waterfalls: always check downstream before launching yourself into the water. Equipment should be waterproofed and bundled as extra flotation. Locate and use any additional flotation you can: large palm leaves bundled together with vine will help. Deep mud and sand can occur along the banks so pick an exit that's achievable and be prepared to spread your weight.

There are often fallen trees across the river, some in the water and some spanning the watercourse. If you use fallen trees in the water always aim for the downstream side. Check that trees above water aren't rotten, and be aware that some may be extremely slippery due to continuous wetting.

Quicksand

If a piece of ground looks suspect then be prepared. Keep spaced out and travel with rope or strong vine at the ready. If you inadvertently start to get drawn down then RELAX. Try to spread your weight and go prone. Use your staff out in front of you to slowly pull yourself up and outwards: aim to go back to where you fell rather than go forward. Use hanging branches, vines or the aid of others to get yourself out.

Hygiene and health

- **Sleep in dry clothes, and sleep off the ground.**
- **Dry your feet at the end of each day and let them air for the night if possible. Attempt to dry socks and boots as best you can. This will avoid Immersion foot and other fungal infections due to having continuously wet feet. Dust in anti-fungal powder if you have it.**
- **Wash your body and clothes regularly.**
- **Air and dry your body whenever you can, particularly your feet. Use anti-fungal powder if possible.**
- **Carry out twice-daily checks for ticks and mites. Keep your hair short.**
- **Purify water. Eat and drink little but often.**
- **Clean eating utensils daily with clean water or boil them at intervals.**
- **A small amount of charcoal paste mixed in water can settle upset stomachs and diarrhoea.**
- **Be careful when using knives and swinging machetes. Treat cuts immediately.**
- **Check clothes and boots in the morning. Something may have crawled in during the night!**
- **Watch where you walk and don't shove your hands into hidden crevasses or holes.**

Taking a jungle bath – bliss!

MOUNTAIN SURVIVAL

Many mountain environments have seasons. Winters can be tough and summer sometimes less so. There can be large variations in topography, climate, flora and fauna. They are often complex areas with high mountains, cliffs, scree slopes, glaciers, raging rivers and dense valley forests. There are often hazards everywhere and there is a daunting atmosphere that often surrounds the multifaceted mountain area. But there are many stories of true survival within this environment and many people venture to the mountains every year. Awareness and sound knowledge can be the key to mountain survival.

Mountain environments

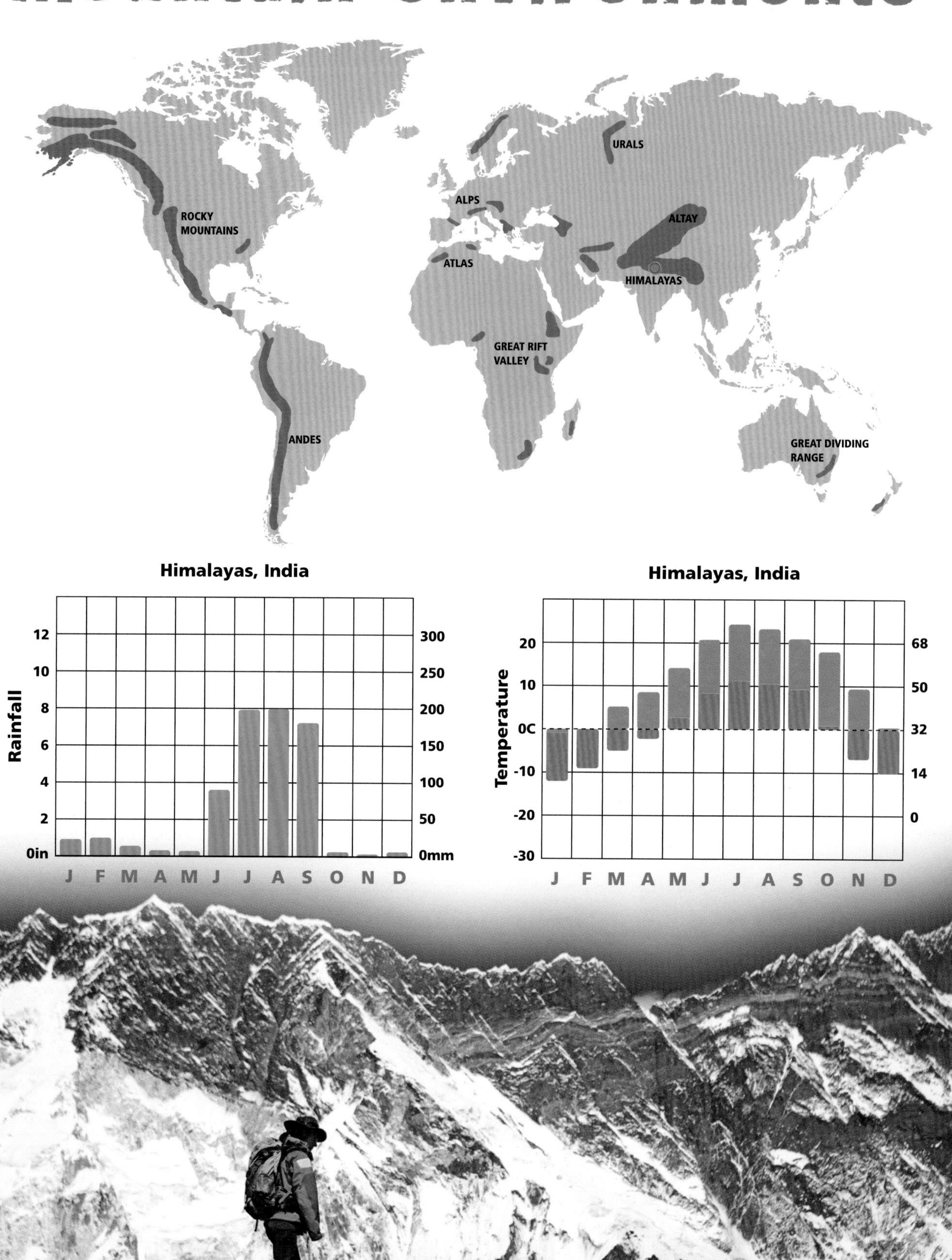

Varying widely in altitude, rock type, snow cover and foliage, there's no simple classification of mountains. A mountain can be less than 1,000m high or it could reach 8,000m. Temperatures can vary from well below freezing to well above freezing; the sun can be reassuring or it can burn terribly. The terrain ranges from gentle tree-covered slopes to wet glaciers to near vertical faces of loose rock where there's potential for avalanche and rockfalls.

The higher you go the colder it becomes. This so-called 'lapse rate' varies depending on whether the air is dry or wet, but in wet air the air temperature will drop approximately 1° for every 200m of height gained. In dry air it drops approximately 1° for every 100m of height gained.

Altitude sickness will affect some individuals at 2,000m, and should you start to venture above 3,000m the altitude can be a killer. The drop in air pressure at altitude makes it harder for your circulatory system to transport oxygen around your body. Although in a survival situation it's unlikely you'll need to travel over the peaks of high mountains, you may need to traverse mountain passes, and some passes (in the Himalaya, for instance) can be over 4,000m.

High mountain air is dry and clean. Nothing much lives above 4,000m and it becomes a very sterile environment.

Protection

In mountain environments the greatest challenge is protection from the combined effects of cold, wet and wind. Having adequate clothing is vital. Rather than a fewer thick layers, it's important to wear a number of thin to medium layers that will retain the air warmed by your body. Layering applies to the feet and hands too, so aim to wear one or two thin socks and a thicker outer, for example.

The outer shell of your clothing should always be a good windproof layer to prevent the wind from whisking away the warm air trapped between the layers. I wear a robust windproof jacket and trousers. I also carry – and wear, if the wind is severe – a thin, lightweight pertex smock as added protection. This packs down to less than the size of a fist and weighs less than 75gm. It provides a sometimes much needed additional layer of protection against the wind.

Much of your body heat will be lost up through your head and down to the ground through your feet. Insulate your head with a good hat and wear the best quality footwear available, since it's often difficult to inspect your feet. The mountain boots I wear today have three pairs of good insoles to insulate my feet from the ground.

Protecting your eyes from the harmful rays of the sun will be a factor, especially if you're amongst snow and ice. Snow blindness is painful, and compromised sight significantly increases the risk if you're a disorientated lone traveller. Wear good-quality 'wrap around' glasses with high UV protection, or goggles. If you lack sunglasses then improvise with cardboard or cloth: a slit cut just large enough to see through will limit the amount of UV light reaching the eye.

Building a shelter

If you can't descend to escape the worst effects of the weather, then finding shelter from the elements must be done quickly and decisively. Look for natural protection from the elements and especially from the wind; boulder fields and trees offer some shelter.

In the treeline

Nature may have done half the work for you, so look out for fallen trees and deadfall. A fallen fir tree, broken just above the stump and leaning at an angle, may provide a half-built shelter.

- Gather branches with needles and lean them against the fallen tree, creating a lean-to.
- Keep the lean-to small enough to crawl into and long enough to lie down in fully.
- Lay as much insulation on the ground as possible. Branches with needles or leaves are good, but use whatever you can. The thicker the better.
- Pile snow on the outside branches of the lean-to for further protection.
- If possible dig a trench around your shelter into which cold air can sink.
- Build a fire as close to the entrance as is safe.
- If you can't build a fire then block the entrance as best you can.

Open-ended lean-to

This works well if you build a long fire running the width of the entrance, arranged so that the heat from the fire circulates into the shelter.

- Locate two living trees that are strong enough to support a crossbar, plenty of foliage and snow. The trees should be just over body-length apart.
- Lash a horizontal crossbar between the trees at about 75cm above the ground.
- Lean branches against the crossbar and down to the ground at about 45 degrees. Leave gaps between each branch that you lay and use deadfall to fill the gaps if possible to save the effort of cutting.
- Lay fir branches over the back covering all gaps, and pile snow on top of this if possible. Lay a thick bed of fir branches in the sleeping area, the thicker the better.
- Make a base for a fire running the width of the shelter. Dig down if necessary.
- Harvest three long logs about the width of the shelter, plus tinder and kindling.
- Create a fire the width of the shelter and approximately a metre from the entrance. The fire should be close enough for the heat to be caught at the top of the shelter to circulate back

down to the sleeping area, but not so close that it sets your bedding alight! The long length of the fire will help to keep your whole body warm.

- Harvest enough wood fuel to keep the fire going all night so that you don't have to keep getting up for it. The fire doesn't have to be raging, so conserve your fuel. But make sure it doesn't go out, as you don't want to have to rekindle it in the cold morning.

Digging a burrow under a conifer

Where there's a significant build-up of snow the makings of a reasonable shelter can sometimes be found at the base of live fir trees.

- The snow will have accumulated to its deepest just outside the perimeter of the branches. A natural recess will hopefully be obvious under the lowest branches.
- Burrow out more snow and cover the outer gaps with branches and snow blocks.
- Lay a good thick bed of insulation.
- Create an entrance and block it as you enter the burrow: use snow blocks or branches.

Be aware that the sleeping area of this shelter is usually lower than the height of the packed snow, so cold will sink into it. Good bedding insulation is the key.

If there's lots of loose powder snow then a snow hole may be the better option for a shelter, even amongst trees.

Emergency snow hole

Snow is a great insulator and if you can get in a snow hole to shelter from a storm your chances of survival increase. In a well-made hole with good ventilation and one burning candle the temperature doesn't drop much below freezing:

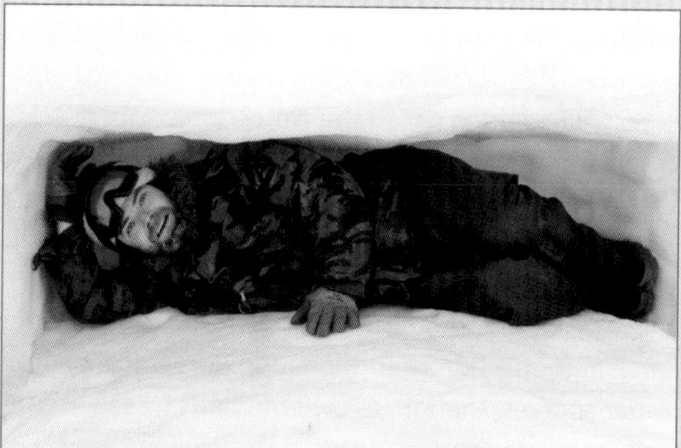

- Snow accumulates on the lee side of slopes. Test the depth with a stick: a shelter can be dug in over 2.5m of depth, depending on the consistency of the packed snow.
- Bearing safety in mind, the steeper the slope the better: on a steep slope the spoil from digging will fall away from the entrance. This results in less effort being needed to clear the entrance as you go deeper.
- Dig in for about half a metre then make a right angle turn to the side. Work hard and fast but try not to sweat. Sweat will cool the body quickly once you've stopped working.
- Try to keep the entrance lower than the hole. As we've seen, cold air sinks so the hole will drain it away.
- Keep the entrance as small as possible. This makes it easier to close it up once you're inside.
- If you're above the treeline then insulate the floor with a rucksack.
- Block the entrance up as best you can but leave a hole about the size of your head for ventilation and observation. On the lee side of a slope the wind tends to decelerate and dump snow; you'll be tired, but you must maintain a ventilation hole to avoid suffocation. Two hours of snowfall could easily take two hours of digging to remove.
- Curl up in a ball, keep wriggling your toes and fingers and stay positive. Spending a night in an emergency shelter with little insulation is tough but your chances of survival are still far better than battling against a blizzard outside.

Mountain basics

Water

It's hard physical work operating in the mountains, so finding water is vital, even in cold climates. Running water is safer than stagnant; particularly water that's running through sphagnum moss. Glacial water will be good to drink but may contain small, gritty particles of moraine. Break the thinner outer ice on lakes and rivers to get to the water: once you've created a hole then re-break it daily to prevent excess ice build-up.

Sucking on icicles and ice is one way of getting water, as is regularly putting small amounts of snow in your mouth or melting it in your hand in small amounts before sucking it up. Be careful of water sources, though, as contaminants freeze and once melted in your mouth can cause illness. Newly fallen snow is a good source as is ice from the high mountains. Although it's more desirable and often less effort to find liquid water, snow and ice nevertheless provide an inexhaustible supply of water, albeit frozen. So if you have fire, you have plenty of water. Melt what you can as often as you can. More dense than snow, ice will provide more fluid once melted. Boiling is the best way to kill any bacteria. A half litre of fresh, fluffy snow will only give approximately a mouth full of water when melted.

If you're venturing on a frozen lake for water be extremely careful. Try to stay on the ground and lean out to break the ice. If you do have to go further out check the thickness of the ice first: in temperatures below zero 6cm or more of solid frozen ice will hold your weight. But take extra precautions, such as spreading your weight by lying or by using a couple of flattish logs. You simply can't afford to fall through the ice; this is especially so if the water is flowing. Underwater springs not visible from the top, can weaken an area of frozen water considerably.

• WISE WORDS •

Once, cutting ice from a frozen river to melt, I looked up to see a dead mountain goat frozen solid upstream. It had clearly fallen from a high cliff above the river. So I went above the animal to collect the ice, but I still boiled the melted ice thoroughly.

Food

Particularly in the treeline, mountains may have an abundance of food in the shape of small mammals, birds and fish. Larger mammals may include bear, moose, elk and deer. Bugs, grubs, ants and termites are all found in the treeline and in the valleys. Storing food in cold climates is as easy as burying it in your natural deep freeze!

Plants

- Pine needles are a good source of vitamin C – eat new shoots raw or boil needles with water for a healthy tea.
- The inner bark of birches and other trees can be cut into strips and eaten raw or cooked and boiled.
- Rosehips and other berries such as wild strawberries can be eaten raw.
- Cattail – peeled roots can be eaten to provide carbohydrates. Young stems can be eaten raw; roast older stems.
- Red, blue, amber or black elderberry – the berries can be eaten raw, but don't eat too many.

Mushrooms

You can fill a book on the different species of fungi so my advice is to avoid them as they offer little nutritional value. If you have no choice, then the safest solution is to only eat ones with pores – not gills – underneath (but avoid any that have orange or red on the pores or stem).

If in any doubt, avoid fungi with gills and go for ones with pores.

Signalling and rescue

An early priority is always to set yourself up for rescue. If you can create fire then use this as your primary means of signalling.

- **If possible find an open area in which to set up your fire or markers. Even within the treeline there's usually an open area to be found, possibly in an area where an avalanche has cleared the trees. Any feature that offers an advantage point with good panoramic views will make for a good signalling location.**
- **Build your 'ready to go' signal fire in the centre of the open area.**
- **Keep your signal fire covered with conifer branches so that any snowfall doesn't badly contaminate the pile of wood fuel. Clear your fire and ground signal markers daily.**
- **Keep a clear trail to your signal fire open and well trodden. This will allow you to move speedily to the area should you hear a rescue aircraft or other aeroplane. Wading through knee-deep snow will slow your progress drastically. It could be the difference between being found and being missed.**
- **Use green conifer branches as your primary source of smoke once the fire is burning well. Pine resin is great to get your fire burning quickly so pile as many lumps as possible at the tinder/spark area of your fire.**
- **Most helicopters that operate in snow conditions have skids. Even so, prepare a good area for landing. Helicopters throw plenty of snow up with their downdraught as they land, so cover up well.**

Mountain travel

To travel through a mountain environment effectively and safely requires persistence, mental strength and good observation of the environment. The weather and terrain can be your friend or your enemy, and knowing when, where and how to travel is one of the key elements to survival in the mountains.

If you're forced to travel through a mountain environment plan your journey well by looking down from a good vantage point. Try to avoid crossing the mountains unless you really have to. You may start out in clear conditions but the weather can change very quickly, trapping you at a higher elevation. If you do have to cross then look for the lowest points on ridges, called cols or passes. These are often windy places as the air is funnelled through the smaller gaps, so travel when there appears to be a period of stable weather. Move slowly but deliberately and take plenty of rests. As a rule you should stop for five minutes every hour.

The decision to travel through or over mountains shouldn't be taken lightly. As you move through the mountains you'll encounter many different types of terrain and potential hazards. There's the ever-changing weather, the risk of heavy snowfall, glaciers and raging rivers.

The distance you travel will be determined by the conditions underfoot, your fitness, the terrain and the route you select.

- You should travel only if you have no alternative: food and water may have been exhausted; there's an unacceptable risk in staying; rescue from your location seems highly unlikely.
- Have a plan and a reason to move in the direction you select. Mountain people inhabit the valleys where there's water, food and protection.
- Observe weather patterns and plan your departure when stable good weather seems likely for some time.
- Take as much food as possible.
- If you're going high take extra insulation and protection, especially for the feet, hands and face.
- Have an equipment and shelter plan for bad weather.
- Know in which direction you're heading and use large, key features as navigational markers. In whiteouts and bad weather stop and make shelter – it's easy to become disorientated and lose your way.
- Don't go any higher than you need to.
- Look for animal travel routes and follow these if practical. Animals will generally take the line of least resistance.
- If necessary make some snowshoes from foliage and branches. Take a couple of strong sticks and something sharp to cut ice and snow.
- If you can take rope or cordage then do so.
- Plan to travel steadily with plenty of breaks. The aim is not to sweat.
- Be prepared to turn back if the risks become too great and to reassess.

High mountains

Although getting to a high point may be useful for observation purposes, don't plan to go to a summit unless it's easily accessible, non-technical and presents few hazards. Gaining a ridge can provide a useful means of skirting hazards and maintaining observation but some are knife-edged and technical. It's safest to aim for the lowest and non-technical features such as cols, saddles and passes. Travel on the wind-sheltered side of slopes but be mindful that the lee side may also have larger quantities of snow. When you can contour around a feature then do so, rather than going up and over it. It may take longer but it will require less effort. Plan your route along the line of least resistance.

Glaciers

Glaciers are slow-moving masses of ice and snow, either advancing or receding, sometimes extending to many square miles. Some are snow covered (wet) while others are mainly ice (dry). Glaciers will have areas to the side, middle and front that may have accumulations of grit, rocks and boulders in various shapes, called moraine. Another key and potentially hazardous feature of glaciers is the crevasse. These are splits in the ice, potentially cavernous, that nearly always go laterally to the direction of the glacier's movement. Crevasses are usually at their most frequent at the snout or as the glacier turns a feature or drops over an edge. Large, often huge lumps of teetering columns of ice called seracs are another dangerous feature of crevasses. Glacial lakes and streams may occur too.

Wherever possible try to avoid travelling on a glacier. If it is your only viable route, you should:

- Keep to the edges and the lateral moraines, or follow obvious safe lines free of crevasses and seracs. Avoid the snout (tip) of a glacier, as these areas are usually hazardous and complicated.
- Wet glaciers will have hidden crevasses. If you can cross as a pair roped together then do so.
- Travel directly up or down a glacier and plan a route that offers the least hazards and least likelihood of crevasses. As crevasses form laterally then crossing laterally increases the risk of falling into one.
- Cross at night or early in the morning when snow and ice bridges are well frozen.
- Use your stick to prod ahead of you for hidden crevasses.
- Glacial streams can be huge and sometimes flow into huge boreholes that the water has created. Be extremely careful crossing glacial streams.
- Throwing grit and small stones on ice will give you grip.
- Cut steps in the ice with any suitable implement.

I've crossed many glaciers around the world, usually to get to a mountain route, and crossing the glacier has often been harder and more hazardous than climbing the mountain!

Deep snow

Travelling in deep snow can be extremely hard work. If you can avoid it then delay your journey until conditions improve and the snow-pack hardens. Snow will generally accumulate on the lee-side of features so consider travel on the exposed side scoured by the wind.

When travelling uphill kick in with the toe and keep your heel slightly higher than your toes. Lean slightly forward and make small kicks. Slowly shift your weight and let it settle before putting all your weight on to the leading leg.

When travelling downhill adopt an almost sitting position with your backside over the back of your heels. Keep your back straight, with the centre of gravity going from your spine to the back of your

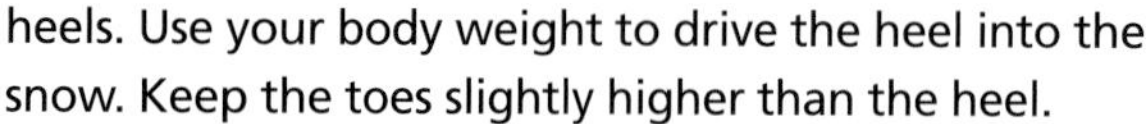

heels. Use your body weight to drive the heel into the snow. Keep the toes slightly higher than the heel.

If you're in the treeline consider making a pair of improvised snowshoes. Evergreen saplings are strong yet flexible. If you have cord then use this to lash the branch into a shoe shape about a metre long. Use cord, animal tendon, shoelaces or whatever you can improvise to weave and lattice within the shaped branch. Improvise a simple foot lashing going over the toe and around the back of the heel.

Alternatively, cut a number of thin evergreen branches that have plenty of foliage. Lash the snapped ends together and use the foliage as your foot base. Improvise a foot harness. If you have spare clothing then use strips to make foot harnesses lashed to the shaped branch.

You can use evergreen saplings and cord for improvised snow shoes.

Hard ice

Hard ice is difficult to negotiate without technical equipment. Bullet-hard ice at any angle is a serious hazard so try and skirt around it. If you have to negotiate sections then throwing gravel on foot placements will give you purchase. Knives and shaped rocks can be used to cut steps. Use handholds as footholds and keeping spacing small. Putting socks over your boots can offer more grip.

Rock fall and scree

Rock fall can occur unexpectedly, particularly in areas that have a large temperature range, like very cold winters and warmer summers. See what lies above and aim to avoid crossing close to or under large, rock-shattered faces. Look for evidence of rock fall and skirt around it if possible. If it is large and obviously hazardous then consider crossing early in the morning when rocks are possibly still frozen in. If a rock is falling, alert others then try and wait to plan its possible trajectory and then move as late as possible as rocks can ricochet randomly.

Scree slopes are areas of smaller, broken rocks that can move when stood on. Some scree slopes can be massive. They can offer a quick way down a slope as they can be somewhat forgiving on the legs if the rocks are small.

When descending scree, moving rocks can dislodge and tumble, hitting those below. Descend and ascend by long, sweeping zig zags. At the 'kick point/switch back point' of the zig zags, the lead person stops and waits for others to join. Then move off on the next trajectory. Always keep an eye on what is coming from above and shout 'BELOW' to alert others.

Avalanches

An avalanche generally occurs when the bonds in the layered snow-pack break and the snow releases down the mountain. Almost anything can trigger an avalanche: sound, movement of an animal, a rock fall, a falling cornice or simply the accumulated weight of snow. The amount of snow, ice and debris released may be colossal and avalanches can be fatal. If you survive the impact of an avalanche and the resultant fall, you may well die from burial and suffocation. Your chances of survival are high if you're dug out within the first 15 mins of being buried. Thereafter they drop radically.

Predicating avalanches is very difficult but there are some warning signs and indicators:

- Look for avalanche damage, indicating avalanche-prone areas. This could take the form of a number of damaged trees all leaning in roughly the same direction. An area with no trees in a wooded region at the base of a snow slope would indicate that regular avalanches don't allow any growth.
- Wherever snowfall accumulates on a slope, assume a high risk of avalanche. Avalanches are experienced in the whole range between 20–60°, but occur most frequently on slopes between 30° and 45°.
- Avalanches will be at their most frequent in the first 24 hours of snowfall.
- Look and listen for other avalanches. If there's a lot of avalanche activity then conditions are ripe.
- Any significant changes in temperature may cause the frequency of avalanches to increase.
- The lee-side of slopes where snow accumulates is high risk.
- Deep, snow-filled gullies are prone to avalanches.

Hesitating about the possible avalanche-prone slopes below.

If you have to cross an avalanche-prone slope:

- Cross one at a time.
- Cross as high as possible.
- Look for islands of safety such as trees and rock outcrops.
- Avoid crossing above cliffs or very steep drops.
- If possible trail a long length of cord, rope or brightly coloured clothing behind you.
- Whether ascending or descending, use the outer flanks.

If you experience an avalanche:

- Watch any victims for as long as possible to try to predict where they'll lie as the avalanche comes to rest. Keeping your own safety very much in mind, move as quickly as possible to the location and dig. Use a stick to probe if necessary to cover a bigger area.
- If you're caught in an avalanche save all your effort until you feel the avalanche coming to a stop, then immediately make an air pocket by cupping your hands in front of your mouth. Fight hard and 'swim' to get as close to the surface as possible or to the flanks.
- I have been buried in snow. The weight on the chest makes it hard to breathe. There is a strong feeling of claustrophobia. If buried, try to relax, control your breathing and wait for rescue if you are in a team.

APPENDIX

Naismith's Rule

Naismith's Rule is a way to estimate how long it will take to complete a walk in the hills. It was calculated in 1892 by William Naismith, an eminent Scottish mountaineer.

Allow one hour for every three miles forward, and half an hour for every 1,000 feet of ascent.

When converted to metric, the rule still works fairly well; three miles is just under five kilometres, and 1,000 feet is close to 300m. People have questioned its accuracy but a study by Leeds University students in 1998 found that it is accurate to within 25% on major routes in Scotland and the Lake District – regardless of weather conditions, terrain or fitness levels.

Time and distance

Distance (m)	Speed (kph)	Time (minutes)
1,000m	2	30
	3	20
	4	15
	5	12
500m	2	15
	3	10
	4	7.5
	5	6
100m	2	3
	3	2
	4	1.5
	5	1.2

Miles to Kilometres

Miles	Kilometres
1	1.6
2	3.2
3	4.8
4	6.4
5	8.0
6	9.6
7	11.2
8	12.8
9	14.4
10	16.1
20	32.1
30	48.2
40	64.3
50	80.4
60	96.5
70	112.6
80	128.7
90	144.8
100	160.9

Kilometres to Miles

Kilometres	Miles
1	0.6
2	1.2
3	1.8
4	2.4
5	3.1
6	3.7
7	4.3
8	4.9
9	5.5
10	6.2
20	12.4
30	18.6
40	24.8
50	31.0
60	37.2
70	43.4
80	49.7
90	55.9
100	62.1

Kilometres to Feet

Kilometres	Feet
0	0.00
0.1	328.083
0.2	656.167
0.3	984.251
0.4	1312.335
0.5	1640.419
0.6	1968.503
0.7	2296.587
0.8	2624.671
0.9	2952.755
1	3280.83
2	6561.67
3	9842.51
4	13123.35
5	16404.19
6	19685.03
7	22965.87
8	26246.71
9	29527.55
10	32808.39
11	36089.23
12	39370.07
13	42650.91
14	45931.75
15	49212.59
16	52493.43
17	55774.27
18	59055.11
19	62335.95
20	65616.79
21	68897.63
22	72178.47
23	75459.31
24	78740.15
25	82020.99
26	85301.83
27	88582.67
28	91863.51
29	95144.35
30	98425.19

Fahrenheit to Celsius

Fahrenheit	Celsius
212	100
203	95
194	90
185	85
176	80
167	75
158	70
149	65
140	60
131	55
122	50
113	45
104	40
95	35
86	30
77	25
68	20
59	15
50	10
41	5
32	0
23	- 5
14	-10
5	-15
- 4	-20
-13	-25
-22	-30
-31	-35
-40	-40
-49	-45
-58	-50
-67	-55
-76	-60
-85	-65
-94	-70
-103	-75
-112	-80
-121	-85
-130	-90
-139	-95
-148	-100

Wind Chill Index

	Temperature (°C)																	
Calm	**4**	**2**	**-1**	**-4**	**-7**	**-9**	**-12**	**-15**	**-18**	**-21**	**-23**	**-26**	**-29**	**-32**	**-34**	**-37**	**-40**	**-43**
Wind (mph) 5	2	0	-4	-7	-10	-14	-17	-21	-24	-27	-30	-33	-37	-40	-43	-47	-49	-54
10	1	-3	-6	-9	-13	-16	-20	-23	-27	-30	-33	-37	-41	-44	-47	-51	-54	-58
15	0	-4	-7	-10	-14	-18	-22	-25	-28	-32	-36	-39	-42	-46	-50	-53	-57	-61
20	-1	-4	-8	-12	-16	-19	-23	-26	-30	-34	-37	-41	-44	-48	-52	-56	-59	-63
25	-2	-5	-9	-13	-16	-20	-24	-27	-31	-35	-38	-42	-46	-50	-53	-57	-61	-64
30	-2	-5	-9	-13	-17	-21	-24	-28	-32	-36	-39	-43	-47	-51	-55	-58	-62	-66
35	-2	-6	-10	-14	-18	-22	-25	-29	-33	-37	-41	-44	-48	-52	-56	-60	-63	-67
40	-3	-7	-10	-14	-18	-22	-26	-30	-34	-38	-42	-46	-49	-53	-57	-61	-64	-68
45	-3	-7	-11	-15	-19	-23	-27	-31	-34	-38	-42	-46	-50	-54	-58	-62	-65	-69
50	-3	-7	-11	-16	-19	-23	-27	-31	-35	-39	-42	-47	-51	-55	-59	-63	-67	-71
55	-4	-8	-12	-16	-19	-24	-28	-32	-36	-39	-43	-48	-52	-56	-59	-63	-67	-72
60	-4	-8	-12	-16	-20	-24	-28	-32	-36	-40	-44	-48	-52	-56	-60	-64	-68	-72

Frostbite times: **30** minutes **10** minutes **5** minutes

Beaufort wind force scale

Beaufort wind scale	Mean Wind Speed		Limits of wind speed		Wind descriptive terms	Probable wave height in metres*	Probable maximum wave height in metres*	Seastate	Sea descriptive terms
	Knots	m/s	Knots	m/s					
0	0	0	<1	0–0.2	Calm	-	-	0	Calm (glassy)
1	2	0.8	1–3	0.3–1.5	Light air	0.1	0.1	1	Calm (rippled)
2	5	2.4	4–6	1.6–3.3	Light breeze	0.2	0.3	2	Smooth (wavelets)
3	9	4.3	7–10	3.4–5.4	Gentle breeze	0.6	1.0	3	Slight
4	13	6.7	11–16	5.5–7.9	Moderate breeze	1.0	1.5	3–4	Slight–Moderate
5	19	9.3	17–21	8.0–10.7	Fresh breeze	2.0	2.5	4	Moderate
6	24	12.3	22–27	10.8–13.8	Strong breeze	3.0	4.0	5	Rough
7	30	15.5	28–33	13.9–17.1	Near gale	4.0	5.5	5–6	Rough–Very rough
8	37	18.9	34–40	17.2–20.7	Gale	5.5	7.5	6–7	Very rough–High
9	44	22.6	41–47	20.8–24.4	Severe gale	7.0	10.0	7	High
10	52	26.4	48–55	24.5–28.4	Storm	9.0	12.5	8	Very High
11	60	30.5	56–63	28.5–32.6	Violent storm	11.5	16.0	8	Very High
12	-	-	64+	32.7+	Hurricane	14+	-	9	Phenomenal

* 1. These values refer to well-developed wind waves of the open sea. 2. The lag effect between the wind getting up and the sea increasing should be borne in mind.

Useful contacts

The Meteorological Office
Tel 0870 900 0100
www.metoffice.gove.uk
enquiries@metoffice.gov.uk

Royal Navy Lifeboat Institute (RNLI)
Tel 0845 122 6999
www.rnli.org.uk

Mountain Rescue
www.mountain.rescue.org.uk

Ramblers Association
Tel 0207 339 8500
www.ramblers.org.uk

British Red Cross
Tel 0844 871 8000
www.firstaid.org.uk

Foreign and Commonwealth Office (FCO)
www.fco.gov.uk/en/travelling-and-living-overseas
Offers useful information for travelling abroad.

London School of Hygiene and Tropical Medicine
Tel 020 7636 8636
www.lshtm.ac.uk/

Index

A

Accident/crash site 116
Alarms 15
Altimeters and barometers 15
Animal tracking 74-75, 133
Antarctica 13, 34, 39
Arctic 9, 12, 34, 39, 105
Arid environments 76, 118, 133

B

Batteries 15
Beachcombing 48
Body heat loss 153
Boots – see Footwear
Buddy-buddy system 111
Bungee straps 19
Buoyancy, improvised 46-47, 49, 117

C

Calorific output 70
Camouflage 74-76, 130
Camps 51
Candles and matches 14
Capsized vessels 116, 121, 125
Catapults 14
Catching animals and fish – see also Traps and snares 25, 76-82, 108, 119-120, 131, 145
Clothing 12-13, 22-23, 67, 116-118, 129
- airing 136
- checking 149
- cold environment 105
- desert 23, 129, 132, 136
- extreme cold 22
- gaiters 20
- jungle 23
- layering 22-23, 129, 153
- mountain environments 153
- period 13, 63
- protective 11-12, 141
- spare 16-17, 141, 160
- thermal underclothes 12
- waterproof 16, 22-23, 141
- wet 45-46, 116-118
- windproof 22, 153

Clouds 124, 132, 141
Coastal (sea) environments 113-125
Cold climates 13, 24, 45, 103-111, 116-117, 121
- storms 111

Compasses 9, 14, 29, 32-33, 42
- improvised 41
- Polar regions 110
- taking bearings 32-33

Condoms 14
Constellations and stars 36-37
Cookers 16
Cooking 13, 57, 87, 122-123
- on ice and snow 13

Cordage 64-65
- para chord 15
- plaiting 65
- rattan palm 146
- using natural sources 64-65

Cotton and needle 14

D

Desert environments 127-137
- dust and sandstorms 129, 136
- lightning storms 130
- travel 136

Drinking water 8, 17, 70-71, 108, 115, 132-133
- bagging vegetation 133
- carrying 136
- contaminated 135
- containers 17, 119-120, 132, 136, 146
- dew 133, 135
- finding and collecting 47, 118-120, 130-135, 144, 156-157
- glacial 156
- icebergs 119
- purifying 14, 135, 144, 149, 156
- rainwater 47, 119, 144
- rationing 118
- reverse osmosis/still 120, 134
- snow and ice 156
- Solar still 120, 134-135
- trickling water 135

Dry climates 24
Duct tape 15

E

Equator 36
Equipment 11-13
- carrying too much 12
- protective 11-12

F

Fire 8, 109
- animal fat fuel 109
- bamboo fire saw 56
- coals and charcoal 55
- collecting fuel 52-53
- flint and striker 14
- friction 57
- fuzz sticks 53
- kindling 53-55, 57
- lighters 16
- lighting 15
- maintaining 52, 55
- making 52-57
- reflectors 53
- tinder 53-55, 57
- transporting 55
- vehicle fuel 57
- wood fuel 53-55, 57, 109

First aid 91-95
- kits 16
- resuscitation (CPR) 92-93

Fish 84-85, 121-122
- freshwater 84
- gutting 84-85, 121
- handling 121
- scaling 27, 85
- toxic test 122
- tropical 84, 121

Fish hooks 15, 121
Fishing 84-85
- at night 121, 123
- bait 84-85, 121, 123
- netting 85
- woven trap 85

Fitness 12
Flash floods 44
Food and drink 8, 16, 25, 69-75, 115, 118, 145, 157
- accessible 16
- barnacles and sea snails 122
- bees, wasps and hornets 73
- berries 71, 109, 157
- birds 89, 145, 157
  - plucking 89
- bivalves 122
- bugs, grubs, insects and maggots 69, 72-73, 131, 145, 157
- carbohydrates 25, 70
- chocolates and sweets 25
- coconuts 144
- crabs and lobsters 122-123
- crustaceans 121, 145
- dehydrated/dried 25
- edibility test 70-71
- eggs 25
- eyes 85, 88, 119-121, 131
- fats 70
- fish 84-85, 120-121, 145
- fruit 25, 145
- fungi (mushrooms) 145, 157
  - cutting 27
- gastropods 122
- honey 73
- large mammals 157
- locusts and grasshoppers 69, 131
- minerals 70
- nuts 25
- octopus and squid 123
- pemmican 25
- plants and vegetation 108-109, 131, 133, 144-145, 157
- preparing animals 86-89
  - bleeding 88
  - boiling 88
  - gutting 87-89
  - skinning 86-88, 145
  - preservation 89
  - drying 89
  - salting 89
  - smoking 89
- protein 25, 70
- purged 72, 122
- rabbit 86-87
- reptiles 89, 131
- rodents 131
- seabirds 121, 123
- searching for 116, 121-123
  - at sea 121
  - in mountains 157
  - in the desert 131
  - on the shoreline 122
- seaweed 121, 123
- shell fish 123
- snakes 89, 131
- storing 67, 76, 88
- termites and ants 145, 157
- triangle 25
- turtles 120-121, 123
- vitamins 70
- wild pig 87

Footprint of location 8
Footwear 20-21, 153
- Arctic 20-21
- boots 13, 20, 22, 45, 129, 153
- high leg 129
- desert 21, 129
- jungle 20-21
- repairs 129
- socks 21-22, 129
- snowshoes 158, 160
- temperate 21
- thermal insoles 20

Frozen lakes 156

G

Glaciers 151, 156, 158-159
- crossing 105, 159

Gloves 20 20

H

Hammocks 19, 62, 142
- bamboo 143

Hats and headgear 15, 23, 116, 141, 153
Helicopters 100, 109, 157
- landing zones (LZ) 100-101, 137, 157

Hot climates 52, 118, 120
Human indicators 147
Hunting in caves 15
Hygiene 67, 110, 116, 121, 132, 141, 149
- snow baths 110
- toilet areas 110, 116

I

Illness, injuries and wounds 15, 86, 91-99, 116, 136, 145
- altitude sickness 153
- bites and stings 98-99, 141, 148
- bleeding 97
- blindness 115
- blisters 99, 129, 136
- burns 99
- butterfly sutures 15
- cold shock 117

constipation 115
cuts 136
dehydration 115-116, 118-119, 132
fractures 94-95
frostbite 97, 111, 115
heat exhaustion 98
heatstroke 98, 115
hypothermia 12, 96, 115-116
infection 91, 97, 116, 141
fungal 99
leeches and parasites 99, 141, 147-148
mosquitoes 148
overheating 98
rabies 98
recovery position 94-95
seasickness 115
shock 96
snow
blindness 153
sores and cracked lips 116
spinal 92
splinters 14, 97
sunburn 15, 115, 132
sunstroke 115
ticks and mites 99,149
trench foot 98
unconscious 92, 96
Inflatable mattresses 24

J

Jungles 7, 12, 26-27, 41, 47, 58, 64, 73, 97, 139-149
hazards 148-149
high 141
primary 141
secondary 141
storms 141, 143
travel 146-147

K

Karabiners 26
Killing animals 86-88, 131
Knives 26-27, 120, 160
care and maintenance 59
flick 27
flint 59, 83
folding 27, 58
improvised 59, 160
lashing to a stick 83
law of the land 27
multi-blade 26
safety 27, 58-59, 86, 149
sharpening 59
sheaths and scabbards 26-27
using 58-59
Knots 60-65

L

Lip salve and sun lotion 15
Lost 9
disorientation 9, 147, 153
in jungle 41

M

Machetes 26, 58-59, 149
Magnifying glasses 15
Mangrove swamps 148
Maps 9, 29, 30, 42
creating models 31
making your own 31
orientating 33
Medical support 12
Mobile phones 9
Moon 37
Mosquito nets 142
Mountain environments 151-161
high mountains 158
rock falls and scree 160-161
travel 158-160
traversing passes 153
Multi tools 26

N

Navigation 8, 29-43
at night 33, 36
by sun 9, 34
GPS 14-15, 110, 115
guidance from nature 9, 38-40
in jungle 146
in the desert 136
in the sea 124
shadow tip method 34-35
using the stars (celestial) 36-37, 110, 136
without map or compass 34
Night travel
in cold environments 105, 110
in deserts 136
North 35
true 36
Northern hemisphere 35-37, 40
Notebooks and pencils 15

O

Overhead cover 18-19, 47, 49, 107, 116, 130, 142-143

P

Polar regions 105, 108, 110-111
Ponchos 18-19, 143
Protection 8, 12, 115-116
from heat and sun 15, 23, 116, 129
in jungle 141
in mountains 153
in water 116-117

Q

Quicksand 149

R

Rafts 47, 115-116
circular 116
paddles 47
sea raft 48-49
Razor blades 14, 41
Rescue 8, 47, 91, 100-101, 109, 115-116, 157
by aeroplane 109
by boat 101, 136
by helicopter 100-101, 109
EPIRBs 115
from cold environments 109
from mountains 157
from the desert 1 36-137
from the jungle 147
from the sea 124
signalling 13, 15, 57, 109, 124, 136-137, 147, 157
fires 137, 147, 157
shapes on the ground 137
Rivers 44-46, 147, 149, 158
crossing 44-46, 149
damming 85
following 146-147
in deserts 44
travelling along 47
wading 44
Rucksacks 16, 46, 155
makeshift 146
packing 17

S

Salt water enemas 120
Sand 38-39, 43, 130
Scott, Captain 13, 25, 63
Sea anchor 116
Sea survival 113-125
finding land 124-125
rip tides 125
Search and rescue
planes 137
teams 147
Shelters 9, 15, 34, 66-67, 105
A-frame 143
constructing 66, 106-107, 141, 154-155
digging a burrow 155
emergency snow hole 155
finding 51, 130
igloos 106
jungle 142-143, 148
lean-to 130, 154-155
mountain 154-155
snow coffins 106
Skis 26
Sleeping bags 24
bivouac 24
Sleeping (roll) mats 13, 24
Snow and ice 38-39, 43, 103, 106-107, 133, 155, 157-161
avalanches 161
deep 160
hard ice 160
sastrugi 39, 109
Southern hemisphere 35-37
Spears 83, 122-123
Speed and distance covered 42-43
bracketing 43
dead reckoning 43
finger method 43
group average 43
judging distance 42
unit of measure 43
Spoons, plastic 15
Sun 34-35, 40, 116, 129
UV light 110, 115
Sunglasses 15, 129
improvised 129
wrap around 153
Survival packs 14-15
Survival
requirements 8
Opportunistic 8
Proactive 8
Resourceful 8
Sweating (perspiration) 12-13, 21-22, 111, 118, 134, 144, 158
Swimming 117
across rivers 44-45
in the sea 117
parallel to the coast 125
under ice 117

T

Tampons 14, 132
Teams 8-9, 12, 29, 43, 46, 125, 147
Temperate climates 40
Tents 18-19
Tent poles 19
Tin mugs 15
Toilet paper 17
Torches 72, 137
fire 145
head 15, 17
improvised 55
Tracking time 35
Traps and snares 14-15.76-82, 121, 145
daisy box trap 81
deadfall traps
figure 4 deadfall trap 80
lift or twitch stick snare 78
Ojibwa bird trap 82
pits 78
running noose 78
spring snares 79
Travelling at night 15, 47, 130, 136
Trees 38, 40, 64, 131, 146-147, 154
deciduous 40
decomposing 72, 145
fallen 149, 154
stumps 131

U

Urinating 67, 118, 132

V

VHF radio 115
Vines 8, 64

W

Water 17, 43-45
fresh water 118-119
immersed in sea water 113, 115
sea water 118-119
submersion in cold climates 111
Waterfalls 23, 45, 146, 149
Waterproofing 17
Way marks 9
Weather conditions 12, 158
Whistle 14
White-out conditions 33, 158
Winds 38-40, 105, 116, 137, 153-154
Wire 15
Wire saw 14
Wood saws 27

Z

Zip ties 15

Credits

Author: Dave Pearce
Managing editor: Louise McIntyre
Copy editor: Ian Heath
Design: Richard Parsons
Illustrations: Dominic Stickland

Photos

Guy Harrop (www.guyharrop.com) Cover (main), pages 11, 14, 15, 17, 17, 18b, 19t, 20, 21, 2, 23, 26, 27, 30t, 31t, 32, 33, 34b, 50, 52, 53, 55t, 56, 58b, 59t, 61, 62, 63, 66, 68, 77, 78, 79, 81, 81, 82, 83t, bl, 86, 87b, 92, 93, 94, 95, 97.
Ross Bowyer 48, 49, 67, 109tr, 160
istockphoto.com 2, 3, 10, 18t, 23, 25, 38, 39, 51, 88, 90, 91, 96, 99r, 100, 101, 104, 105, 109br, 110t, 111tr, 112, 114, 115, 118, 120, 121, 124, 125, 126, 129r, 135b, 136, 137, 148t, 152, 153b, 155r, 156, 159
wikimedia commons 19, 73, 75, 89, 97l, 99l, 122l, 148b, 157tl, 157tr
dreamstime.com 103, 117t, 119
All other photos from Dave Pearce's library

The author would like to thank the following people for their contributions.

Ross Bowyer, Dr Pete Carr, Bear Grylls, Jane Pearce, Andrew 'Woody' Wood (www.bushcraftexpeditions.com), The Royal Marine Commandos.